T0299088

This book measures and explains the performance of major competitor countries in international financial services. Covering the markets for foreign exchange, mergers and acquisition advice, syndicated loans, Eurobonds, international equities, Eurocommercial paper, and Euro medium-term notes, the author assesses performance on the basis of the shares of the major institutional players in the United States, Japan, the United Kingdom, and Europe. Explanations for the contrasts in national performance are sought through interviews with senior officials of financial institutions operating in selected markets. The role and importance of a number of explanatory factors are then examined, including the structure of national banking sectors, capital inputs, technology, regulation, and domestic economic conditions. The book concludes by asking how the banking sectors of different countries are likely to fare as international trade in financial services is liberalised.

THE NATIONAL INSTITUTE OF
ECONOMIC AND SOCIAL RESEARCH

Occasional Papers
XLV

INTERNATIONAL FINANCIAL
MARKETS

The performance of Britain and its rivals

INTERNATIONAL FINANCIAL MARKETS

The performance of Britain and its rivals

ANTHONY D. SMITH

CAMBRIDGE
UNIVERSITY PRESS

CAMBRIDGE
UNIVERSITY PRESS

University Printing House, Cambridge CB2 8BS, United Kingdom

Cambridge University Press is part of the University of Cambridge.

It furthers the University's mission by disseminating knowledge in the pursuit of education, learning and research at the highest international levels of excellence.

www.cambridge.org
Information on this title: www.cambridge.org/9780521431033

© Cambridge University Press 1992

First published 1992

A catalogue record for this publication is available from the British Library

Library of Congress Cataloguing in Publication data

Smith, Anthony D.
International financial markets: the performance of Britain and its rivals /Anthony D. Smith.
p.   cm. – (Occasional papers / the National Institute of Economic and Social Research; 45)
Includes bibliographical references and index.
ISBN 0-521-43103-4 (hardback)
I. Financial institutions – Great Britain.   2. Financial institutions – United States.   3. Financial institutions – Japan.
4. Financial institutions – European Economic Community countries
5. International finance.   I. Title.   II. Series: Occasional papers
(National Institute of Economic and Social Research); 45.
HG186.G7S59   1992
332.1 – dc20   92-5882   CIP

ISBN 978-0-521-43103-3 Hardback

CONTENTS

LIST OF TABLES

SYMBOLS IN THE TABLES
.... not available
—— nil or negligible
n.a. not applicable

PREFACE

This study is one in a series undertaken by the National Institute over a period of many years which focuses on inter-country sectoral comparisons. The first of the line, *Comparative Productivity in British and American Industry*, relating to prewar conditions, was produced by L. Rostas. This was succeeded in the postwar period by a number of other such international comparisons which concentrated essentially on manufacturing and industrial activities mainly in advanced economies.

Recently the National Institute's work in this field was extended to the service economy with the publication of *Productivity in the Distributive Trades: A Comparison of Britain, America and Germany*, by A. D. Smith and D. M. W. N. Hitchens. The present study reflects the burgeoning interest in tertiary activities by broadening this new line of research to cover the international performance of national financial service industries (essentially commercial banks, investment banks and security houses) which supply major global capital markets. It is hoped that its findings, particularly those relating to the United Kingdom's performance, will be especially apposite against the current background of deregulation and liberalisation of financial markets.

Initial research, undertaken during the first half of 1989, took the form of a pilot study funded by the Bank of England. The aim of this pilot study was to select those international financial markets which would be subject to scrutiny and to identify ways in which the performance in these markets of the financial service sectors of different countries could be compared. The main study, carried out between mid-1990 and mid-1991, was financed by contributions from: the Bank of England, HM Treasury, the Department of Trade and Industry, Barclays Bank, Lloyds Bank, the Midland Bank, the National Westminster Bank, Ernst and Young and Daiwa Europe. To these sponsors and to the many officials of the large number of financial institutions who provided, during the course of interviews and otherwise, information on which the study has freely drawn, the National Institute and the author express their sincere gratitude.

I would like to acknowledge especially the contributions to the study provided by members of the Institute: Alan Shipman for his work on the foreign exchange and mergers and acquisitions sections of Chapter 3; and David Wilkinson for collecting, processing and preparing the data on which Chapter 5 is based. From inception to completion of the project Andrew Britton provided both advice and, equally important, encouragement. In its final form the book has also benefited greatly from detailed, and constructive, comments supplied by Christopher Johnson and E. P. Davis. I would also like to thank Fran Robinson for helping to prepare the manuscript for publication and Chris Moore for compiling the index. Ultimate responsibility for the views expressed and conclusions drawn rests, of course, with the author.

ANTHONY D. SMITH
Consultant at the National Institute
November 1991

1

INTRODUCTION

The origins of this project are to be found in the projected liberalisation of the European Community in 1992. When the United Kingdom acceded to the European Economic Community in 1973, concern was expressed about the relative efficiency of British manufacturing industry and how that sector would fare in the Common Market. It was appreciated that with the full liberalisation of the Community's internal market in 1992, attention would need to be focused on the competitiveness of Britain's financial service industries relative to those of other countries. Interest in this question has also been stimulated by the fact that negotiations in the Uruguay Round of GATT trade negotiations are directed largely towards liberalisation of international trade in services.

This interest in the impact of 1992 on the Community's financial service industries has been reflected in debates about a wide variety of relevant aspects. These include the nature of the financial and prudential regulatory regimes to be implemented by individual member countries, the extent to which member countries' tax regimes will influence the location of financial services, and the implications of the international integration of financial markets for exchange controls and monetary policy. It is clear, however, that an especially significant ingredient which needs to be taken into account when gauging the impact of market integration and service trade liberalisation on the performance and development of national financial service industries is their relative competitiveness. It is with this issue, and especially with Britain's comparative performance, that this study is essentially concerned.

The objective of the study is to determine and explain the comparative efficiency of certain British owned and managed financial service institutions, regardless of whether the operations in question are conducted from the United Kingdom or are based overseas. It is not directly concerned with comparisons of financial centres in an attempt, for example, to identify the relative strengths and weaknesses of the City of London as a base for financial operations. The results should make it easier to assess how British financial institutions are likely to fare in competition with foreign

1

owned and managed companies, wherever they are located, when trade in financial services is liberalised.

Until recently – perhaps on account of the pre-eminent position which the City was assumed to occupy as the leading European financial centre – it was generally thought that with the advent of full market integration, and in sharp contrast to expectations for UK manufacturing in 1973, British financial service industries would 'clean up' at the expense of their overly-protected, less efficient, and smaller continental competitors. Moreover the possibility has been raised that some recent developments affecting British financial services (technological changes associated, *inter alia*, with the Big Bang, sharper competition resulting from both the diversification of British financial sectors and also the arrival of overseas financial groups) may have further enhanced the efficiency of British financial service activities. However the comparative position of British financial services is currently regarded in a more circumspect fashion, partly as a result of the impact of the 'prudential' regulations to which they have recently become subject.

Whilst interest in the question of the comparative efficiency of British financial services was thus triggered by the advent of 1992, initial work on the project indicated that its scope would need to be widened in some important respects. In particular it was quickly appreciated that given the major roles which they play in international financial markets, coupled with relatively free access which they may enjoy in Community markets, the financial sectors of such countries as the United States, Japan and Switzerland would need to be included and examined alongside those of the United Kingdom and other member countries.

The scope of the study also needed to be enlarged in order to encompass a review of the appropriate methodology for quantifying inter-country comparisons of sectoral competitiveness and comparative advantage. In contrast to the position with international studies of manufacturing industry, the methodology for such comparisons has barely reached beyond the embryonic stage in the case of service industries.

Chapter 2 of this study is devoted to a review of possible approaches and the identification and selection of a measure that is suitable and practicable for the present purpose. The various approaches have been examined in a critical fashion and all were found wanting in one or more critical aspects. In the case of those measures which are based on international productivity/cost/price comparisons, the principal weaknesses are as follows. First, they fail to distinguish between the foreign-owned segment of a country's financial sector (frequently large) and the performance of domestic financial institutions. Second, little or no attention is paid to capital inputs (again very important in financial services) as opposed to labour resources. Finally, the analyses are invariably highly aggregative, typically relating to the whole of a country's financial service industry. In each of these cases the problems are attributable, *au fond*, to data limitations for which there appears to be no prospect of any immediate improvement.

Chapter 2 also reveals that data restrictions, too, impair the usefulness of some of those international comparisons of the performance of financial service industries which are based on revealed comparative advantage: the extent to which financial services feature in a country's exports and the share of global exports of financial services gained by a given country. The data which are available in the standard national and international compilations of trade information are such that, again, comparisons can be made only for service sectors as a whole and not for individual financial service industries. More fundamentally, the revealed comparative advantage approach based on *direct* trade flows fails to take any account of the trade implications of foreign direct investments, the role of which can be of paramount importance in the case of financial services.

More positively, Chapter 2 serves to emphasise that a sharp distinction must be made when analysing the competitiveness and performance of financial institutions between their ownership and location. Another lesson which is drawn is that, ideally, any quantitative analysis needs to be conducted at a disaggregated level and also take full account of foreign direct investment in financial facilities.

In the event the shares of selected financial markets obtained by the relevant financial institutions have been aggregated on a nationality basis to yield the basic measure for comparison between countries. To some extent this is a form of the revealed comparative advantage approach, though one which is designed to avoid weaknesses in methods hitherto attempted, and is best suited to the data available. Since inter-country contrasts in such shares reflect not only the efficiency differentials of national financial institutions but also the influence of formal and informal barriers to domestic and global markets, the resulting measures are best regarded as indicators of comparative performance, one of the most important influences on which will be national contrasts in the inherent efficiency of the financial service industries.

Chapter 2 also sets out criteria for the selection of those financial markets for which country shares are measured and analysed. To make the research manageable, consideration is first restricted to the general ambit of the operations of security houses, investment banks, merchant banks and the non-retail activities of commercial banks. At a second stage individual markets were selected on the basis of a variety of criteria: market size; participation by all banking types; the coverage of both old and new markets; and data availability.

In the event country shares have been measured and analysed for the following markets: the market for foreign exchange; the market for merger and acquisition advice; the market for syndicated bank loans; the Eurobond market; the international equity market; the Eurocommercial paper market; and the market for Euro medium-term notes. As can be seen, market selection has been strongly biased in favour of international rather than domestic arenas since these tend to be large, less regulated and have few entry barriers, so that the financial institutions of all countries compete on an equal footing.

Preliminary work on the project also made it apparent that merely to assess, by whatever means, the comparative efficiency of the financial service industries of different countries as it is at present would fail to provide an adequate basis for judging comparative performance after 1992. Clearly it is equally important to know in which direction, relative to other countries, Britain's performance has been changing. This requires that considerable attention be devoted to recent and longer-term developments in country market shares, a task undertaken in Chapter 3 where each of the selected markets is allocated a sub-section tracing the manner in which the shares of countries participating in that market developed during the 1980s.

This historical chapter also opens the search for explanations of the size of market shares obtained by British financial institutions and their principal rivals. This quest is pursued in Chapter 4, which comprises a more detailed analysis of the selected markets for 1989. Each country's share in each market is explained in terms of the number of its financial institutions active in the market, the number of financial units produced per firm, and the average value of these units. Britain's performance relative to its competitors is then compared for each of these share-determining factors, first *vis-à-vis* the United States and second relative to other countries. Country shares have also been aggregated across markets, an exercise which suggests that, in terms of this study's product coverage, the United Kingdom ranks second overall, after the United States. An important by-product of this 1989 market analysis is a Schedule of Market Participation, which lists, by nationality, all the financial institutions which held significant shares in 1989 in one or more of the selected markets. This list, which runs to almost a hundred institutions, has been further exploited in this study.

First it forms the basis of a statistical comparison of national banking sectors which is presented in Chapter 5. Data derived from the 1989 annual reports and accounts of these financial institutions have been grouped and aggregated by nationality and then compared between countries in an attempt to determine whether there exist specific national characteristics which may influence the performance of a nation's financial institutions in international markets. These inter-country comparisons relate to average firm size, factor ratios, income components, cost structures and personnel remuneration.

Secondly, this same list of participating financial institutions constituted the framework for a series of interviews undertaken to identify the causes of inter-country contrasts in the performance of financial institutions. This facet of the research was facilitated by the fact that virtually all firms on the list had branches, subsidiaries or other kinds of representation in London. An approach by letter yielded 36 such interviews. Country coverage was good, with institutions from most of the major players (the United Kingdom, United States, Japan, Switzerland, Germany, France, Canada and the Nordic Group) participating. There was also full cross-sectional representation of the financial service sector, with the inclusion of commercial banks, investment banks, merchant banks and security houses. The bulk of the interviews took place in London but some were conducted in Paris, Geneva and Frankfurt.

The information and views recorded in these interviews constitute the main basis (though other sources have also been drawn upon) of Chapter 6. This chapter extends the search for, and identification of, the factors which do most to explain the relative performance of Britain's financial institutions and their principal rivals. Among the explanatory factors which have been considered and analysed are: human resources, capital, levels of technology, innovation and the more significant regulatory parameters.

Another set of influences on the comparative performance of national financial sectors, discussed at length, are those associated with economies of scope and scale in banking operations of the type covered in this study. It was felt necessary to pay special attention to the impact on comparative performance of the structures, and changes therein, which characterise the banking industries of different countries, in particular to mergers within commercial banking and investment banking sectors, and between commercial banks and investment banks, in each case both domestic and cross-nationality.

The impact and relevance of domestic conditions on relative performance is also explored in Chapter 6. Whilst the study is essentially concerned with competitiveness in international financial markets, it emerged that the nature of domestic markets, their size and accessibility, is highly relevant to the performance in these markets of a country's financial institutions, as are interest-rate levels and the international role of the domestic currency.

The salient findings are assembled in Chapter 7, where special attention is directed towards the comparative performance of the British financial sector and to its competitive prospects in the immediate, post-1992, future. The timing of this project requires that great care must be exercised when gauging future developments. The research extended over the period 1989 to 1991, when the financial markets upon which attention has been focused were for the most part severely depressed and characterised by excess capacity in the financial sectors which served them. For this, and a variety of other reasons amongst which bad debt provisions rank high, the national banking sectors which are the central focus of this study were in general experiencing difficult trading conditions. As the study was being concluded there were indications, primarily in the operational results of American investment banks though rather less so in the case of commercial banks, that a corner was being turned. An attempt has been made when assembling the results of the study to minimise and look beyond the relatively short-term vicissitudes of this period in the search for an assessment of Britain's underlying comparative performance.

2

ASSESSING THE COMPARATIVE PERFORMANCE OF FINANCIAL SERVICES

An article which analyses the impact on the British economy of the 1992 initiative to remove barriers in a single European market begins in the case of the financial service industries: 'It is generally accepted that the UK has a comparative advantage in the provision of financial services' (Lloyds Bank, 1989). Below we survey and assess the kind of evidence which hitherto has been used to gauge the comparative efficiency and performance of national financial sectors and devise a measure which, against this background and taking account of data availability, can be pressed into use for the purposes of this study.

THE COMPARATIVE SIZE OF FINANCIAL SERVICE SECTORS

At one end of the analytical spectrum the comparative efficiency of different countries' financial sectors has been inferred very simplistically from the attitudes of their respective governments to the liberalisation of trade in financial services. The support for freedom of competition and international establishment in banking which tends to be a feature of the policy, for example, of the United States and the United Kingdom, is thought to imply and reflect the fact that these countries 'enjoy a comparative advantage in banking relative to nearly all other nations in the world'. Thus 'one reflection of the belief in United States comparative advantage in service industries is the strong effort the United States has been making to reduce barriers to what is referred to as trade in services'. In contrast a predominance, at least until recently, of protectionist attitudes in countries such as Canada, Sweden, Australia, Brazil and Taiwan has been seen to indicate the absence of such comparative advantage (Kravis and Lipsey, 1988, and Gray and Walter, 1983).

In a somewhat more sophisticated fashion attention is frequently drawn to the size of a country's financial sector as a positive indicator of its efficiency. In some cases attention is focused on the absolute scale of activities, an approach based in part on expectations of the internal and external economies which may in consequence arise. Thus in support of the above assertion about the superior efficiency of British financial services emphasis was placed *inter alia* on the fact that 'daily foreign exchange turnover is estimated to be roughly twice as high in London as in New York or Tokyo' and that 'London has 56 per cent of the international market for insurance'; the external economies associated with the scale of financial activities in the City were also stressed (Lloyds Bank, 1989). The importance of size, both of individual firms and whole sectors, in the context of international banking has received a great deal of attention (Revell, 1985).

More frequently, however, interest is directed towards the size of a financial sector in relation to the total economy of the country in question. Although no rationale for such an approach may be explicitly cited there is an expectation, based on international trade theory, that activities in which a country enjoys a comparative advantage will bulk relatively large in the economy. Another, again implicit, reason for focusing attention on proportionate industry size is that, assuming each developed country has approximately the same (proportionate) domestic need for financial services, there is a presumption that the surplus output will be exported from those countries where the financial service sector is relatively large, and this in turn is taken to be a reflection of the comparative efficiency of financial services in that country.

For thirteen countries Oulton has collated and presented data for the relative sizes of the financial services sectors (Oulton, 1986, table 2.3). Based on OECD sources the results reveal that in 1983 value added in British financial services constituted 15.6 per cent of total GDP, somewhat greater than the (unweighted) average of 12.9 per cent registered for all the selected countries. The individual proportions in descending order were: United States 22.3 per cent, France 17.4 per cent, Japan 16.9 per cent, United Kingdom 15.6 per cent, Denmark 14.5 per cent, the Netherlands 14.3 per cent, Belgium 14.0 per cent, Canada 12.8 per cent, Germany 11.4 per cent, Spain 9.5 per cent, Portugal 7.7 per cent, Greece 7.3 per cent and Ireland 4.5 per cent. A feature of such comparisons which emerged in the above exercise is the difficulty of ensuring international compatibility in the definition of the financial services sectors being measured. Whilst in principle the above measures relate to 'finance, insurance, real estate and business services', in the case of Canada, Greece, Japan and the United Kingdom business services were excluded and for Germany, Ireland, Portugal and Spain, business services and real estate, wholly or in part, were left out of account.

This source shows that, for the same year and again based on OECD data, when measured by the proportion of the occupied population, the relative size of the British financial services sector, 8.7 per cent, is somewhat larger than the (unweighted) arithmetic average for 12 countries, 6.5 per cent, and in fact ranks third from the highest after the United States, 11.8 per cent, and Canada, 9.7 per cent (Oulton, 1986, table 2.5).

The 'Cecchini Report' contains a similar analysis but one based on European Community statistics for 1985 and defines the financial service sector as 'credit and insurance institutions'. This shows that compared with an unweighted average of 7.3 per cent (weighted 6.4 per cent) for eight principal members of the Community, value added in the British financial service sector constituted 11.8 per cent of total GDP. In descending order the relative sizes of the sector in these countries were: Luxembourg 14.9 per cent, United Kingdom 11.8 per cent, Spain 6.4 per cent, Belgium 5.7 per cent, Germany 5.4 per cent, Netherlands 5.2 per cent, Italy 4.9 per cent and France 4.3 per cent (EEC, 1988).

Apart from suggesting that the relative size of the British financial sector is large compared with that of its major continental competitors these data emphasise, as much, the discrepancies in results which can arise using different statistical sources and alternative definitions of financial services. In the case of the six countries for which the comparison is feasible (Belgium, Germany, Spain, France, the Netherlands and the United Kingdom) there is a negative correlation between the sizes of their financial service sectors as measured on the basis of OECD and EEC value added data and definitions.

Other indicators assembled in the Cecchini Report also suggest that the British financial services sector may be comparatively large: Britain emerges as top of the above eight member countries in terms of insurance premiums as a percentage of GDP, second on the basis of bank loans (headed by Luxembourg), and third using stock market capitalisation (after Luxembourg and the Netherlands).

INTERNATIONAL PRODUCTIVITY COMPARISONS OF
FINANCIAL SERVICES

For both goods and service industries there are two broad approaches to the comparison and assessment of international competitiveness. On the one hand the cost-based approach focuses, in particular, on such variables as relative labour productivity, unit labour costs and export prices. On the other attention can be directed to revealed comparative advantage using data for export values and market shares. Here we consider the first of these approaches in the context of financial services and return to the latter in the following section.

Over the past two or three decades a whole economic discipline has

developed around international productivity comparisons for manufacturing industries, especially those for labour productivity. Such
analyses are still rare in the case of service activities principally, but
not entirely, because of practical difficulties associated with output
measurement.

Two methods have been favoured for making international productivity comparisons in industrial activities. The first, normally based
on census data, seeks to compare between countries for a given
activity, physical output per person employed or per man-hour, with
different units being aggregated on the basis of suitable value weights.
Whilst there is no record of this approach having been applied to
financial services, the development of inter-temporal output measures
based on numbers of service output units suggests that it is an avenue
which might be fruitfully explored in an inter-spatial context. It has
been found practicable in the case of both the British banking and life
insurance industries to base inter-temporal output measures on
changes in numbers of the various kinds of accounts, transactions and
insurance policies, new and in existence (Smith, 1989). It might prove
feasible to extend this methodology to international output and
productivity comparisons using national statistical sources equivalent
to those drawn upon in the United Kingdom, or in the case of
banking, the type of data collected periodically by the Bank for
International Settlements (BIS, 1985).

A second method used for making international labour productivity
comparisons in the case of goods-producing industries involves
deflating to a common currency, using appropriate purchasing power
parities, the value added per unit of labour for a given industry in
different countries. Some use has been made of this kind of approach
for international labour productivity comparisons in the distributive
trades (Smith and Hitchens, 1985) and more recently it has been
essayed by the National Economic Development Council (NEDC,
1988) in the case of financial services.

The results of this latter exercise suggest that if real value added per
employee in the British banking and insurance sector is taken as unity
then corresponding productivity levels in major continental rivals are
lower at: Italy 0.85, Germany, 0.62, France 0.52, Belgium 0.46 and
the Netherlands 0.45.[1] Results which are similar in nature, though not
numerically identical since the approach obviates the use of purchasing power parities, can be derived from combining the proportions of
value added with those for manpower shares of the financial sectors
presented in the 'Cecchini Report'.[2] If in each country the sector's
share of value added is divided by its manpower share the following
results emerge: Belgium 1.50, Germany 1.80, Spain 2.29, France 1.54,

Italy 2.72, Luxembourg 2.61, the Netherlands 1.41 and the United Kingdom 3.19. Two features of these results merit attention. First the fact that all the ratios are greater than unity demonstrates that in each country labour productivity in financial services lies above the average for the economy as a whole. Secondly, if the result for the United Kingdom is taken as unity, the comparative productivity performance of financial services in other countries emerges as: Italy 0.85, Luxembourg 0.82, Spain 0.72, Germany 0.56, France 0.48, Belgium 0.47 and the Netherlands 0.44. Not unexpectedly, given the methodological similarity and overlap in the data sources, these results are close to those obtained by the NEDC. Nevertheless confidence in the reliability of either set of findings is hardly inspired by the high ranking with which Italy's financial sector emerges.

For a variety of reasons such measures are far from satisfactory as indicators of comparative levels of national efficiency in the provision of financial services. It has been demonstrated that the results vary with the data sources used but these methods are also flawed in other, more fundamental ways.

First, a major weakness is that, relating as they do to the whole financial sector, the measures are much too highly aggregative to be very instructive. Secondly, and even more important, the national income data on which they are based (sectoral contributions to GDP and labour force data) are such that the measures reflect not only the scale and productivity of domestically-owned financial service organisations in a given economy but also embrace the activities of foreign-owned units which are located in the same country. The implications of this distinction between nationality of ownership and location of financial services for international efficiency comparisons are especially significant in the case of financial services. Particularly in the case of Britain, the comparatively large size of the financial service sector reflects to a substantial extent the presence in the City of a large number of foreign-owned financial institutions. To the extent that the measures of comparative efficiency cited above place the United Kingdom in the upper part of any league table, it is possible that its position may be due to the location in it of many highly efficient but foreign-owned financial service organisations rather than to the performance of domestically-owned institutions. Thirdly, measures of this kind fail to take account of capital inputs.

An analysis of data collected on an international basis for the world's largest banks goes some way towards dealing with the problems raised by both aggregation and nationality. Information about shareholders' capital, total assets, profits and employment are collected and published annually for the largest banks by both

Table 2.1 *Bank assets per employee, by country*

Country	1986[a]				1987[b]	
	No. of banks	Assets ($bn)	No. of employees ('000)	Assets per employee ($mn)	No. of banks	Assets per employee ($mn)
Japan	70	3716.8	358.9	10.4	107	11.6
Switzerland	14	326.6	68.2	4.8	15	6.0
Germany	39	1086.7	228.8	4.7	44	5.9
Sweden	6	115.2	25.4	4.5	7	5.6
Austria	7	115.7	26.5	4.4	9	5.7
Belgium	9	208.0	58.2	3.6	9	4.6
Italy	35	697.8	226.8	3.1	33	3.7
Norway	3	42.1	13.8	3.0	4	2.5
Denmark	8	78.9	29.5	2.7	8	2.8
France	13	869.6	350.6	2.5	20	3.1
Netherlands	4	226.2	96.4	2.3	5	3.0
Finland	5	66.0	29.0	2.3	5	3.1
United States	121	1956.9	1058.6	1.8	87	1.9
Canada	7	285.1	156.7	1.8	7	1.9
Spain	12	184.7	136.9	1.3	13	1.9
United Kingdom	18	546.7	454.6	1.2	15	1.3
Ireland	2	19.3	17.7	1.1	2	1.6
Australia	7	132.3	160.2	0.8	7	1.0

[a] *Euromoney*, June 1987: data presented in this source for Luxembourg banks suggests assets per employee of $5.1 million.
[b] *The Banker*, July 1988.

Euromoney and *The Banker*. Table 2.1 shows the outcome of grouping these banks on a country basis and comparing internationally the levels of assets per employee.[3] Since only the world's largest banks are covered in this list then those allocated to each country are essentially domestically owned.[4] The table suggests that when ranked on the basis of assets handled per employee these eighteen developed countries fall into four groups whether regard is paid to the *Euromoney* series for 1986 or *The Banker* series for 1987. Isolated at the top of the table stands Japan with assets per employee running at more than $10 million. There follows a group of four European countries, Switzerland, Germany, Sweden and Austria, with comparatively high per capita asset levels, though no more than half those managed on average by Japanese bank employees. A third group of countries, Belgium, Italy, Norway, Denmark, France, the Netherlands and Finland, have ratios which centre around the (unweighted) average for all these national banking sectors, about $3 million in 1986 and $3.5 million in 1987. Finally a group of six countries, the United States, Canada, Spain, United Kingdom, Ireland and Australia, lie at the foot of the table with per capita assets in the region of $1 to $2 million.

The volume of assets handled per employee is at best a very crude indicator of comparative international productivity levels in banking. As calculated above it is a measure which for instance is arbitrarily affected by changes in exchange rates *vis-à-vis* the US dollar. Even more substantively this measure will be influenced by the balance which obtains, in the case of each country, between commercial retail banking, for which assets per employee are relatively low, and wholesale banking where per capita asset levels tend to be high.[5] Thirdly, banks with low assets per employee may derive a relatively high proportion of their income from fees. Nevertheless, the international contrasts in table 2.1 and the low position of the United Kingdom are sufficiently marked to invite further analysis and speculation in an exercise undertaken in Chapter 5.

Whilst the use of asset levels as a surrogate output indicator may be questioned (in Chapter 5 bank income is used for this purpose) the practice of focusing only on labour inputs in the above, and all the preceding productivity measures, is equally open to challenge. To assess comparative international efficiency, what is ideally required is a measure, for the specified activity, of total factor productivity. Even in the case of manufacturing, where international comparisons of labour productivity have become commonplace, few attempts have been made to measure international total factor productivities differentials. Yet the relative capital intensity which characterises the production of financial services requires, *a fortiori*, that to be relevant for assessing international competitiveness, inter-country comparisons of productivity should take account of capital as well as labour inputs.

Given the data limitations which have restricted manufacturing studies to labour productivity comparisons, there seems little immediate prospect of international comparisons of financial services being based on levels of total factor productivity. Inter-country comparisons of the prices charged for specified goods and services avoid the difficulties associated with comparative assessments based on productivity levels but only by raising other problems. Whilst in principle price comparisons automatically take account of international productivity differentials as well as country differences in factor prices, the extent to which they also reflect, *inter alia*, monopoly and protectionist elements means that they too are imperfect indicators of comparative international efficiency and competitiveness.

Using data compiled by Price Waterhouse the Cecchini Report compares the prices charged for a range of financial services in eight

Community countries (EEC, 1988 and Price Waterhouse, 1988). The comparisons relate to seven banking services, five insurance products and four activities associated with security transactions. In each case the price applicable in each country is expressed as a percentage of the average of the four lowest observations. British prices emerge as fourth lowest in banking, third lowest in security transactions and second lowest in insurance. Overall, on this criterion, the Netherlands would seem to possess the most competitive financial services sector with average prices 9 per cent above the base, followed in second place by the United Kingdom with a 13 per cent differential, and then in turn Luxembourg 17 per cent, Belgium 23 per cent, France 24 per cent, Germany 25 per cent, Italy 29 per cent and Spain 34 per cent. Little consistency is to be found in the country patterns between the results obtained for the three separate financial services. The position of Italy and Spain reinforces the view that these comparisons may reflect monopoly elements which exist in each country as a result of regulations effectively protecting the domestic market as well as contrasts in operational efficiency.[6]

REVEALED COMPARATIVE ADVANTAGE IN SERVICES

For a variety of reasons (difficulties associated with measuring service outputs, the inadequacy of labour productivity measures and the failings of price comparisons) the productivity/cost based approach towards assessing international competitiveness does not readily lend itself to financial service industries. Therefore attempts have been made to apply an alternative approach which has been used with some success in the case of goods-producing industries and is based on what has become known as revealed comparative advantage. This method 'which can be termed the specialisation approach, stems from the observation that, as a result of countries exploiting their competitiveness in certain products . . . each country's exports should be dominated by these products in which its degree of comparative advantage is significant' (Petersen and Barras, 1987).

Petersen and Barras have adopted this method in a study of exports of a single, broadly defined, group of tradeable services from 22 countries, developed and undeveloped. Included, for each country, are 'shipment, other transportation and passenger services, travel and tourism and other private services'. For each country they calculate the share of this service category in total exports and adjust for the size of each economy as measured by GDP and also for the 'openess' of the country as reflected in the ratio of total exports to GDP. The authors acknowledge that the results of the exercise are in some respects 'odd'. It emerges, for example, that low comparative advantage is a feature of services supplied by the United States, Germany, Japan, Canada, Australia, South Africa, Brazil and Bangladesh; whilst Spain, Austria, Mexico, Greece and Egypt are the countries enjoying, on this criterion, the highest comparative advantages in services. The United Kingdom features in an intermediate group.

As the authors recognise, such intuitively unconvincing results may well be due to the fact that an aggregative analysis of this kind conceals authentic underlying differences in competitiveness which exist at the level of individual service industries. Oulton went some way towards remedying this deficiency by analysing revealed international comparative advantage separately for 'Freight and Insurance' and 'Other Private Services', the latter category including banking and non-merchandise insurance activities (Oulton, 1986). His data show that the British share of fifteen developed countries' exports of 'Freight and Insurance' fell from 42 per cent in 1959/60 to 15 per cent in 1979/80; the United States' share also declined over this period, whilst the performance of France, the Netherlands and Japan, measured in this way, improved. At the same time the United Kingdom's share of the fifteen countries' exports of 'Other Private Services' declined from 25 per cent to 14 per cent; in this case the United States' performance again deteriorated, whilst Belgium/Luxembourg, Denmark, Germany and Japan improved their positions. Measured against total British exports the share of 'Freight and Insurance' declined from 9 per cent to 4 per cent at a time when the share of 'Other Private Services' remained approximately unchanged at about 8 per cent (Oulton, 1986, tables A5.2, A5.5, A5.9 and A5.12).

Oulton computes two measures of comparative advantage for these service complexes in the fifteen developed countries. First a measure referred to as 'competitiveness' is derived from the trade balance standardised by GDP, that is for each service and each country:

$$(\text{Exports} - \text{Imports}) / \text{GDP} \times 100$$

Secondly, he measures revealed comparative advantage (RCA) by:

$$\frac{\text{share of country } j \text{ in (all countries') exports of product } i}{\text{share of country } j \text{ in (all countries') exports of all products}} \times 100$$

$$= \frac{\text{share of product } i \text{ in country } j\text{'s total exports}}{\text{share of product } i \text{ in total (all countries') exports}} \times 100$$

This is Balassa's measure of revealed comparative advantage, originally applied to manufacturing (Balassa, 1965), which in turn is equivalent to the revealed comparative advantage measure adopted by Petersen and Barras (1987).

In the case of 'Freight and Insurance' the first measure suggests that in 1979/80 Britain was just competitive (with a small positive result) and that its competitiveness has declined over time; on this score Denmark returned the best performance. The revealed comparative advantage indicator yields a more favourable British result though again one which deteriorated over time. On this basis the United Kingdom was bettered only by Denmark and Japan. For 'Other Private Services' the first measure suggests that British competitiveness has improved somewhat over the period whilst still lagging behind Switzerland, Greece, Belgium/Luxembourg and Denmark. The revealed comparative advantage result for this group of services points to a fairly stable British performance over the years but one which is inferior to Greece, Belgium/Luxembourg, Switzerland and Denmark (Oulton, 1986). It would seem from these measures, in the case of both 'Freight and Insurance' and 'Other Private Services', that at the beginning of the 1980s Britain had a comparative advantage relative to its major European competitors, Germany, France and Italy, and also to the United States and Japan, though one which had tended to decline over the years.

Yet doubts must remain about how realistic such results are for two bundles of activity that are still highly aggregative and combine very different types of service. For example the collapse in the share of 'Freight and Insurance' in Britain's exports may be largely due to developments in the shipping market, although export earnings of the United Kingdom's insurance underwriting have also fallen. Yet both national and international systems for compiling and presenting service trade flows are such that further disaggregation is virtually impossible.

In short, an application of the revealed comparative advantage method to these service trade flows is severely impaired by statistical shortcomings. The above measures were derived from trade data which had been standardised and compiled using the IMF classification. Whilst this source is suitable for the broad-based, aggregative, service trade analysis undertaken by Oulton it is totally inadequate for identifying international trade flows in financial services as a whole let alone for those of individual financial service industries. The reason for this is that financial service trade flows are spread among several categories of the IMF classification and for no individual classification do they account for the whole flow: merchandise insurance is included as an indistinguishable element along with freight, in category 2; fee income of banks and other financial institutions is lumped together with trade flows in a wide variety of other services in the portmanteau category 6 'Other Goods, Services and Income: Private and Other'; whilst net interest receipts of banks, that is margins between borrowing and lending rates, are hidden in part of category 5, 'Other (Private) Investment Income'.

This, for the present purpose, highly unsatisfactory statistical treatment of trade flows in financial services, reflects national practice. The British balance of payments accounts show for insurance, banking and brokers a separate figure of credits for services, that is commissions, fees and premiums (less claims) net of any expenses incurred by the institutions concerned (CSO, 1988, tables 3.6 and 6.1). However it is impossible to identify as a separate category the equivalent payments by United Kingdom residents to overseas suppliers of the same services[7] so that no measure is available for the trade balance of this group of financial services as a whole, and certainly not for banking, insurance and brokerage separately.

An inspection of balance of payments statistics not only confirms the practical handicaps faced by the application of revealed comparative advantage analysis to financial services, it also reveals that the approach itself is deficient by failing to take account of additional relevant international financial flows. Other elements of major importance in the balance payment statistics, namely inward and outward foreign direct investment, together with the credit and debit income flows associated with them, reflect to a substantial degree the activities and performance of domestic and overseas financial service institutions. As Petersen and Barras write, 'countries may exploit their comparative advantage by extending their operations into other countries' economies. In cases such as this export data could be unreliable because the export earnings, which are supposed to 'reflect' comparative advantage, would accrue to the country of location rather than the country of origin' (Petersen and Barras, 1987).

Whilst much might be deduced about the past, present and future competitiveness of a country's financial service industries from the extent and international patterns of its foreign direct investment in these activities, such an approach has been rejected in this study in favour of a modified form of revealed comparative advantage.

THE ANALYSIS OF COUNTRY MARKET SHARES

It is clear from the contents of the previous section that attempts to apply revealed comparative advantage to financial services have been marred not so much by inherent defects in the method itself but by the nature of, and weaknesses which characterise, the nationally and internationally compiled trade flows to which it has been applied. First the trade flows in question are much too highly aggregated to yield very useful results. Secondly by including, on the one hand, some offshore activities of non-national firms whilst, on the other, excluding offshore activities of national firms, these basic trade data fail to measure even approximately the performance of national financial sectors.

The data contained in league tables which record the performance of individual financial institutions in certain financial markets, and which are compiled by, and appear on a regular basis in journals and the financial press, are entirely free from these two major deficiencies. First the data are available for specific self-contained, essentially homogeneous, financial markets and products. Secondly all the operations of a given financial institution are in principle included whether they are conducted from a national or overseas base. By aggregating the shares obtained in a specific market by the financial institutions of a given nationality the performance in this sense of the country in question may be measured and compared with the shares, similarly calculated, won by other countries' financial institutions in the same market. This approach has been adopted in this study as the principal means of measuring relative performance and to provide a framework for the analysis of the major factors which give rise to inter-country differences in performance as quantified in this way.

The method can be illustrated by applying it to the market for worldwide merger and acquisition (M&A) advice in 1989. The relevant league table compiled by *Euromoney* shows, for each of the top 40 financial institutions active in this market, the total value (and number) of M&A deals in which they participated. When these institutions are grouped, and their results aggregated, on the basis of nationality of ownership and control, it emerges that this market was shared between the major countries in the following manner: United States 71.2 per cent, United Kingdom 19.0 per cent, France 4.4 per cent and Canada 3.7 per cent.

It is useful to recapitulate what this approach seeks to achieve and, by inference, to identify those aspects of international competitiveness with which it is not primarily concerned. The basic objective, as set out above, is to illuminate the performance of certain financial institutions functioning under British ownership and control, wherever they operate, in comparison with institutions of other nationalities, again regardless of their location. For this purpose it is appropriate to aggregate market shares, as shown in the relevant league tables, on the basis of nationality of institution. In sharp contrast an assessment of the comparative advantage of undertaking business in, say, London as opposed to other financial centres is not the purpose of the study. This does not imply that the latter question is of no importance – indeed it is currently the subject of a major research project[8] – nor that there is no overlap between these two facets of international competitiveness in financial services.

Nevertheless the relative performance of national financial sectors is quite distinct from the relative attractions of different financial centres and their individual implications for a country's national income, balance of payments and employment levels are quite different. For instance the location and operation of a foreign-owned bank in the City brings substantial benefits to the United Kingdom in the form of income and employment generation and also, to the extent that it engages in offshore activities, to the British balance of payments. On the other hand the fruits of the successful overseas operations of a British bank are largely identified with the impact on the United Kingdom national income and balance of payments of repatriated profits.

The distinction between these two facets of international competition in financial services is reflected in a comparison of, on the one hand, banking assets broken down by nationality of bank and, on the other, their geographical (country) location. Data provided by the Bank for International Settlements show that Japanese, American, German, French and British banks own most assets with shares in the total of respectively 36.1 per cent, 12.4 per cent, 9.0 per cent, 8.7 per cent and 4.8 per cent. A geographical analysis carried out by the Bank of England reveals asset shares held in these countries, irrespective of nationality of ownership, to be, respectively, 16.8 per cent, 13.5 per cent, 3.6 per cent, 4.7 per cent and 10 per cent (BIS, 1990 and *Bank of England Quarterly Bulletin*, August 1991, table 13.1). Clearly the total of banking assets held in the United Kingdom is much larger than the total held worldwide by British banks.

It also merits emphasis that, since much of the ensuing analysis is based on market shares as measured in the above merger and acquisition advice example, then the resulting revealed performance will be influenced by a wide variety of factors (including industrial structure, regulatory regimes and domestic economic conditions) as well as by the intrinsic efficiency of the financial institutions in question. However, as shown in the following section, by focusing attention on those international financial markets where operating conditions are similar for all participating institutions, it is believed that comparative institutional efficiency will play a substantive part in shaping the national market shares that emerge.

Alongside such conceptual parameters within which this study is confined, some practical limitations should also be noted. First the tables embrace only those institutions with the largest shares though it emerges that with the relatively high degree of concentration which typically characterises the financial markets in question, the bulk of the market is covered in most cases. In practice this deficiency means that the larger country shares tend to be somewhat overstated whilst minor country shares may not be registered. The results of sensitivity tests that have been carried out and which are reproduced at a later stage suggest that any distortion in the pattern of country market shares which may arise in consequence of this weakness is not very significant.

Secondly, there are one or two instances of ambiguity about the nationality of a given financial institution, though the scale of this problem proves to be less than might have been anticipated. Specific cases are noted in Chapter 4, where it becomes clear that these uncertainties are not such as to distort the results.

Thirdly the value data on which these country shares are based do not relate to the earnings which the financial institutions derived from these markets but rather to the value of deals or issues with which they are associated. This is taken into account when an attempt is made in Chapter 4 to aggregate country shares across markets to obtain a picture of the global performance of the major players. This latter exercise is affected by a third deficiency: the fact that the requisite league tables are not compiled for all financial markets.

THE CHOICE OF MARKETS

The type of market for which this kind of league table data are available effectively restricts the general ambit of the study to the operations of security houses, investment banks and certain non-retail activities of commercial banks. This initial narrowing of the scope of the enquiry still leaves a plethora of services, markets and 'products' for which such financial institutions are responsible and from which the final choice needs to be made. A second stage selection procedure has therefore been based on a variety of criteria. First, since complete market coverage is impracticable, it is necessary (to enhance the representativeness of the results) to ensure that among those activities to which attention is directed there should be a significant number of absolutely large global markets. Secondly, again to promote representativeness, the cross-section of selected markets should be such that the activities of all the relevant industry sub-sectors – commercial banks, investment banks, merchant banks and security houses – are somewhere captured. Thirdly it is desirable that new as well as long-standing international markets be analysed. They are relevant because of their future growth potential and for revealing the alacrity, or lack of it, with which the financial institutions of different countries respond to new opportunities.

The choice of market has been strongly biased in favour of financial services that are traded in international rather than domestic arenas. Euromarkets in particular have been favoured in the selection process. First such markets are intrinsically interesting because of the size they have attained or promise to attain. Secondly, and even more significantly, Euromarkets are essentially unregulated in such a way that the financial institutions of all countries may compete on an equal footing. The field is essentially level for all players, especially those operating from London, although domestic loyalties still play an important role.[9] In short, country shares of such markets should prove a superior guide to the inherent competitiveness of their respective financial institutions than do domestic financial markets where for a variety of reasons, regulatory or less formalised, national institutions enjoy advantages that owe nothing to their intrinsic efficiency.

The strength of such influences in shaping market shares is evident from the fact that in contrast to expectations about the inroads which foreign competitors would make into United Kingdom equity markets when the 1986 Big Bang opened regulatory doors, by 1990 no more than three British houses, Smith New Court, Warburgs and BZW, continued to control between them as much as 45–70 per cent of the market (*The Banker*, May, 1990). As a consequence of favouring Euromarkets in our analysis it is anticipated that the conditions which characterise them should help to isolate and identify the impact of pure institutional efficiency on the market shares won by the financial institutions of different nationalities.

On the basis of these criteria seven markets have been selected for special scrutiny and are examined in Chapter 3 in a sequence based broadly on their age: the market for foreign exchange, the market for merger and acquisition services, the market for syndicated bank loans, the Eurobond market, the international equity market, the Eurocommercial paper market and the market for Euro medium-term notes. The first two of these markets are long established, the following two are essentially post-World War II phenomena whilst, to all intents and purposes, the latter three were born in the 1980s.

Apart from its longevity the major relevant features of the market for foreign exchange are its size, in terms both of gross flows and institutional earnings, and its concentration among commercial banks: the same two features are also common to the market for syndicated loans. Longevity and market size are characteristics of merger and acquisition advisory services but this activity has been the perquisite principally of investment and merchant banks. Whilst the Eurobond market is very large and that for Eurocommercial paper substantial, the nascent markets for medium-term notes and international equities are as yet comparatively small. In the case of the first three of these markets participants are to be found alike amongst the ranks of commercial banks, investment banks and security houses, though the market for international equities is essentially the preserve of the latter.

This choice of activities is reasonably representative of the full range of traded financial services. The classification scheme postulated by Walter prescribes the following types: (a) deposit taking (demand and time deposits of residents and non-residents in foreign on-shore accounts and Euro-deposits in offshore accounts); (b) international trading and dealing in foreign currencies, forward exchange contracts, financial futures and options and so on; (c) international trade services (trade documentation, letters of credit); (d) international lending; (e) international securities business; and (f) other investment banking activities such as merger and acquisition advice and financial advisory services (Walter, 1988). Our particular selection of markets means that activities under headings (a) and (c) are excluded from consideration: (b) is represented by the foreign exchange market, (d) by syndicated loans, (e) by Eurobonds, international equities and Eurocommercial paper and (f) by merger and acquisition advice.

Besides leaving out of account retail banking activities, the study excludes derivative markets, for example futures and options, a range of domestic markets, such as the markets for equities and commercial paper, and secondary markets, even in the case of Eurobonds, international equities and Eurocommercial paper. Also excluded are fund management and private banking activities.

3

CHANGES IN COUNTRY SHARES OF SELECTED FINANCIAL MARKETS

INTRODUCTION

The previous chapter identified specific markets for financial services for which country shares can be measured and analysed. Such an analysis is carried out in some depth for a single year, 1989, in Chapter 4. Early stages of the research suggested, however, that much could also be learned about the comparative performance of the financial institutions of different countries by tracing the manner in which country shares of the selected markets have changed over time. The present chapter is addressed to this task.

Each of the seven selected markets is allocated here a section which, as far as possible, follows a common format: a description of the financial instrument in question and of the market's origins; the tabular presentation of, and commentary on, the country market shares which emerge and their changes over time; the identification of specific factors (historical, institutional, product size, currency structures and nationality of market users) which may have helped to determine these market shares; together with a brief assessment of possible future market trends. Special attention is paid throughout to the role and performance of individual financial institutions.

The salient findings, with special reference to the performance of British banks, are summarised in a final section.

THE FOREIGN EXCHANGE MARKET

Though financial institutions have always exchanged currency in return for commission for the finance of trade this market grew substantially when the industrialised countries switched to floating exchange rates in the early 1970s. A new range of financial instruments was then developed for corporate clients seeking to hedge against exchange-rate movements and reduce the cost of raising foreign capital. The simplest of these instruments are forward contracts, options, and currency swaps. Since contracts and options are tradeable, secondary markets have developed. In connection with the foreign exchange market some banks also sell forecasting services.

The appearance of this range of instruments, the continued growth in the need for foreign exchange that is associated with an increase in international trade and the major currency requirements more recently associated with the mushrooming international investment flows of portfolio investors, life insurance companies and pension funds have all combined to yield a rapid growth in the market for foreign exchange. A survey by the Federal Reserve Bank of New York suggests that, over a ten-year period, the United States foreign exchange market alone has expanded twelve fold (Cross, 1988). It has been estimated that by the end of 1989 the market was running at a level of more than $400 billion per day (*Euromoney*, January 1990).

The relative fixing of some European exchange rates through the ERM and bilateral exchange rate pegging by some other countries has done little to restrain market growth because the most heavily traded currencies (the yen, Deutschmark, dollar) continue to float against one another. Coordinated central bank efforts to realign certain currencies have been generally unsuccessful and so do not seem to have disturbed private sector currency trading.

Innovation in the market appears to have been supply-led with financial institutions developing new instruments for sale to corporate treasurers. This same growth in new instruments has so far compensated for a narrowing of margins consequent upon interbank competition so that foreign exchange earnings were responsible for an increasing proportion of many banks' profits in the 1980s. On the negative side large multinational corporations now rely mainly on their own currency dealing rooms.

Foreign currencies are mostly traded in six world financial centres: London, New York, Frankfurt, Bahrain, Singapore and Tokyo. At the beginning of 1986 the Bank of England conducted a survey which suggested that London's share stood at about 40 per cent (*Bank of England Quarterly Bulletin*, September 1986). Now that currency trading continues round the clock, London gains from being favourably placed among time zones; all the main operators have dealing rooms there. The same survey found that 90 per cent of transactions were between banks and that less than 10 per cent involved corporate clients directly. Commercial banks continue to dominate the market but some American investment banks, notably Goldman Sachs and Salomon Brothers, have recently established a presence. For the most part however the foreign activities of investment banks, merchant banks and security houses are directed towards their internal operations, oiling the machinery of the deals and issues which they undertake.

The total volume, institutional and national shares of foreign

Table 3.1 *Country shares of total foreign exchange transactions, 1980–89[a]*

Percentages

	1980	1981	1982	1983	1984	1985	1986	1987	1988	1989
United States	34.0	18.9	29.4	28.5	30.4	35.7	22.0	25.4	15.7	20.5
Japan	0.4	—	1.0	1.4	1.0	2.4	—	—	5.3	2.5
United Kingdom	1.2	2.8	4.4	3.6	7.7	10.5	8.0	7.1	5.9	9.5
Germany	—	3.6	1.3	2.0	—	—	—	—	—	—
France	6.9	—	1.0	2.0	1.3	5.2	—	—	1.4	—
The Netherlands	—	0.9	—	1.5	—	—	0.5	—	2.1	—
Switzerland	9.7	2.9	5.2	1.9	2.2	3.1	0.8	—	—	—
Canada	1.0	4.9	1.6	4.8	6.2	2.7	2.8	1.4	3.5	2.9
Australia	—	—	—	—	—	—	1.0	2.2	6.9	5.4
Sweden	0.7	3.5	1.0	1.4	—	3.0	0.7	0.6	—	—
Percentage of market covered	53.9	37.5	44.9	47.1	48.8	62.6	35.8	36.7	40.8	40.8

Source: Euromoney, April 1979, September 1980, August 1981, August 1982 and May 1983, 1984, 1985, 1986, 1987, 1988, 1989, 1990.
[a]As explained in the text the 'country shares' as shown in this and similar tables presented later refer to nationality of activity, based on an aggregation of the market shares of financial institutions of a common nationality, and not to the geographic location of the operations in question.

exchange trading, is difficult to establish because of the geographical dispersion of the activity and often short-term nature of the deals. Since 1979 *Euromoney* has compiled a league table of banks involved in the market based on the 'votes' accorded by an international panel of corporate treasurers. It has also published the estimated market share held by the top twenty players, the coverage of which it is believed averaged 41 per cent of total transactions between 1979 and 1989. Table 3.1 is based on this series but in effect has a somewhat enlarged statistical coverage: because most of the relevant *Euromoney* tables are backdated three to four years the past market shares of new entrants to the foreign exchange market have also been included.[1]

Table 3.2 constitutes an attempt to make these shares more comparable across years by expressing the shares listed in table 3.1 as a proportion of the market coverage of the same table. The implicit assumption is that national shares of the non-covered market are the same as those revealed for the covered market. Information presented at a later stage for other financial markets suggests that whilst this assumption does not greatly distort the underlying global state of affairs, the largest percentages in table 3.2 tend to overstate the shares of the countries in question and more complete market coverage would introduce some minor country shares into the picture.

On this basis United States institutions were the most important

Table 3.2 *Country shares of covered foreign exchange transactions, 1980–89*

Percentages

	1980	1981	1982	1983	1984	1985	1986	1987	1988	1989
United States	63.1	50.4	65.5	60.5	62.2	57.0	61.5	69.2	38.4	50.2
Japan	0.7	—	2.2	3.0	2.0	3.8	—	—	13.0	6.1
United Kingdom	2.2	7.5	9.8	7.6	15.8	16.8	22.3	19.3	14.5	23.3
Germany	—	9.6	2.9	4.2	—	—	—	—	—	—
France	12.8	—	2.2	4.2	2.7	8.3	—	—	3.4	—
The Netherlands	—	2.4	—	3.1	—	—	1.4	—	5.1	—
Switzerland	18.0	7.7	11.6	4.0	4.5	5.0	2.2	—	—	—
Canada	1.9	13.1	3.6	10.2	12.7	4.3	7.8	3.8	8.6	7.2
Australia	—	—	—	—	—	—	2.8	6.0	16.9	13.2
Sweden	1.3	9.3	2.2	3.0	—	4.8	2.0	1.6	—	—
Total	100	100	100	100	100	100	100	100	100	100

Source: table 3.1.

players in the market throughout this period although their combined share fell from about three fifths in 1980 to a half in 1989. Germany, Sweden, France and Switzerland all commanded shares of the market in the early years of the decade, in the case of the latter country substantial ones, but by 1989 none of these countries features in table 3.2. In contrast, Britain's share grew steadily throughout the period to a point where it accounted for almost a quarter of the market in 1989 and Australian institutions have also participated to a substantial extent in recent years. Japan is amongst the countries where market shares have tended to increase whilst Canada has held significant shares throughout.

With twenty financial institutions regularly handling an estimated 40–50 per cent of all foreign exchange transactions this market is relatively highly concentrated by most standards though, as will be seen, some financial markets exhibit even higher degrees of concentration. Table 3.3 shows the number of firms in each country which contributed to the national shares presented in table 3.1. Both the numbers and the firms they represent are fairly constant. For the United States Citicorp (formerly Citibank), Chemical Bank, Chase Manhattan, Bank of America, Morgan Guaranty and Bankers' Trust consistently feature in the lists. Citicorp has retained the largest single market share though Chemical has been closing the gap since 1982. The United Kingdom is normally represented by three or four of the 'Big Four' clearing banks plus Standard Chartered: Barclays consistently holds the largest market share among British firms and is second only to Citicorp globally. Typically a single bank appears for

Table 3.3 *Number of top financial institutions by country, 1980–89*

	1980	1981	1982	1983	1984	1985	1986	1987	1988	1989
United States	10	8	10	9	10	9	10	11	7	9
Japan	1	—	1	1	1	2	—	—	4	2
United Kingdom	2	2	3	2	4	3	4	5	2	5
Germany	—	2	1	1	—	—	—	—	—	—
France	3	—	1	1	1	2	—	—	1	—
The Netherlands	—	1	—	1	—	—	1	—	1	—
Switzerland	1	1	2	1	1	1	1	—	—	—
Canada	2	3	1	3	2	2	2	1	1	1
Australia	—	—	—	—	—	—	1	2	4	3
Sweden	1	3	1	1	1	1	1	1	—	—

Source: as table 3.1.

other countries: Royal Bank of Canada for Canada, WestPac for Australia, Bank of Tokyo for Japan, Swiss Bank Corporation for Switzerland and Skandinaviska Enskilda for Sweden.

Absolute size appears to be an advantage in this market given the prevalence of commercial banks among the top dealers. Banks derive much of their foreign exchange business from long-standing corporate clients and must be able to hold large stocks of currencies on their books. So far only in the case of American institutions have investment banks become large enough to deal effectively.

The strength of United States banks in this market can to some extent be explained by the dollar's continued use as the main currency for international trade. As in other markets firms' shares of deals in non-national currencies might afford a better indication of their relative competitiveness. Should the United States hold a comparative advantage in foreign exchange dealing its firms ought to rank among the larger dealers in currencies other than the dollar even though, because of their closer relations with the corporate buyers and sellers of the national currency, domestic financial institutions are likely to enjoy some advantage.

Unfortunately no breakdown of firm shares in individual currency markets is readily available. *Euromoney* (see May, 1990) periodically resorts to a poll of banks and corporate treasurers asking them to identify their 'favourite' dealer in cross deals between major currencies. It is unclear how representative these results are. Although choices are weighted by the asset size of the voting institution this will not necessarily relate to the volume of transactions the company carried out in the market under scrutiny (even if the firm stayed loyal to the financial institutions it identified); nor is it clear to what extent the voting panel is representative of all banks or clients in the particular market.

The results suggest that in deals involving sterling, Swiss francs and French francs (normally 'crossed' with the dollar), preference is given to a bank of the same nationality – usually Barclays leading in Britain, Swiss Bank Corporation and UBS in Switzerland and BNP in France: the main American institutions rank immediately below them. In deals involving Deutschmarks and yen 'local' names come some way down the list and the main American banks are accorded preference.

For currencies with less international significance the following pattern emerges: a 'local' bank is preferred in Australia, New Zealand, Canada, the Netherlands, Italy, Scandinavia, Eire and Hong Kong; a United States bank is preferred in Belgium, Mexico, Saudi Arabia and Brazil; and a British bank is preferred in Spain, Malaysia, Nigeria, Singapore and South Africa.

Where the local banking system is relatively undeveloped preference is given to American or British institutions, in the latter case based on reputations which often derive from colonial involvement. Standard Chartered and Barclays feature consistently as the British banks best recognised for dealing in minor currencies, especially in southern Africa and Asia where they have long-standing experience. Though many of the instruments traded in the foreign exchange market are comparatively new, national market shares clearly owe much to the participants' histories and reputations. The substantial shares held by British banks are due in part to their success in former colonial markets.

In the case of American institutions the names which feature in these lesser markets tend to be those which rank at the top of the global league: Citicorp, Chase Manhattan, Chemical and Bank of America. It seems that a primary strength of these United States banks is their ability to secure very large transactions which require a substantial asset base and are often mediated through dollars even when two other currencies are involved in the final exchange (*Euromoney*, August 1982).

There can be no guarantee that in the future the market for foreign exchange will continue to grow at rates which have been sustained in recent decades. Whilst further trade liberalisation is being pursued through a variety of mechanisms, such as the GATT Uruguay round of negotiations, much has already been attained in the post-World War II period. Similarly, whilst global market deregulation, especially the abolition of capital and exchange controls, has a bearing on the demand for foreign exchange, much has now been achieved. The move to a common European currency will inevitably retard the future growth of the foreign exchange market.

It seems equally likely that, as in the case of other financial markets, the shares held by Japanese institutions will eventually expand beyond their current modest size. In part this will reflect the emergence of the yen as the second most widely traded non-dollar currency (Cross, 1988). Furthermore the relationship between market shares as analysed above and profitability is unclear: in several of the years surveyed the highest return to foreign exchange dealing (in terms of profit on turnover) went to firms which did not rank high in the league tables. This suggests that some firms prefer building market shares by means of narrow margins, a tactic successfully adopted by Japanese institutions in other financial markets.

THE MARKET FOR MERGER AND ACQUISITION ADVICE

The process of mergers between, and the acquisition of, companies is a long-established feature of capitalist economies: equally long-standing is the provision of financial services in connection with this process. The distinguishing features of this activity during the last decade were the sharp increase in the number of deals concluded, the rising value of the real assets involved, and an escalation in the cross-border share of total transactions. Correspondingly the collection and publication of aggregate data on M&A activity has become more systematic in recent years.

Financial institutions derive revenue from M&A activity in two main ways. They may offer advice and information (for instance about target selection and financing arrangements) and they can also become financially involved in the deal by providing loans or underwriting bond issues to finance the acquisition. Large deals tend to be associated with both types of involvement. Therefore, although purely advisory agents such as management consultancy and accountancy firms may engage in small-scale M&A deals, it is generally the larger commercial and investment banks which feature in national and international M&A league tables. Such firms are employed both by the bidders and by the recipients of bids. The task of the first group is to ensure that the right price is being paid for the right target company while the second group may seek to deter the bid, improve the terms or find a more sympathetic buyer.

The recent rapid growth of the M&A market, and particularly the cross-border market, reflects the operation of a variety of factors. The internationalisation of economic activity, and especially the move to a single European market, has compelled many industrial and service sector firms to merge globally in a search for economies of scope and scale and to acquire overseas firms in order to raise market shares and bypass protective national barriers. Rapid structural change, producing sharp falls in profitability in previously strong sectors, has also left an increasing number of big, cash rich, firms seeking to diversify into new markets by acquisition. The 1980s saw large financial surpluses accumulated by American, German, Japanese and British companies, the most profitable application of which often lay in overseas acquisition. At the same time the deregulation of banking activities made available new M&A financing instruments including loans and bond issues secured on the expected future value of the firms and assets acquired. The greater accessibility of world stock markets to foreign buyers has also promoted the international purchase of publicly-quoted companies.

A league table of institutions supplying advice on M&A has been compiled by *Euromoney* since 1986 using information about the number of deals handled and the asset values involved. The data for both deals and values are subdivided into cross-border and domestic activity; and for 1988 and 1989 league tables have been produced ranking advisers by deals completed in the principal national markets and for main nationalities of client.

Though the method of compilation is consistent across these years, the principal tables being based on the top 25 institutions throughout, the data must be treated with caution. Some institutions do not provide full information. For example, Morgan Grenfell, formerly one of Britain's biggest operators, has never provided details of its overseas operations; Citicorp did not reply to the survey in 1985; and in 1987 Goldman Sachs featured consistently in the top three for main industrial sectors yet is absent from both main tables. The number of 'undisclosed' deals has also been growing and it is not always clear whether information on these has been included in the summary figures for individual institutions. Inevitably estimates of the assets involved and their conversion into United States dollars are subject to some margin of error.

Because data relating only to the top 25 institutions are presented in the following tables, the total M&A market is understated although the bulk of deals and asset values will be included. For instance, extending the coverage to the top 40 firms, as is possible in 1989, raises the total of assets covered by no more than 5 per cent from US$964.2 billion to US$1,013.3 billion. Nor should the shorter cut-off greatly distort the pattern of country market shares. Based, again for 1989, on the top 20 and top 40 firms the respective country shares are United States 73.3 and 71.2 per cent, United Kingdom 17.5 and 18.6 per cent, and other countries 9.2 and 10.2 per cent. Despite these qualifications, the picture derived from the tables should provide a

Table 3.4 *Country shares of M&A advisory services, 1985-9*[a]

	1985 US$bn	%	1986 US$bn	%	1987 US$bn	%	1988 US$bn	%	1989 US$bn	%
United States	222.0	75.5	271.5	74.9	298.4	73.8	530.1	72.6	707.0	73.3
United Kingdom	63.7	21.7	85.3	24.3	102.6	25.4	193.4	26.5	168.8	17.5
Other	8.3	2.8	5.7	0.9	3.2	0.7	6.7	0.9	88.4	9.2
Total	294.0	100.0	362.5	100.0	404.2	100.0	730.2	100.0	964.2	100.0

Source: Euromoney, February, 1986, February, 1987, February, 1989 and March, 1990.
[a] Based on data relating to the top 25 M&A advisors.

Table 3.5 *Number of M&A deals, 1985-9*[a]

	1985 No	Ave size US$mn	1986 No	Ave size US$mn	1987 No	Ave size US$mn	1988 No	Ave size US$mn	1989 No	Ave size US$mn
United States	825	269.0	1,106	245.4	1,082	275.8	1,411	375.7	1,313	538.5
United Kingdom	553	115.1	805	106.0	875	117.2	1,014	190.7	567	297.7
Other	35	237.1	61	93.4	20	160.0	32	209.4	222	398.2
Total/Average	1,413	208.1	1,972	183.8	1,977	204.4	2,457	297.2	2,102	458.7

Source: table 3.4.
[a] Based on data relating to the top 25 M&A advisors.

broad indication of the relative sizes of country shares in the M&A market as well as their development over time.

A final word about the statistics relates to an apparent substantial discrepancy between the total asset values given in table 3.4 for 1989, US$964 billion, and the total value of all deals worldwide, US$355 billion, registered for the same year.[2] The former figure substantially exceeds the latter because the value of a deal may be included twice as reported by the advisors of both the acquirer and the acquired. In some deals more than one advisor may be retained and advice tendered in the case of unsuccessful deals is also included.

It is plain from tables 3.4 and 3.5 that American and British institutions dominated this market throughout the period surveyed. The United States has consistently retained about three quarters of the market whilst the United Kingdom's share, though wilting somewhat in 1989, approximated a fifth to a quarter of the market in the latter half of the 1980s. In 1989 the major United States players, all investment banks or security houses, in order of assets handled, were Morgan Stanley, Credit Suisse First Boston (CSFB), Shearson Lehman, Goldman Sachs, Wasserstein Perella, Drexel and Merrill Lynch. In the case of Britain, S. G. Warburg, Schroders, Kleinwort Benson,

Table 3.6 *Country shares of cross-border M&A advisory services, 1985–9* [a]

	1985 US$bn	%	1986 US$bn	%	1987 US$bn	%	1988 US$bn	%	1989 US$bn	%
United States	35.0	72.2	38.1	72.9	67.1	69.1	154.9	64.4	163.0	57.7
United Kingdom	9.8	20.2	13.6	26.1	28.0	28.8	78.1	32.5	88.7	31.4
Other	3.7	7.0	0.5	1.0	1.9	2.0	7.5	3.1	30.6	10.8
Total	48.5	100.0	52.2	100.0	97.1	100.0	240.5	100.0	282.3	100.0
% of global market		16.4		14.4		24.0		32.9		29.3

Source: table 3.4.
[a] Based on data relating to the top 25 M&A advisors.

Table 3.7 *Number of cross-border M&A deals, 1985–9* [a]

	1985 No	Ave size US$mn	1986 No	Ave size US$mn	1987 No	Ave size US$mn	1988 No	Ave size US$mn	1989 No	Ave size US$mn
United States	188	186.1	166	229.5	237	283.1	331	468.0	338	482.2
United Kingdom	153	64.1	178	76.4	229	122.3	316	247.2	248	357.7
Other	8	462.5	5	100.0	33	57.6	29	258.6	76	402.6
Total/Average	349	139.0	349	149.6	499	194.6	676	355.8	662	426.4

Source: table 3.4
[a] Based on data relating to the top 25 M&A advisors.

Morgan Grenfell and Barings were the investment banks responsible for the larger market shares. In the 'other country' group, which raised its relatively small share in 1989, France (with Lazard Frères) and Canada (with the Royal Bank of Canada) figured most prominently; Japan, the Netherlands and Switzerland held only tiny shares.

Shares of the global M&A market are an inadequate guide to the relative efficiency of different countries' M&A advisors because they include national markets of variable size in which domestic financial institutions may enjoy inherent advantages. These can arise where the parties to M&A deals may have imperfect information about foreign financial institutions or face transaction costs and possibly regulatory restraints when employing them. Therefore to point up inherent competitiveness attention is focused on that arena where the institutions in question compete essentially on equal terms: cross-border M&A activity. *Euromoney* defines a cross-border merger or acquisition as one in which the advised company was taking over, merging with, being acquired by, or resisting acquisition by a company with headquarters overseas.

Tables 3.6 and 3.7 reflect development of the cross-border M&A

Table 3.8 *Country shares of cross-border sub-sector M&A advisory services, 1989*

Direction of purchase	Number of firms	Value US$mn	Percentage share		
			United States	United Kingdom	Japan
Europe into US	15	58,329	82	18	—
US into Europe	9	11,217	69	31	—
UK into US	10	59,959	62	38	—
US into UK	5	24,658	87	13	—
Europe into UK	5	21,916	37	63	—
UK into Europe	5	7,853	57	43	—
Japan into US	6	6,676	68	—	32

Source: Euromoney, February 1990.
Note: Europe refers to European Community excluding the United Kingdom.

market and of the principal country shares. It can be seen that measured thus this sub-market expanded faster than domestic M&A activity so that by 1989 it accounted for 29 per cent of the global market compared with 16 per cent in 1985. Again the market is dominated by American and British firms but two features distinguish their shares in this market from their shares in the global market. First, although the United States share is still the largest, it is comparatively smaller and has declined from 72 per cent in 1985 to 58 per cent in 1989. In contrast the British share is larger than in the global market and increased from 20 per cent in 1984 to 31 per cent in 1989. Whilst about a fifth of total United States business derives from cross-border markets for the United Kingdom the fraction is as high as a half.

There are no surprises among the institutions which led for the United States (Morgan Stanley, Goldman Sachs, Wasserstein Perella, CSFB, Shearson Lehman, and J. P. Morgan), nor among those which performed for Britain (Schroders, Kleinwort Benson, S. G. Warburg and Morgan Grenfell). In the 'other' country group only Canada (principally through Royal Bank of Canada and Wood Gundy), Switzerland (with UBS) and France (Lazard Frères) held notable market shares.

Table 3.8 shows country shares in the more significant cross-border sub-sectors. It can be seen that these sub-markets are dominated by a small number of firms to an even greater extent than the overall cross-border market. Only in the case of Japanese companies buying into the United States (a small market) does a country other than the United States or Britain hold a substantial share, thanks to small-scale activities by three Japanese banks: Sanwa Bank, Long Term Credit Bank and the IBJ group. For the rest, the United States takes

Table 3.9 *International patterns in cross-border M&A activity, 1989*

US$ million

Selling region	Buying region			
	European Community	North America	Rest of world	Total
European Community	23,963	13,072	8,471	45,506
North America	32,907	11,733	22,952	67,592
Rest of world	2,673	2,646	2,845	8,164
Total	59,543	27,451	34,268	121,262

Source: KPMG, *Deal Watch: International Mergers and Acquisitions*, March 1990, p. 20.
Note: These data are compiled on different bases to those in tables 3.4–3.8; see text.

the lion's share of the two largest markets, Continental Europe and the United Kingdom buying into the United States, and also the United States buying into the United Kingdom. However British institutions play the lead role where Continental European countries buy into the United Kingdom.

Several factors can be identified which confer competitive advantages on British and American firms in the provision of cross-border M&A advisory services. First a strong home market in M&A activity gives domestic advisors a chance to acquire experience and build a reputation which can be used to secure similar business abroad. Both the American and British domestic markets have been very large. In 1989 the highest ranking ten advisors for domestic United States M&A activity recorded deals to the value of US$328.2 billion or approximately a third of the global (domestic plus cross-border) market; corresponding figures for the British domestic market were US$172.7 billion and a fifth. National institutions account for virtually all domestic M&A activity in the United States though in 1989 the domestic United Kingdom market was almost equally divided between British and American institutions, almost certainly the latters' performance owing much to their strong presence, on the doorstep, in London.

A second type of advantage enjoyed by the United States and the United Kingdom can be traced to the international pattern of cross-border M&A activity. The United States is favoured by the fact that the largest inter-regional flow contained in table 3.9 relates to the European Community buying into North America, since it has already been noted that United States institutions retain the major slice of advisory services for this sector. The second largest market for inter-country M&A activity, that within the European Community, mainly reflects Continental countries buying into the United Kingdom where British institutions, followed by the United States, handle the bulk of the work, and British firms buying into Continental Europe, a market shared between British and American firms. In some respects the Anglo-Saxon dominance of these markets can be traced to the disabilities which characterise potential rivals. Much of the success of American and British institutions in this market is attributable to the fact that unlike most 'universal' Continental banks they are not closely associated with particular industrial groupings so that for them fewer conflicts of interest arise in M&A situations. Additionally they have developed substantial international networks which greatly facilitate cross-border deals (*The Economist*, 20 January 1990). Japanese institutions are hindered in cross-border M&A aspirations by the virtual absence of this corporate strategy in Japan, in turn a reflection of dislike for the loss of face associated with takeovers and the low esteem with which in consequence they are regarded.

A factor that might play a role in the comparative effectiveness of United States and British firms is to be found in differences in the sizes, as measured by average values, of the deals with which they are associated. It is clear from tables 3.5 and 3.7 that for both markets, global and cross-border, in each year the average size of deal handled by American institutions has been much larger than the average serviced by their British counterparts. However there is evidence that this disparity has tended to narrow over time. In the case of the global market the average British deal was only 43 per cent of the size of the typical United States deal in 1985 but had risen to 55 per cent by 1989; for the cross-border market the corresponding proportions were 34 and 74 per cent. Such disparities in the size of deals have implications both for the kind of financial institutions which are in a position to undertake them and also for the profitability of the business.

After enjoying a decade of rapid growth in the M&A market the participating financial institutions are finding, as are those in most other financial markets, that currently 'there is simply not enough business to go round' (*The Economist*, 20 January 1990). The weakening of the market largely reflects a downturn in takeover activity in the United States and the United Kingdom as a consequence of the demise of junk bond financed leveraged buy-outs, banks' current reluctance to finance takeovers and weaknesses in the equity markets, all underscored by recessional tendencies in the two economies and the impact of the Gulf crisis.

The depressed state of these domestic markets will to some extent be offset by continued buoyancy in cross-border merger activity in Western Europe. In 1989 there were almost 1,300 such deals and 'spurred on by the European Community's single market project, companies are indulging in an unprecedented shopping spree'.[3] Intra-European Community M&A activity appears to have survived the recent downturn experienced elsewhere in cross-border M&A.

It is difficult to anticipate the extent to which this structural shift in the M&A market and the emergence of Western Europe as the principal battleground will have implications for institutional and national market shares. Certainly, given their track record, American and British firms will continue to capture substantial shares of this market: for the United States, Goldman Sachs and Morgan Stanley are expected to do well; and for Britain, Schroders and S. G. Warburg are usually cited in this context. Also 'the Lazards triangle of investment banks in New York, London and Paris ... means that it is well placed too'.[4]

Nevertheless Continental firms will inevitably benefit to some degree from these market developments. Whilst such Continental institutions as Mediobanca in Italy and Paribas in France focus primarily on domestic markets, others are certainly looking towards an expansion of their international presence. The Deutsche Bank now owns an M&A arm in the shape of Morgan Grenfell which in turn has recently entered into a joint venture with the United States specialist M&A practitioner, Gleacher and Company. The French investment bank Indosuez is engaged in a similar joint M&A venture with the American firm Blackstone. In this latter connection it is relevant that French industrial companies currently head the list of acquirers in Western European cross-border deals. There are few signs that cross-border M&A advisory services provided by Japanese institutions are set to grow substantially though, for instance, the IBJ has recently initiated a small scale M&A operation in the United States.[5]

THE MARKET FOR SYNDICATED BANK LOANS

The syndication of bank loans is a financial practice of more than twenty years standing. In effect it is an extension, in the form of a term loan, of a much longer-established form of financing: the granting of overdraft facilities by individual banks. Like many other major financial instruments its origins are to be found in the United States, where it was developed as a device to circumvent the regulations which restricted the loan activities of a bank to its state of operation (*Euromoney*, January 1990). Syndication effectively became internationalised in the late 1960s and early 1970s when loans based on

Eurodollars appeared. As with essentially domestic syndications such loans enable sovereign or multinational borrowers to obtain funds from a group of banks which in turn sell parcels of loans to smaller banks (KPMG, 1989).

The leading institutions involved in a syndicated loan comprise one or more lead managers, co-managers and other participants. Their revenue accrues in the form of a management fee for arranging the loan and assembling the syndicate, an agency fee for administering the loan and a commitment or facility fee paid to the banks guaranteeing the life of the loan. The maturity of syndicated loans ranges up to seven years and interest payments are normally based on a floating rate related to Libor.

Developments in this market both in terms of overall growth and loan structure have been largely dominated by a switch in type of borrower from sovereign borrowers in the 1970s and early 1980s to corporate borrowers in more recent years. Sovereign lending, largely to European and Latin American borrowers, declined sharply in the early 1980s as a consequence, especially, of the Mexican default in 1982. The level of syndicated loans fell from US$184.1 billion in 1981 to US$101.2 billion in 1983, since when it has grown almost continuously to US$414.2 billion in 1988. This expansion is attributable to a rapid increase in corporate borrowing through this medium partly for project finance but more significantly to fund acquisition programmes.

The switch in loan structure has potentially substantial consequences for institutional and therefore national shares in this market. It is generally accepted that syndication activities in connection with loans to sovereign borrowers, involving essentially coordination activities, were relatively uncomplicated and the demands on the loan arrangers correspondingly modest. In contrast the required operations (negotiation, syndication, prospectus preparation, timetabling, pricing, structuring, and above all credit analysis) associated with corporate loans are more complex and require financial intermediaries with higher levels of skills and resources than was the case a decade ago (*Euromoney*, January 1990).

Tables 3.10 and 3.11 show changes over the period 1980–89 in country shares of the syndicated loan market based on data relating in each year to the top twenty lead manager/arrangers. That this method yields a reasonably accurate picture of country shares can be demonstrated by comparing, for 1989, these results based on the top twenty firms with those derived from the top fifty firms. The shares recorded on these two bases, respectively, are: United States 74.9 and 66.2 per cent; United Kingdom 16.4 and 15.9 per cent; France 1.6 and

Table 3.10 Country shares of the syndicated loan market, 1980–89[a]

US$ million

	1980	1981	1982	1983	1984	1985	1986	1987	1988	1989
United States	22,064	74,077	35,306	29,805	108,935	109,189	102,585	165,221	222,769	298,754
Japan	1,290	4,251	8,435	5,927	4,857	4,657	6,251	7,671	6,974	—
United Kingdom	5,916	13,940	14,058	4,904	6,916	13,474	13,137	37,056	56,482	65,252
Germany	3,309	—	—	—	—	—	—	—	—	—
France	3,759	3,721	2,106	—	1,575	—	2,869	3,312	5,779	6,422
Switzerland	—	—	—	—	—	4,028	2,686	4,955	10,298	6,096
Canada	6,814	10,481	7,160	5,468	7,249	13,541	6,100	—	4,771	14,769
Other	1,202	—	—	3,621	2,154	—	3,262	3,481	4,189	7,378
Total: top 20	44,354	106,470	67,065	49,725	131,686	144,889	136,890	221,696	311,262	398,670
Total: syndicated loans	89,580	184,060	159,460	101,160	199,430	230,640	215,950	328,050	414,210	
Percentage coverage	49.5	57.8	42.1	49.2	66.0	62.8	63.4	67.6	75.1	

Source: Euromoney, 20th Anniversary Supplement, June 1989, pp. 163 *et seq.*; and *Euromoney*, Annual Financing Report, March 1990, p. 24.
[a]Based on data relating to the top twenty lead managers/arrangers in each year.

Table 3.11 *Country shares of the syndicated loan market, 1980–89*

Percentages

	1980	1981	1982	1983	1984	1985	1986	1987	1988	1989
United States	49.7	69.6	52.6	59.9	82.7	75.4	74.9	74.5	71.6	74.9
Japan	2.9	4.0	12.6	11.9	3.7	3.2	4.6	3.5	2.2	—
United Kingdom	13.3	13.1	21.0	9.9	5.3	9.3	9.6	16.7	18.1	16.4
Germany	7.5	—	—	—	—	—	—	—	—	—
France	8.5	3.5	3.1	—	1.2	—	2.1	1.5	1.9	1.6
Switzerland	—	—	—	—	—	2.9	2.0	2.2	3.3	1.5
Canada	15.4	9.8	10.7	11.0	5.5	9.3	4.5	—	1.5	3.7
Other	2.7	—	—	7.2	1.6	—	2.4	1.6	1.3	1.9
Total	100.0	100.0	100.0	100.0	100.0	100.0	100.0	100.0	100.0	100.0

Source: table 3.10.

3.1 per cent, Switzerland 1.5 and 1.6 per cent; and Canada 3.7 and 3.5 per cent. Additionally, the more comprehensive coverage afforded by fifty firms gives Japan a 4.7 per cent share, Germany 1 per cent, Italy 0.7 per cent and Australia 1.2 per cent. Whilst therefore coverage discrepancies do little to disturb the broad picture, a restricted firm coverage tends to exaggerate the largest country shares and to under-record very small country shares.

The United States has always accounted for the lion's share of this financial market: at the beginning of the last decade American banks captured about half the total and by the end they were taking substantially more. Chase Manhattan, Citicorp and Bank of America played major roles throughout the period. In more recent years they have been joined by other large banks: Manufacturers Hanover, Bankers Trust, Chemical Bank and J. P. Morgan. In addition, at some stage during the 1980s, six other American financial institutions were substantially active in the syndicated loan market: Morgan Guaranty, CSFB, Merrill Lynch, Shearson Lehman, Continental Illinois and First National Chicago.

It is apparent from the experience of the United States and, as will be seen other countries too, that the major players in this market are commercial banks rather than investment banks or security houses. This simply reflects the fact that, in the case of syndicated loans, financial institutions provide not only the kind of intermediate service which is a feature of many financial operations but also supply much of the finance itself.

Taking the period as a whole, second position in the market for syndicated loans has been unequivocally occupied by the United Kingdom with an annual share typically in the range of 10–20 per cent. It is difficult to discern from tables 3.10 and 3.11 any tendency for this share to rise or fall. Each of the 'Big Four' banks played important roles throughout the period; the Standard Chartered Bank and, especially in recent years, Warburgs, have also been substantively active.

The share of Japanese institutions has rarely been better than modest and, unlike the country's performance in other markets, has if anything tended to wane. Those Japanese banks (the Bank of Tokyo, IBJ, the Fuji, Mitsubishi and Sumitomo Banks) which have functioned in this market have never met with the success that their compatriot security houses achieved in the Eurobond market.

Canada, which recorded substantial shares in the early part of the period, has seen its share dwindle in recent years typically to less than 5 per cent. The principle participant banks have been the Bank of Montreal, the Canadian Imperial Bank of Commerce, the RBC, Bank of Nova Scotia and Toronto Dominion Bank. Of the other countries in tables 3.10 and 3.11 the shares of both France and Switzerland, following their institutions' participation in recent years, have typically remained below 5 per cent. In the case of the former country the major responsible banks were Credit Lyonnais, Société Générale, Banque Nationale de Paris and Banque Paribas and, for the latter country, SBC and Credit Suisse.

The large share of the market captured by American banks owed much to the fact that the practice of loan syndication was effectively born in the United States. That this share has actually risen is attributable mainly to the extent to which in recent years loan syndication was undertaken principally for the benefit of corporate borrowers. In particular the dominance of the market by a handful of United States banks largely reflects the importance of this source of funds for the acquisition and leveraged buyout activity of American firms (*Euromoney*, March 1989).

This raises the question of the extent to which contrasts in country shares of this market may be associated with differences in the nationality of the borrowers. Table 3.12, which displays borrowing country shares of syndicated loans, suggests that this factor may well be important in determining market shares. Apart from confirming that during the last decade loans to developing countries were comparatively small (OECD borrowers received no less than 84 per cent of the total), the table reveals that the two countries with the largest market shares, the United States and the United Kingdom, were also the main customers for this type of loan, taking 42 per cent and 12 per cent of the total respectively. The market share of American borrowing is somewhat below that captured by United

Table 3.12 *Borrowing country shares of syndicated loans, 1981–8*

	US$ billion	Share, %
United States	758.8	42.0
United Kingdom	222.6	12.3
Australia	109.8	6.1
Canada	104.3	5.8
France	57.0	3.2
Italy	52.3	2.9
Total above	1304.8	72.2
Total other OECD	217.4	12.0
Total OECD	1522.2	84.2
Total OPEC	44.3	2.5
Total non-OPEC LDC	210.2	11.6
Comecon	31.0	1.7
Total	1807.7	100.0

Source: Euromoney, 20th Anniversary Supplement, June, 1989.

States banks whilst Britain's demand for syndicated loans is roughly in line with its banks' share of the market. That a causal relationship may exist between a country's demand for syndicated loans and the share of the market taken by its financial institutions should hardly occasion surprise. Such a relationship may reflect the operation of financial regulations which makes it difficult for foreign banks to compete domestically; it may also be due to the close commercial ties which exist between domestic borrowers and banks.

A review of the average size of the syndicated loan managed by the banks of each country is relevant in two respects. First it provides a rough indication of the relative sizes of the resources which a country's banks can bring to bear and thus of the competitive edge which may stem from this. Secondly, *ceteris paribus*, a high unit loan size should be relatively more profitable than a small one to the banks in question. Over the full period 1980–89 the average value of the syndicated loans covered by tables 3.10, 3.11 and 3.13 was US$110 million. In the case of three countries, Japan, Switzerland and the United States, their banks managed loans which on average were well in excess of this figure, respectively US$288 million, US$176 million and US$155 million. The average loan size associated with British banks was significantly below these levels at US$83 million and those associated with Canadian and French banks were lower still at US$60 million and US$50 million respectively.

When judging the competitiveness of non-American banks in the market for syndicated loans it is instructive to compare the extent to

Table 3.13 *Number of syndicated loans, 1980–89*

	1980	1981	1982	1983	1984	1985	1986	1987	1988	1989
United States	411	866	817	622	876	738	676	622	874	1059
Japan	49	166	401	407	252	116	201	119	40	—
United Kingdom	206	392	491	173	307	191	233	223	262	296
Germany	88	—	—	—	—	—	—	—	—	—
France	141	142	79	—	87	—	45	21	49	29
Switzerland	—	—	—	—	—	36	31	29	33	31
Canada	157	266	197	132	220	178	50	—	18	65
Other	37	—	—	176	79	—	27	16	42	30
Total	1089	1832	1985	1510	1821	1259	1263	1030	1318	1510

Source: See table 3.10.

which they have been able to penetrate the United States market. This can be done by measuring country shares of syndicated loans for American borrowers based on the top fifty arrangers/lead managers for the United States market during the period 1980–89.[6] The largest non-US share, 4.1 per cent, was in fact acquired by five Canadian banks, followed by Japan with 3.1 per cent from eight banks, the United Kingdom with 2.9 per cent from four banks, Switzerland with 2.2 per cent and France 0.8 per cent in each case from three banks, Germany 0.5 per cent from one bank and the Netherlands with 0.2 per cent also from one bank.

For the immediate future at least further growth in this market will hinge substantially on corporate financial requirements for merger and acquisition purposes. Although such activity is expected to hold up in Europe in anticipation of the projected liberalisation of the Community, the pace has now slackened in both the United States and the United Kingdom. In the longer term 'it is likely that international loan syndications will eventually be replaced by a securitization technique' (Gart, 1989), even though the fees payable on a syndicated loan are usually lower than those incurred in a bond issue (*Euromoney*, January 1990).

The past decade has been marked by a substantial increase in the degree of institutional concentration in the market, a trend which shows no sign of abating: table 3.10 reveals that the top twenty lead managers accounted for 75 per cent of the total market in 1988 compared with only 50 per cent in 1980. This is likely to favour the major operators in the market, especially the big American 'players' who possess the resources to syndicate very large loans as well as the sophisticated skills necessary for dealing with the complex requirements of corporate borrowers.

THE EUROBOND MARKET

The Eurobond market, along with that for syndicated loans, was among the earliest of the international capital markets to emerge in the postwar period. It owes its existence largely to two developments: the appearance of substantial financial funds in the form of Eurodollars, and American financial regulations which were introduced to strengthen the dollar.

Eurodollars comprise dollar deposits held outside the United States, principally in Europe and especially in London. The origin of these funds is to be found in dollar deposits held in Europe in the immediate postwar period by Communist bloc countries seeking to avoid their possible sequestration in the United States. They were substantially bolstered as a result of continuing United States balance of payment deficits and by large volumes of petrodollars attributable to the oil price increases of the mid-1970s.

From the very early 1960s large international borrowers (sovereign, supra-national and corporate) had every incentive to tap this supply of funds. In 1963 an interest equalisation tax, along with other financial regulations, was introduced in America to strengthen the dollar by dissuading foreign borrowers from using the United States foreign bond market which, prior to this action, had been a principal source of their funds. The Eurobond emerged when these borrowers redirected their attention to the Eurodollar market. It is generally accepted that the first Eurobond issue was for the Italian Autostrade road group in 1963.

A Eurobond is thus a bond denominated in any currency held outside the borrower's domestic market by a non-resident of the country's currency.[7] Whilst originally this currency was Eurodollars, large Eurobond issues have for some years been dominated in other such Euro currencies, Deutschmarks, French francs, sterling, ECUs, Canadian dollars, Australian dollars, yen, and so on. The bonds which may be of five to thirty year maturity are issued on behalf of borrowers by syndicates of banks and security houses comprising lead managers, co-managers and underwriters based mainly in London which manage and underwrite the securities and then sell them to other banks, institutions and private individuals. These financial intermediaries are rewarded by management fees, underwriting fees and selling concessions.

The Eurobond market grew rapidly and consistently between 1963 and 1986 from a total new issue value of US$148 million to US$179,881 million, that is, by an annual average rate of 36 per cent. Numbers of issues, which are perhaps a better measure of the 'real' growth of the market, increased by an average of 23 per cent per annum. The instrument's advantages to borrowers which stemmed from American financial regulations have already been touched upon but additionally the market offered a diverse investor base, the facility to float loans (especially relevant for governments and supra-national bodies) in excess of those which could be comfortably launched on a single domestic market, the choice of a wide variety of currencies, and a method of raising capital which, typically, is more efficient and quicker than that provided by domestic markets.

For investors, particularly private individuals, a major attraction of this instrument has been the fact that it is not registered but exists in bearer form. In addition to the receipt of interest without deduction of withholding, or any other taxes, this facility provides the lender with complete anonymity. It is a market over which no single central bank or monetary authority has jurisdiction and this absence of regulation has contributed substantially to the concentration of the market in London. Of the 127 reporting dealers of the Association of International Bond Dealers (AIBD),[8] as many as 89 are to be found in London, followed by Paris six, Amsterdam and Luxembourg five, Copenhagen four, Brussels and Helsinki three, Zurich and Frankfurt two, and one each in Basle, Bergen, Hong Kong, Lausanne, Milan, Singapore, Turin and Vienna (Walmsley, 1988).

Other background factors also favoured the growth of this market. Especially important among these has been the general drift towards 'securitisation', the trend for bank loans to be replaced by tradeable instruments, a development which received impetus from the international debt crises which detrimentally affected syndicated loans.

However, perhaps the most significant element in the long-term growth of the Eurobond market is the degree to which it lends itself to product innovation. One *summary* of the modifications which, over the years, have been introduced to vary, *inter alia*, the interest paid, life of the bond, proceeds received on maturity, issue price and bondholder entitlements runs to eighteen pages (KPMG, 1989). That such new trading techniques have evolved in line with those required by the market is largely due to its lack of formal regulation. Among the more significant of these product innovations have been the floating rate note, which pays a variable rate of interest normally tied to Libor, and convertible bonds and bonds with equity warrants, which in effect provide a lender with the right to buy shares at a future date at a fixed price. Perhaps the two most significant recent variations are asset-backed Eurobonds (often credit card backed) and the fixed price reissue technique.

The historical series for country shares of the Eurobond market set

Table 3.14 Country shares of the Eurobond market, 1980–89[a]

US$ million

	1980	1981	1982	1983	1984	1985	1986	1987	1988	1989
United States	4,950	9,387	16,919	16,868	37,177	59,523	60,738	26,151	44,736	46,939
Japan	955	1,819	1,729	1,120	5,131	10,224	38,768	46,991	46,810	87,943
United Kingdom	1,467	2,294	1,560	2,106	2,891	7,311	2,734	6,061	7,090	5,576
Germany	3,352	2,006	8,966	10,971	8,743	10,072	14,555	12,829	19,383	13,290
France	1,780	1,965	3,111	3,295	4,537	3,356	9,841	3,589	6,029	8,947
Switzerland	655	1,200	2,822	803	1,275	6,257	7,700	5,463	8,280	3,417
Canada	405	546	799	1,477	1,163	2,930	—	—	—	—
Netherlands	—	—	924	719	—	—	—	—	—	—
Total: top 20	13,564	19,217	36,830	37,359	60,917	99,673	134,336	101,084	132,328	166,112
Total: all Eurobonds	18,827	25,582	47,863	47,592	79,289	132,595	179,881	135,023	175,760	
Percentage market coverage	72.0	75.1	77.0	78.5	76.8	75.2	74.7	74.9	75.3	

Sources: 1980–88, Euromoney, 20th Anniversary Supplement, June 1989; and 1989, Euromoney, Annual Financing Report, 'Markets into the 1990s', March 1990.

[a] Based on top 20 book runners in each year.

Table 3.15 *Country shares of the Eurobond market, 1980–89*

percentages

	1980	1981	1982	1983	1984	1985	1986	1987	1988	1989
United States	36.5	48.8	45.9	45.2	61.0	59.7	45.2	25.9	33.8	28.3
Japan	7.0	9.5	4.7	3.0	8.4	10.3	28.9	46.5	35.4	52.9
United Kingdom	10.8	11.9	4.2	5.6	4.7	7.3	2.0	6.0	5.4	3.4
Germany	24.7	10.5	24.3	29.4	14.4	10.1	10.8	12.7	14.6	8.0
France	13.1	10.2	8.4	8.8	7.4	3.4	7.3	3.6	4.6	5.4
Switzerland	4.8	6.2	7.7	2.1	2.1	6.3	5.7	5.4	6.3	2.1
Canada	3.0	2.8	2.2	4.0	1.9	2.9	—	—	—	—
Netherlands	—	—	2.5	1.9	—	—	—	—	—	—
Total	100.0	100.0	100.0	100.0	100.0	100.0	100.0	100.0	100.0	100.0

Source: table 3.14.

out in tables 3.14 and 3.15 are based on the issue values of the top twenty book runners in each year which accounted for about three quarters of the market. That the results represent a reasonably accurate picture for the whole market and developments therein is supported by a comparison of the country shares shown for 1989 in table 3.15 with those, for the same year, based on the top fifty book runners. These shares are, respectively: Japan 53 and 46 per cent; United States 28 and 25 per cent; Germany 8 and 9 per cent; France 5 and 9 per cent; United Kingdom 3 and 4 per cent; and Switzerland 2 per cent in both cases. In addition the more comprehensive coverage allocates minor market shares, totalling 5 per cent, to Italy, the Netherlands, Belgium, Canada and the Nordic Group. Clearly the Eurobond market is currently dominated by Japanese (especially) and American institutions. Significant but much smaller shares are held, in the following order, by Germany, France, the United Kingdom and Switzerland.

Focusing attention on changes in country shares over the period 1980–89, the most striking feature of the table is the growth of that part of the market captured by Japanese financial institutions. From a mere 7 per cent share in 1980 Japan's share increased to 53 per cent by 1989, with most of this growth concentrated in the latter half of the decade. In contrast to the relatively small roles played by three Japanese security houses in 1980 (Daiwa, Nomura and Yamaichi), by 1989 six institutions (these three together with the Industrial Bank of Japan (IBJ), Nikko and the Long Term Credit Bank (LTCB) all held substantial market shares.

In terms of market shares the major country loser, even though it continues to hold the second largest share, has been the United States.

Although the 28 per cent registered for 1989 is not much below the 37 per cent of 1980, it is way down on the three-fifths market share held by American financial institutions in the mid-1980s prior to the Japanese surge. The security houses CSFB, Goldman Sachs, Merrill Lynch, Morgan Stanley and Salomon Bros have enjoyed significant market shares throughout the period. Recently they have been joined by two banks, J. P. Morgan and Bankers Trust.

Table 3.15 reveals that the shares of the other significant participating countries were also squeezed over the period. In 1980 Germany held 25 per cent of the market, France 13 per cent, the United Kingdom 11 per cent and Switzerland 5 per cent, representing in each case shares substantially in excess of those currently held, whilst Canada has effectively been removed from the market. At the beginning of the period four German institutions (the Deutsche Bank, Dresdner Bank, Commerzbank and Westdeutsche Landesbank Group) played significant roles in the market but by 1989 only the former two featured among the top twenty each with substantially diminished shares. Whilst at some stage over this period five French institutions (Paribas, Credit Lyonnais, Banque Nationale de Paris, Société Générale and Credit Commercial de France) appeared among the top twenty, by 1989 representation was restricted to the first two. For Switzerland both the Swiss Banking Corporation and Union Bank Swiss were normally present in the list but by 1989 this distinction was held by the latter only. Out of six British institutions (S. G. Warburg, Hambros, Samuel Montagu, National Westminster, Lloyds and Baring Bros) which at some time during this period played a role, the prime and most consistent performance was achieved by S. G. Warburg, which featured in the top twenty in each of the ten years. Yet even in the case of this British house its league position declined steadily from fourth place in 1980 to fourteenth in 1988.

American investment houses such as Kuhn Loeb, White Weld, First Boston, Dillon Read, Lehman Bros and Goldman Sachs were among the first institutions to exploit the Eurodollar capital pool and so establish a major original stake in the market for the United States.[9] The role of Germany, still substantial in 1980, was even more significant in earlier years with the Deutsche Bank being the major German institution in the market in both the 1960s and the 1970s and the Dresdner Bank also featuring high on the list. This reflected in part the comparative advantage enjoyed in the early Eurobond market by the universal banks of Continental Europe: the advantage associated with joint experience of two basic requirements, underwriting securities and, for distributive purposes, retail banking (Hamilton, 1986).

Table 3.16 *Number of Eurobond issues by country, 1980–89*[a]

	1980	1981	1982	1983	1984	1985	1986	1987	1988	1989
United States	59	117	171	112	255	422	379	206	286	308
Japan	22	33	30	16	77	131	377	367	385	455
United Kingdom	18	23	20	28	29	43	24	53	67	62
Germany	51	23	92	118	103	107	124	115	138	79
France	18	28	39	39	37	55	94	38	46	65
Switzerland	7	14	24	9	14	49	70	51	72	29
Canada	7	12	10	26	19	51	—	—	—	—
Netherlands	—	—	14	10	—	—	—	—	—	—
Total	182	250	400	358	534	858	1068	830	994	998

Sources: 1980–89, *Euromoney*, 20th Anniversary Supplement, June 1989; and *Euromoney*, Annual Financing Report, 'Markets into the 1990s' March 1970.
[a] Based on top 20 book runners in each year.

Table 3.17 *Average issue value of Eurobonds, 1980–89*

US$ million

	1980	1981	1982	1983	1984	1985	1986	1987	1988	1989
United States	84	80	99	151	146	141	160	127	156	152
Japan	43	55	58	70	67	78	103	128	122	193
United Kingdom	81	100	78	75	100	170	114	114	106	90
Germany	66	87	97	93	85	94	117	112	140	168
France	99	70	80	84	123	61	105	94	131	138
Switzerland	94	86	118	89	91	128	110	107	115	118
Canada	58	45	80	57	61	57	n.a.	n.a.	n.a.	n.a.
Netherlands	n.a.	n.a.	66	72	n.a.	n.a.	n.a.	n.a.	n.a.	n.a.
All	75	77	92	104	114	116	126	122	133	166

Sources: See tables 3.14 and 3.16.

For the United Kingdom S. G. Warburg, which attained the rank of fourth in the overall league table for the period 1963–72 and third for 1972–7, was an outstanding performer. This individual success was largely attributable to marketing techniques developed jointly with the Wall Street house, Kuhn Loeb and Co, and to Warburg's leading the 1963 Italian Autostrade issue. S. G. Warburg has also been cited, along with White Weld, as a pioneer of an important variant of the Eurobond, the floating rate note.

For more recent years the factors which help to explain contractions in the market shares of American, German, French, British and Swiss financial institutions are a mirror-image of those which lie behind the expansion of the Japanese share, namely: the rising value of the yen and the development of the Euro-yen market; some reluctance on the part of American corporations to issue Eurobonds; a declining use of the perpetual floating rate note much favoured by United States issuers; and the growth of equity warrant bonds in which Japanese houses specialise (Bowe, 1988).

It is relevant to consider whether such factors as average issue value, currency structure of issues, type of Eurobond and nationality of borrowers play any role in shaping contrasts in country market shares of the Eurobond market. Table 3.17 shows for each country changes over the period 1980–89 in the average value of the Eurobond issues led by its financial institutions. High market shares acquired by the United States have been associated in most years by issue values which were broadly similar to, or significantly above, the market average. Comparatively low Japanese market shares in the early part of the period were accompanied by low average value issues and the recent rapid growth in that country's share, especially in 1989, has been associated with relatively high average values. Broadly speaking, and taking the period as a whole, the average issue values handled by German and French institutions have rarely differed to a great extent from the global average.

In contrast Swiss and British issue values have tended to fall relative to the average. This has been especially marked in the case of the United Kingdom where, as the table shows, there has been a decline in issue values since the mid-1980s, not only relatively but also, unlike the case in any of the other countries, in absolute terms too. As a consequence the average issue value, US$90 million, registered by British institutions in 1989, was lower than that associated with any other country. Whether or not this reflects developments in the scale of the resources which the relevant United Kingdom institutions can bring to bear on this market, as well as its use by quite small British building societies, the resulting low issue values have clear detrimental implications for these British financial services. First, *ceteris paribus*, low issue values have a direct negative impact on Britain's share of the Eurobond market. Secondly it is likely that such a development impairs the profitability of these British financial institutions relative to that of their competitors.

Another factor systematically influencing country market shares may be associated with the currencies in which bonds are issued. If it is the case that a country has a predominant share in those which are denominated in its own currency then, clearly, its overall share of the market will be affected by the currency pattern of issues.

The data presented in tables 3.18 and 3.19 for the top ten lead managers in each currency sector in 1989[10] suggest that there is indeed a tendency for this condition to hold. Measured in this fashion

Table 3.18 Country shares by currency, 1989[a]

	US$ million	Yen billion	DM million	ECU million	£ million	Can$ million	Aus$ million	Ffr[b] million	Sfr[c] million
United States	21,497	149	1,400	2,350	4,701	4,121	1,960	—	1,430
Japan	73,045	1,548	670	—	—	—	225	—	2,395
United Kingdom	—	—	24,710	—	5,055	—	1,859	—	1,260
Germany	3,500	—	—	550	—	550	610	—	—
France	—	—	—	3,745	—	1,877	420	29,070	1,415
Switzerland	—	—	—	1,316	940	890	—	—	20,211
Canada	—	—	—	—	—	2,844	—	—	—
Australia	—	—	—	—	—	—	1,022	—	—
Belgium	—	—	—	451	—	—	—	—	—
Total	98,042	1,697	26,780	8,412	10,696	10,282	6,096	29,070	26,711
Total market	120,593	2,110	28,580	11,050	12,060	13,110	8,230	29,070	30,390
Percentage market covered	81.3	80.5	93.7	76.1	88.7	78.4	74.1	100.0	87.9

Source: Euromoney, March 1990 Supplement, Annual Financing Report, pp. 16–20.

[a] Based on data for top ten lead managers in each market sector.

[b] Top eight lead managers.

[c] Relates to Swiss franc foreign bonds.

Table 3.19 *Country shares by currency, 1989*

Percentages

	US$	Yen	DM	ECU	£	Can$	Aus$	Ffr[b]	Sfr[c]
United States	21.9	8.8	5.2	27.9	44.0	40.1	32.2	—	5.4
Japan	74.5	91.2	2.5	—	—	—	3.7	—	9.0
United Kingdom	—	—	—	—	47.3	—	30.5	—	4.7
Germany	3.6	—	92.2	6.5	—	5.3	10.0	—	—
France	—	—	—	44.5	—	18.3	6.9	100.0	5.3
Switzerland	—	—	—	15.6	8.8	8.7	—	—	75.7
Canada	—	—	—	—	—	27.7	—	—	—
Australia	—	—	—	—	—	—	16.8	—	—
Belgium	—	—	—	5.4	—	—	—	—	—
Total	100.0	100.0	100.0	100.0	100.0	100.0	100.0	100.0	100.0

Source and notes: See table 3.18.

French financial institutions accounted for all French franc issues, German institutions for 92 per cent of DM issues, Japanese institutions for 91 per cent of yen issues and Swiss institutions for 76 per cent of the Swiss franc foreign bond market. The British hold on the sterling sector is less strong, but with 47 per cent of the market it nevertheless retains the largest share. Another striking feature is the revelation that Japan, not the United States, won the bulk (74 per cent) of the US dollar sector, whilst American institutions hold shares across the board, very substantial ones in the case of US dollars, ECUs, sterling, Canadian and Australian dollars. The lion's share of the ECU market, 44 per cent, was claimed by France.

It can be seen therefore that Japan's current domination of the Eurobond market largely reflects the lead role of its institutions in US dollar issues (mainly due to its domination of dollar denominated warrant bonds), which in 1989 accounted for about half the total market rather than its 91 per cent share of the yen sector. In contrast America's large market share is associated with a spread of its institutions' activities across the various currency sectors. The substantial overall market shares obtained by Germany and France are also associated with own currency specialisation coupled with the fact that each of their currencies accounted for roughly a tenth of the market. The comparatively low degree of domination by British institutions of the sterling sector coupled with the fact that they hold significant shares in only two other sectors (the Australian dollar and Swiss franc), contributes to their relatively small overall share of the market. Longer-term trends in currency shares of the Eurobond market point towards a decline (proportionately) in US$ issues and growth for the ECU, Can$, sterling and yen (*Euromoney*, June 1989, Supplement).

The above exercise can be repeated for the Eurobond market divided into sub-sectors which reflect the type of bond issued. The relevant data, again for 1989, are set out in tables 3.20 and 3.21 which distinguish the four main types of bond (fixed rate issues, floating rate issues, Eurobonds with warrants and Euro-convertibles) as well as data for three comparatively new variants, fixed price re-offerings, asset-backed Eurobonds and Eurobond repackagings. Although the shares in this table are again based on the top lead managers it can be seen that in each sector market coverage is high.

In the case of the straightforward fixed rate issues which constitute about half the total market, America and Japan appropriate the largest shares accounting for some two thirds of the sub-market with Germany and France taking a further tenth each. The share of British institutions in this, the largest Eurobond market, is small. Japan's overall share of the Eurobond market is further boosted by its virtual monopoly of the second largest market, bonds with equity warrants, and America's large overall share is supported by its domination of floating rate issues. The only market sector where the United Kingdom plays a substantive role, with an 18 per cent share, is Euroconvertibles, one of the smallest segments of the Eurobond market.

Explanations of Eurobond market shares may also be sought in the nationality pattern of borrowers. The following series for 1989 make rough comparisons between, respectively, market supply shares (based on table 3.15) and the proportions of the market accounted for by the borrowers of each country: Japan 53 and 38 per cent; United States 28 and 6 per cent; Germany 8 and 3 per cent; France 5 and 5 per cent; United Kingdom 3 and 9 per cent; and Switzerland 2 and 0.3 per cent.[11] It would appear from these data that the United States especially, but also Germany, Switzerland and Japan, hold shares of the global market in excess of their domestic demand, whilst the opposite applies to British institutions.

A perusal of market operations reveals that where a Eurobond is issued by a domestic borrower in the domestic currency the chances are very high that the bond will be lead managed by a financial institution of the same country, though this rule holds less strongly in the case of British issues and sterling than in the case of other market sub-sectors.

A slackening in 1989 and 1990 of growth in the Eurobond market has been associated with fierce competition between, and lack of profitability amongst, the major players, together with the closure by

Table 3.20 *Country shares by type of Eurobond, 1989*[a]

US$ million

	Fixed rate issues	Floating rate issues	Eurobonds with warrants	Euro convertibles	Fixed price re-offerings	Asset-backed Eurobonds	Eurobond repackaging
United States	32,666	11,675	330	2,128	7,253	4,284	70
Japan	22,941	476	62,575	900	650	931	1,549
United Kingdom	1,972	1,330	—	796	473	1,049	—
Germany	10,607	2,008	2,189	538	1,050	—	—
France	9,729	1,311	425	—	572	605	—
Italy	—	1,178	—	—	—	—	—
Netherlands	—	—	467	—	—	85	—
Switzerland	2,854	500	—	—	549	325	100
Austria	—	890	—	—	—	—	—
Canada	1,584	—	—	—	64	—	—
Total	82,353	19,368	65,986	4,362	10,611	7,279	1,719
Total market	116,150	21,690	66,990	5,260	10,611	7,279	1,719
Percentage market covered	70.9	89.3	98.5	83.0	100.0	100.0	100.0

Source: Euromoney, Annual Financing Report, March 1990, pp. 12–16.
[a] Based on top lead managers as follows: fixed rate and floating rate, top 20; warrant and convertibles, top 10; fixed price re-offerings, top 19; asset backed, top 17; and repackagings, top 11.

Table 3.21 *Country shares by type of Eurobond, 1989*[a]

Percentages

	Fixed rate issues	Floating rate issues	Eurobonds with warrants	Euro convertibles	Fixed price re-offerings	Asset-backed Eurobonds	Eurobond repackaging
United States	39.7	60.3	0.5	48.8	68.4	58.9	4.1
Japan	27.9	2.4	94.8	20.6	6.1	12.8	90.1
United Kingdom	2.4	6.9	—	18.2	4.5	14.4	—
Germany	12.9	10.4	3.3	12.3	9.9	—	—
France	11.8	6.8	0.6	—	5.4	8.3	—
Italy	—	6.1	—	—	—	—	—
Netherlands	—	—	0.7	—	—	1.2	—
Switzerland	3.5	2.6	—	—	5.2	4.5	5.8
Austria	—	4.6	—	—	—	—	—
Canada	1.9	—	—	—	0.6	—	—
Total	100.0	100.0	100.0	100.0	100.0	100.0	100.0

Source: See table 3.20.

some financial institutions (perhaps as many as thirty) of their London-based Eurobond operations. The Gulf War precluded any immediate recovery in the market. Superimposed on these short to medium term developments is a general expectation that, in the longer term too, the prospects for growth in this market are not bright.

This view is based on the probability that the regulations affecting domestic markets which initially gave rise to the development of Eurobonds will be eroded and eventually rescinded thus undermining the *raison d'être* of the market. As early as 1986 Hamilton noted that 'many of the laws and rules that once made the Eurobond market so distinct a European phenomenon have been abolished' (Hamilton, 1986). By 1989 it was being confirmed that whilst the Eurobond market developed because of regulatory barriers in the world's domestic bond markets these barriers have been gradually removed: 'if this process continues the Eurobond market won't have a reason for living anymore' (*Euromoney*, September 1989). Also it is believed that when withholding taxes are removed, the Eurobond market, though it will retain some advantages, may retire gracefully at least in its current form. The beneficiaries will be the domestic bond markets: should Glass–Steagall be repealed then US dollar issues for all borrowers may gravitate to their natural home in the United States since American commercial banks will then be able to underwrite corporate bonds in New York (*The Economist*, 23 June 1990). The structure of the market is currently being influenced by a dearth of private investors and a domination by institutional lenders who prefer Eurobonds issued by governments and supra-national organisations rather than those offered by corporates.

Whatever the fate of the total market the manner in which it is apportioned between the major participating financial institutions will be greatly influenced, as in the past, by their respective innovative capabilities. In this context data contained in tables 3.20 and 3.21 relating to new techniques and 'products' is revealing. It shows that in the case of the very rapidly growing new style asset backed Eurobonds American institutions are leading the way, though Britain's share, thanks to S. G. Warburg, Barclays and Samuel Montagu, along with Germany's, is significant.

On the other hand Britain's performance in the fixed price re-offering sector, representing an issuing technique which involves an undertaking on behalf of syndicate members not to sell bonds to investors above or below a fixed price during the syndication process, is not encouraging. The bulk of this new market is accounted for by American institutions, no doubt reflecting the fact that the technique was developed in the United States domestic market, with Britain, up to now, attaining, thanks to S. G. Warburg and Barings, little more than a toe-hold. Indeed, following the initial use of this technique in the Eurobond market by Morgan Stanley in August 1989, no British financial institution featured among those which immediately took it up, namely: Deutsche Bank, Salomon Bros, Société Générale, UBS, CSFB and Banque Paribas. Britain has no significant presence in the Eurobond 'repackaging' sector which is controlled almost exclusively by Japanese institutions.

THE MARKET FOR INTERNATIONAL EQUITIES

Two significant features of this international financial market are its newness and the potential which it offers for substantial growth from its current modest size. This activity comprises the underwriting and distribution of equity securities to investors in markets outside a company's home market. The operation, which may also include some placements in the domestic market, is usually performed under a lead manager by a syndicate of international banks and security houses. These syndicates operate in two forms: as a Euro-equity syndicate whose members may sell stock to any client; and as a geographically targeted syndicate in which a member may sell only in a specified region to avoid multiple solicitation of clients (Walmsley, 1988).

For a company seeking additional equity capital an international issue offers several advantages over a domestic issue (*Euromoney*, November, 1986). First it provides an instrument which broadens the company's investor basis. Secondly, in the case especially of large issues, an international placement is likely to be more easily absorbed than one focused on a single domestic market. Thirdly, the net proceeds to the issuer are frequently significantly higher than what can be achieved in the home market. For the investor, particularly the institutional investor, the international equities market provides an opportunity to diversify beyond domestic equity holdings with, perhaps in addition, superior yields and capital appreciation possibilities. As for the intermediary institutions, banks and security houses, syndicating the issues, they 'have found this profitable as they can charge fees of 3–5 per cent compared with 1.75 per cent on typical Eurobond issues' (KPMG, 1989).

This new financial market had little substance prior to 1984 when there were US$1.2 billion issues compared with US$0.2 billion in the previous year. The market grew rapidly in its formative years with new issue values totalling US$3.7 billion in 1985, US$11.5 billion in 1986, and US$20.2 billion in 1987. Following the stock market crashes in the latter year, international equity issues fell back to US$8.8 billion in 1988 from which level there was some recovery to US$9.8 billion in 1989. By comparison with other international financial markets the international equity market cannot even now be considered at all large.

This market is hardly one which can trace its origins to innovation, or the appearance of a new financial instrument: as early as 1956 Goldman Sachs placed some shares abroad for the Ford Motor Company (*Euromoney*, January, 1990). Rather can its recent growth be traced to worldwide deregulation of markets and in particular to the dismantling of restrictions which hampered cross-border flows of equity capital.

Its development has been greatly facilitated by the pre-existence of a highly developed system for underwriting and distributing debt securities to international investors: the Eurobond market. Indeed some twenty years after the start of the latter the international equity, or Euro-equity, market closely parallels the Eurobond market. In the first place the Euro-equity market makes much use of the same clearance systems, Euroclear and Cedel, which sustain the Eurobond market, though unlike Eurobonds Euro-equities are listed on and traded in domestic stock exchanges. Moreover since it is essentially modelled on the Eurobond market the Euro-equity market is largely centred in London. The use and popularity of convertible bonds and bonds with equity warrants also forge close links between the Eurobond and Euro-equity markets.

In brief 'the Euro-equity market has begun to take shape twenty years after its predecessor the Eurobond market. After companies became accustomed to satisfying their debt financing requirements all over the world, becoming totally indifferent as to whether they borrow in dollars, Swiss francs, Japanese yen, or Australian dollars ... the logical next step is to seek equity capital from international investors' (Walmsley, 1988).

Tables 3.22 and 3.23 show for years during the period 1983–9 the country shares based on issue values of the top ten lead managers for international equity issues. This procedure yields a market coverage ranging from about 60 to 80 per cent. For some of the countries which appear in this table no share is registered for certain years, in part reflecting a lack of complete market coverage but also the fact that during this period the market was relatively small, with few participating institutions, so that the short-term fortunes of those that did play a role determined whether or not a country registered a share. Even in the case of the United States[12] no more than six financial institutions featured in the market at some time during this period: CSFB, Goldman Sachs, Merrill Lynch, Morgan Stanley, Salomon Bros and Shearson Lehman. Japan has three participants, Daiwa, Nomura and Yamaichi. Two representatives appear for France,

Table 3.22 *Country shares of international equity issues, 1983–9* [a]

US$ million

	1983–85	1986	1987	1988	1989
United States	1,779	4,000	6,751	3,849	3,517
Japan	403	—	977	1,702	1,764
United Kingdom	—	—	1,011	—	—
Germany	1,516	4,002	619	320	—
France	—	567	983	—	—
Switzerland	783	665	999	557	—
Canada	306	—	747	—	—
The Nordic Group	214	382	—	—	—
Other	—	—	—	363	656
Total top 10	5,001	9,616	12,087	6,791	6,723
Total international equities	7,200	11,530	20,170	8,790	9,790
Percentage coverage	69.5	83.4	60.0	77.3	68.7

Source: Euromoney, May 1986, pp. 105–7; and *Euromoney*, Annual Financing Reports.
[a] Based on top ten lead managers.

Table 3.23 *Country shares of international equity issues, 1983–9*

Percentages

	1983–85	1986	1987	1988	1989
United States	35.6	41.6	55.9	56.7	52.3
Japan	8.1	—	8.1	25.1	26.2
United Kingdom	—	—	8.4	—	11.7
Germany	30.3	41.6	5.1	4.7	—
France	—	5.9	8.1	—	—
Switzerland	15.7	6.9	8.3	8.2	—
Canada	6.1	—	6.2	—	—
The Nordic Group	4.3	4.0	—	—	—
Other	—	—	—	5.3	9.8
Total	100.0	100.0	100.0	100.0	100.0

Source: See table 3.22.

Banque National de Paris and Banque Paribas, for Switzerland, SBC and UBS, and for Canada, McLeod, Young and Wood Gundy. The other countries, the United Kingdom, Germany, Italy, the Netherlands, Belgium and the Nordic Group, had only a single participant each in this top group, respectively, S. G. Warburg, Deutsche Bank, Mediobanca, Nederlandsche Middenstandsbank, Général Bank and Skandinaviska Enskilda Banken.

To some extent the 'patchiness' of tables 3.22 and 3.23 can be remedied if attention is directed more widely in table 3.25 to market

Table 3.24 *Number of new equity issues, 1983–9*

	1983–85	1986	1987	1988	1989
United States	20	64	66	56	71
Japan	4	—	4	16	6
United Kingdom	—	—	12	—	9
Germany	2	7	5	3	—
France	—	4	11	—	—
Switzerland	14	13	11	4	—
Canada	5	—	6	—	—
The Nordic Group	8	2	—	—	—
Other	—	—	—	1	3
Total	53	90	115	80	89

Source: See table 3.22.

Table 3.25 *International equities: market shares of top 20 lead and co-lead managers, 1985–9*

Percentage shares

	1985	1986	1987	1988	1989
United States	17.3	31.3	49.0	51.0	45.7
Japan	10.7	7.3	8.6	24.3	15.9
United Kingdom	12.4	—	8.3	4.7	13.0
Germany	19.4	24.7	7.2	8.4	3.5
France	4.8	9.2	7.7	—	7.6
Italy	0.7	5.7	—	3.1	—
The Netherlands	—	1.5	—	—	7.4
Switzerland	30.9	11.1	11.8	5.1	7.0
Canada	2.2	1.2	7.4	2.0	—
The Nordic Group	—	1.7	—	—	—
Other	1.5	6.2	—	1.4	—
Total	100.0	100.0	100.0	100.0	100.0

Source: Euromoney, Annual Financing Reports.
Note: For the value totals ($mn) from which these percentage shares are derived each issue is allocated equally between lead and co-lead managers.

shares based on the activities of co-lead managers as well as lead managers, an extension which also benefits from the fact that for this group historical data are available for the top twenty participants in each year.[13] This approach serves to embrace additional participating institutions: for the United States, Drexel Burnam and Prudential Bache; for Japan, Nikko; for the United Kingdom, Kleinwort Benson, Morgan Grenfell and Schroder Wragg; for Germany, Commerzbank, Dresdner Bank and Westlandbank; for France, Banque Indosuez, Banque Paribas and Credit Commercial; for Italy, Banca Commerciale Italiana and Banco di Roma; for the Netherlands, Amsterdam–Rotterdam Bank and Algemene Bank Nederland; for Switzerland, Bank Leu; and for Canada, Dominion Securities and Scotia McLeod.

Taken together tables 3.23 and 3.25 are sufficient to reflect the broad development of country shares in the international equity market. Both tables confirm that the United States' share has been the largest and that, if anything, it has tended to grow over time to a point where the country accounts for about half the market in international equities. Japan's share has also been enlarged to the point where it is now the second biggest. Substantial shares which appear to have been fairly stable over the life of the market are held by the United Kingdom (with about a tenth over the period) and France. In contrast, although both German and Swiss financial institutions remain significant participants, their shares are now substantially below the levels registered at the market's inception.

Whilst product innovation by individual institutions played little role in the development of this market America's consistently high share must to some extent be associated with the experience acquired by United States financial institutions as major players from the outset. It is claimed that the first significant separate syndication of shares outside the home country of the issuer was undertaken by CSFB in 1984; Morgan Stanley and Salomon Bros also functioned in this field in the very early years.

A second factor bearing on a country's share of the market stems from the close relationship, identified above, which exists between the market for international equities and the Eurobond market. In 1989 no fewer than six American financial institutions played major roles in both these markets, namely: CSFB, Goldman Sachs, Merrill Lynch, Morgan Stanley, Salomon Bros and Shearson Lehman. Three Japanese institutions, Daiwa, Nomura and Yamaichi, also had significant stakes in both market places. For the United Kingdom, S. G. Warburg alone operated in a substantial way in both markets. Indeed out of the top twenty lead arrangers of international equities only five (Prudential Bache (US), Robert Fleming (UK), Nederlandsche Middenstandsbank (Netherlands), Général Bank Group (Belgium) and Skandinaviska Enskilda (Nordic)) failed to feature also among the top fifty lead managers for Eurobonds. It is conceivable that the comparatively poor performance of Britain's financial institutions in the Eurobond market may have had a detrimental impact on their share in international equities.

It is relevant to enquire, as in the case of other international capital markets, whether there is any association between the country pattern of 'demand' for international equities and countries' financial sectors

shares in supplying the market. Taking the country shares presented
in table 3.25 as a measure of the latter and national percentages based
upon the turnover of the top 300 foreign equities aggregated by
nationality of the issuing corporation as a measure of the former, the
results for 1989 are, respectively: United States 46 and 11 per cent;
Japan 16 and 11 per cent; United Kingdom 13 and 19 per cent;
France 8 and 7 per cent; the Netherlands 7 and 7 per cent; and
Switzerland 7 and 2 per cent.[14]

The most striking feature of these data is the extent to which, in this
sense, the United States has a 'surplus' of supply over domestic
demand, though to a lesser extent Japan and Switzerland are in a
similar position. In contrast there appears to be a 'deficit' between the
extent to which British corporations use the market for international
equities and the share of the market held by British financial
institutions.

There is general agreement about the major features which an
investment bank or security house should possess if it is to win a
substantial stake in the international equity market. First, it must
have accumulated relevant experience in underwriting debt and
equity securities. Secondly, for placement purposes it needs to have a
global presence and, especially, substantial operations in the principal
investor countries. Thirdly, it helps to win such business if an
institution has successfully provided other financial services for the
issuer.[15]

The average size of international equity issues underwritten by a
country's financial institutions is significant in several relevant
respects. Almost by definition international equity issues are large,
often very large, and if a country has no financial institution, or only a
few, with the necessary capital muscle and distributive facilities to
lead manage such issues its market share will be correspondingly
restricted. At best such countries can but hope that their banks and
security houses will play a secondary role as syndicate members. Also
the ability to play leading roles in large issues can be especially
remunerative for financial intermediaries. On the one hand, as in the
case of many financial operations, the input resources required are
generally not proportionate to the 'output' as measured by the value
of the 'product' say the new issue value (Smith, 1989). In contrast the
fees earned by the financial institution normally vary with the new
issue value.

When ranked by the average size of the issues lead managed by
their financial institutions the countries concerned fall into two fairly
distinct groups. The first comprises Germany with seventeen issues
during the period 1983–9 at an average value of US$380 million and

Japan with thirty issues of US$160 million. There follows, at a distance, a group which includes: France, fifteen issues at US$103 million; Canada, eleven at US$96 million; the United Kingdom, 21 at US$86 million; the United States, 277 at US$72 million; Switzerland, 42 at US$72 million; and the Nordic Group with ten issues having an average value of US$60 million (see tables 3.22 and 3.24).

When short-term market vicissitudes, including the retrenchment in international equity issues following the 1987 stock market's collapse and the Gulf crisis, are left out of account there is every reason to suppose that this market is set for substantial growth during the 1990s. It is as yet young and small in comparison with other capital flows. Indeed in many respects its current position corresponds with the embryonic state of development reached by the Eurobond market a couple of decades ago: 'the most impressing thing about the global market for shares is its prospects. The pace of growth has been brisk these past few years, starting from a small base' and 'although the overwhelming amount of securitized instruments consists of bonds and notes, the equity composition is rising' (Garten, 1989).

More specifically investment funds in the United States as yet typically hold proportionately small portfolios in foreign stocks so that a substantial future demand for international equities may well stem from this source. Relevant EC directives should also ease current investment restrictions faced by European funds. At the same time efforts being made to balance the budgets of major western economies could detrimentally affect the 'supply' of government securities.

The long-term growth of this market will be facilitated by technological developments affecting the trading and clearing of international equities. A screen-based system for these activities perhaps provided by the National Association of Securities Dealers, is anticipated for the near future. Indeed it is expected that the only significant restrictions on the market's growth will be associated with a lack of efficient systems for clearance and settlement, an absence of effective global, as opposed to national, regulatory systems, and the lack of common international standards for company accounting and financial disclosure (Kaushik, 1989).

In anticipation of this growth some principal 'players' (CSFB, SBC, UBS and Deutsche Bank though no British institutions) have been noted as switching their resources and operations towards the international equity market (*Euromoney*, July 1989). Whilst the scale of operations and especially global representation are a prerequisite for a financial institution's success in this market there will inevitably be much product specialisation in the sense that individual banks and security houses may focus their underwriting and trading activities on particular types of equity. As in the case of Eurobonds the future growth of the market for international equities will be characterised by innovations relating both to product types and techniques. The market shares of individual financial institutions, and thus of countries, will be crucially influenced by the banks' and security houses' abilities in these areas.

THE MARKET FOR EUROCOMMERCIAL PAPER

The nature of commercial paper is best conveyed by distinguishing it from the two financial instruments to which it is closely related, certificates of deposit and note issuance facilities.[16] A certificate of deposit is a negotiable instrument which a bank may provide for a depositor and which can be traded to change ownership of the deposit. A note issuance facility is an arrangement by which a bank or group of banks agree to act as managers underwriting a borrower's issue of short-term paper as and when required and to back the facility with medium-term bank credit should the notes not find a market (Bullock, 1989, Heller (Ed.), 1988 and Hamilton, 1986). Note issuance facilities also have much in common with syndicated loans in that they may require direct lending by a consortium of banks to the borrower; they differ in that they involve securitisation and the provision of a borrowing facility only part of which is taken up at any time.

Commercial paper is a form of securitisation but differs sharply from a note issuance facility in that typically it results in direct borrowing by the issuer from an (often non-bank) end investor. A financial institution acts as an agent and places these short-term securities rather than being itself a lender. Thus unlike the position with note issuance facilities there is no commitment of bank funds, though it may still benefit from a bank guarantee. In effect this characteristic feature, a dealer acting as a financial intermediary to place the commercial paper with other investors, means that the market, in contrast to those for note issuance facilities and syndicated loans, is open to investment banks and security houses with smaller asset bases than those possessed by commercial banks.

As with other financial markets that have been examined the Eurocommercial paper (ECP) market had its origins in United States regulations, in this case those introduced in 1968 which restricted overseas borrowing by United States firms. As a consequence of these restrictions United States financial institutions led by the investment bank Goldman Sachs tapped the Eurocurrency markets through the medium of Eurocommercial paper programmes. In doing this they enjoyed two competitive advantages over possible rivals: experience of operations in a well developed domestic market for commercial paper; and a demand from their domestic customers for a solution to this funding problem.

Modification of the relevant United States regulations led to the effective termination of the original market in 1974. Its re-emergence in the mid-1980s can be directly traced to developments in Euronote issue facilities: 'the ECP market is an offshoot of the underwritten Euronote market which itself developed as an alternative to the syndicated credit markets in the early 1980s' (*Bank of England Quarterly Bulletin*, May 1988). A relevant feature of the Euronote market, which grew dramatically throughout the early years of the 1980s, was the predominant role played from the outset by American banks. The 'invention' of the note purchase facility is generally attributed to the Citicorp International Bank (the investment bank arm of Citicorp), a lead which was immediately followed in 1980 by Credit Suisse First Boston and the Swiss Banking Corporation (Bullock, 1987). By 1985 it had been recognised that a decoupling of the underwriting process from note placement functions, the distinguishing feature of commercial paper, ensured that this instrument enjoyed both distribution and placement advantages over Euronote issuing facilities and in general offered a more efficient and flexible medium. As a result the weight of activity switched away from the latter and in favour of the former instrument. Over the last decade the number of Euronote facilities and of ECP programmes have developed, respectively, in the following fashion: 1980, 7 and 1; 1981, 19 and 4; 1982, 26 and 1; 1983, 30 and 3; 1984, 74 and 2; 1985, 225 and 51; 1986, 171 and 313; 1987, 152 and 326.

From the investor's point of view commercial paper offered better yields than could be obtained on bank deposits yet was frequently issued by corporations which, following the failure of many syndicated loans, had higher credit ratings than some commercial banks. Once again American financial institutions led the way in the revival of this market. The basic feature of the new market as in the case of the original one is that the issuer appoints a dealer, or dealers (typically numbering up to four) who arrange an ECP programme which is uncommitted in the sense that it is not coupled with any commercial bank underwriting and whose responsibility is to place the notes with the end investor. The dealers are committed to an ECP programme only insofar as they will be prepared to make a bid offer to an investor (Bullock, 1987). Dealer income derives essentially from the spread between their bid for paper and the price at which they sell to investors, typically three base points. Eurocommercial paper constitutes essen-

Table 3.26 *Country shares of the Eurocommercial paper market, 1986–9*[a]

	1986		1987		1988		1989	
	US$mn	%	US$mn	%	US$mn	%	US$mn	%
United States	17,918	83.3	32,332	72.8	32,849	65.0	27,373	63.4
Japan	—	—	3,285	7.4	5,494	10.9	5,279	12.2
United Kingdom	1,093	5.1	4,508	10.1	6,335	12.5	2,916	6.8
Germany	—	—	—	—	—	—	1,216	2.8
France	1,200	5.6	769	1.7	—	—	—	—
Italy	—	—	—	—	—	—	1,500	3.5
The Netherlands	—	—	—	—	—	—	—	—
Switzerland	—	—	2,325	5.2	3,752	7.4	1,656	3.8
Australia	500	2.3	707	1.6	1,155	2.3	—	—
Canada	610	2.8	—	—	264	0.5	—	—
The Nordic countries	200	0.9	500	1.1	400	0.8	3,210	7.4
Other	—	—	—	—	300	0.6	—	—
Total	21,521	100.0	44,426	100.0	50,548	100.0	43,150	100.0

Source: The Bank of England.
[a] Based on data relating to the top thirty arrangers.

tially a short-term form of borrowing having maturities ranging from 7–364 days and interest related to Libor.

Table 3.26 shows changes in country shares of the ECP market for the years from 1986, when it first reached substantial proportions, to 1989. The tables are based on the market shares gained in each year by the top thirty arrangers. Some impression of the market coverage represented by these top dealers is conveyed by the fact that in 1989 they accounted for US$43.1 billion issued paper compared with US$47.7 billion handled by the top fifty arrangers. Again country patterns do not greatly change when attention is switched from the top thirty to the top fifty (though more countries are embraced by the latter) the respective country shares for 1989 being: United States 64 and 60 per cent; Japan 12 and 13 per cent; United Kingdom 7 and 8 per cent; Germany 3 and 3 per cent; France 0 and 1 per cent; Italy 3 and 3 per cent; Switzerland 4 and 4 per cent; Australia 0 and 1 per cent; and the Nordic countries 7 and 7 per cent.

The tables show that at its inception this market was supplied almost wholly by American financial institutions accounting as they did for more than four fifths of the total in 1986. Their share has since fallen continuously though in 1989 it was still by far the largest at about 63 per cent. This decline has been accompanied by a decrease in the number of American institutions featuring in the top thirty, from twenty in 1986 to thirteen in 1989. Those which have disappeared from the list include Security Pacific, Chemical Bank, Morgan Stanley and First Interstate.

Nevertheless a group of United States firms, Citicorp (which headed the league in all four years 1986 to 1989), Morgan Guaranty, CSFB, Shearson Lehman (in its early years as Shearson Loeb and Lehman Brothers), Merrill Lynch and Chase Manhattan, dominated the market both at the beginning and end of this period. It should be noted that both commercial and investment banks feature in this list for, although the Federal Reserve has only recently allowed security affiliates of American commercial banks to arrange domestic commercial paper programmes, in Europe by contrast the commercial banks have been in the forefront of the market (Heller, 1988).

After American firms only British and French institutions held shares of any substance at the market's inception, each country possessing about a twentieth of the total. The early British entrants, Warburg, Barclays, Samuel Montagu and Lloyds, together with the help of County Natwest, Morgan Grenfell and Kleinwort Benson, raised the British share in the middle years, though by 1989 it had declined to about 7 per cent with the disappearance from the top thirty of all but National Westminster, Warburg and Morgan Grenfell.

Repeating a familiar picture, alongside the contraction in America's share that of Japan has risen from, effectively, zero in 1986 to 12 per cent in 1989. The institutions responsible for this, which as in the case of American and British players include commercial banks, investment banks and security houses, are Daiwa, Nomura, IBJ, Nikko, Bank of Tokyo, Mitsubishi International Finance and Yamaichi.

After their early participation French institutions, Société Générale and Paribas, have fallen by the wayside as top arrangers though Swiss banks, SBC and UBS, have performed creditably obtaining combined market shares of 5, 7 and 4 per cent in, respectively, 1987, 1988 and 1989.

Other financial institutions which have from time to time attained the ranks of the top 30 are the Canadian Imperial Bank of Commerce, the Australia and New Zealand Banking Group, Westpac, the Saudi International Bank, the Union Bank of Finland, Enskilda, the Kansallis International Bank and Svenska Handelsbanken, the latter three combining to give the Nordic group of countries a 7 per cent share of the 1989 market.

It is clear that American domination of this market, though less complete than it once was, owes much to historical factors: to the early pioneering attempts of American institutions in the ECP market and to the experience of United States institutions, especially Citicorp, in note issuance facilities, an activity from which the ECP market stemmed. Another important historical consideration is to be

Table 3.27 *Average amount of Eurocommercial paper arranged per firm,*
1986–9

US$ mn

	1986	1987	1988	1989
United States	896	2,155	2,346	2,106
Japan	—	1,095	1,373	754
United Kingdom	219	751	1,056	972
Germany	—	—	—	1,216
France	600	769	—	—
Italy	—	—	—	1,500
The Netherlands	—	—	—	—
Switzerland	—	2,325	1,876	828
Australia	500	707	1,155	—
Canada	610	—	264	—
The Nordic countries	200	500	400	1,070
Other	—	—	300	—
Average	717	1,481	1,685	1,438

Source: Based on data supplied by the Bank of England.

found in the know-how which is associated with the very early
establishment of a domestic paper market in the United States. Such
domestic markets were developed in competitor countries at much
later dates: New Zealand, 1982; Hong Kong, 1983; France, 1985; the
United Kingdom, Finland and the Netherlands, 1986; and Japan,
1987 (Heller, 1988). Until recently the Swedish commercial paper
market was among the more important.

There is evidence which suggests that these historical considerations are underpinned by fundamental competitive factors which
have contributed to the large market share won by American
institutions. In particular table 3.27 reveals that on average the scale
of operations, as measured by the average value of ECP arranged by
United States firms is greater, usually significantly so, than that
which characterises their rivals. In 1989, for instance, this value for
the thirteen American institutions was as high as US$2,106 million,
the next largest figure, US$1,216 million, being reached by Ger-
many's lone 'player', the Deutsche Bank. The average value arranged
by the three British institutions, National Westminster, Warburg and
Morgan Grenfell, was US$972 million, some way below the overall
figure for the top thirty firms, US$1,438 million.

As with other financial markets it is relevant to enquire whether
there is any evidence that the nationality of ECP issuers has
influenced country market shares. On the basis of the data presented
in table 3.28 the conclusion must be that if such an association exists it

Table 3.28 *Eurocommercial paper outstanding by nationality of issuer,*
December 1989

	All issuers		Non-bank issuers	
	US$mn	Percentage	US$mn	Percentage
Australia	11,957	20.5	5,665	15.4
United Kingdom	8,132	13.9	5,226	14.2
United States	7,210	12.3	5,222	14.2
France	4,059	6.9	3,812	10.4
Sweden	3,504	6.0	2,531	6.9
Italy	3,348	5.7	755	2.1
Denmark	2,645	4.5	1,027	2.8
Finland	2,224	3.8	1,398	3.8
Cayman Islands	1,854	3.2	1,854	5.0
Spain	1,313	2.2	979	2.7
Norway	1,097	1.9	562	1.5
Austria	1,025	1.8	—	—
Other	10,067	17.2	7,707	21.0
Total	58,435	100.0	36,738	100.0

Source: Bank for International Settlements, *International Banking and Financial Market Developments,*
Basle, May 1990, table 9.

can hardly be a strong one. Heading the list of issuers in 1989 was
Australia, the financial institutions of which have played only a minor
role in this market. In contrast to the market dominance of United States
institutions, American issuers accounted for little more than a tenth of
the total. Equally revealing is the fact that Japan, Switzerland and
Germany all fail to appear in this list of the largest issuers even though
their financial institutions won significant market shares. British issuers
acounted for 14 per cent of the total compared with about 7 per cent of the
market captured by the country's financial institutions.

Two features currently dominate the ECP market. First, as with
many other financial markets, but perhaps to an even greater extent,
it is widely agreed that it is characterised by over-capacity in terms of
the number of participants relative to the amount of paper being
issued. Secondly, the market contracted sharply between 1988 and
1989 (in these years there were 326 and 144 programmes respectively), whilst in 1990 growing concern about the creditworthiness of
corporations which have issued, or wish to issue, ECP has caused
continued stagnation in the market.

The very narrow margins which in consequence emerged have led
to the withdrawal from the market of two principal American players,
Merrill Lynch and Bankers Trust (*Euromoney*, March 1990), a path
recently followed by one of the few remaining British participants,

Warburgs (*The Financial Times*, 22 October 1990). Bankers Trust remains active in the markets for Euro certificates of deposit, Eurobonds and medium-term notes (*The Financial Times*, 13 July 1989) and the Warburg ECP team has been redeployed to the new medium-term note market.

THE MARKET FOR EURO MEDIUM-TERM NOTES

The international market for medium-term notes evolved only in 1986 though, as table 3.29 reveals, it grew rapidly over the next two years. The story of its development is a familiar one. Originally initiated by General Motors in 1972 there developed an active domestic United States market for medium-term notes during the early years of the 1980s prior to its extension into the European arena (Walmsley, 1988).

Within the spectrum of financial instruments medium-term notes fit between bonds and commercial paper programmes. They differ from the former in that they are issued under programmes which ensure their availability on a continuous basis and have a relatively short maturity. Compared with commercial paper, however, their maturity is relatively long, from nine months to ten years. Interest rates may be fixed or floating, typically relative to Libor. A financial institution acts as an agent on the issuer's behalf making no underwriting provisions.

Table 3.29 paints a picture of a market dominated by American

Table 3.29 *Country shares of the market for medium-term notes, 1986–9*

	1986		1987		1988		1989	
	US$mn	%	US$mn	%	US$mn	%	US$mn	%
United States	1,750	94.6	8,775	93.1	13,918	85.6	9,225	87.8
Japan	—	—	—	—	300	1.8	—	—
United Kingdom	—	—	400	4.2	450	2.8	—	—
Germany	—	—	—	—	—	—	1,001	9.5
France	—	—	—	—	49	0.3	75	0.7
Italy	—	—	—	—	—	—	154	1.5
The Netherlands	—	—	—	—	133	0.8	52	0.5
Switzerland	—	—	—	—	900	5.5	—	—
Australia	—	—	—	—	500	3.1	—	—
The Nordic countries	100	5.4	250	2.7	—	—	—	—
Total	1,850	100.0	9,425	100.0	16,250	100.0	10,507	100.0
No of arrangers	6		8		17		13	

Source: Based on data supplied by the Bank of England.

institutions.[17] Though the United States' share shows a marginal contraction over this period, by 1989 American firms still held almost nine tenths of the market compared with a virtual monopoly at its inception. Merrill Lynch has perhaps been the most consistent player for the United States but CSFB, Shearson, Goldman Sachs, Citicorp, Morgan Guaranty and Morgan Stanley have also been substantively active in this market.

Table 3.29 suggests that only a handful of other countries have participated to any significant extent, and then sporadically: the United Kingdom (S. G. Warburg), Germany (Deutsche Bank), Switzerland (SBC and UBS), France (Société Générale), the Netherlands (Algemene Bank Nederland), Italy (Instituto Bancario San Paulo di Torino), Australia (Australia and New Zealand Banking Group), Sweden (Enskilda Securities) and Japan (Nomura).

It is plain that the continuing dominance of the American institutions reflects the expertise and experience acquired in their more mature domestic market for medium-term notes. This advantage is further boosted, and profitability no doubt enhanced, by their ability to arrange much larger programmes than their global competitors. The average value of medium-term notes handled per participating American institution over the period 1986–9 was US$1,161 million compared with US$291 million for their rivals.

Until quite recently there were expectations that the market for medium-term notes was about to take off, probably at the expense of the ECP market and in much the same way that the latter instrument displaced earlier note issuance facilities. It has been noted how some ECP teams have been redeployed to medium-term note markets. Such a switch may hold attractions for the financial intermediaries concerned since, 'in contrast to the competitive bidding system in the ECP market, the structure of fixed commissions in the market for medium-term notes has ensured a higher level of profitability for intermediaries' (BIS, 1990). However, given the recent depressed nature of international capital markets, such expectations of rapid growth for the medium-term note market can be discounted in the immediate future.

SUMMARY

The salient feature of recent developments in these selected financial markets is the extent to which they have been dominated by American financial institutions. With hardly any qualification the United States obtained the largest shares of these markets at both the beginning and end of the periods in question,[18] and its share has been greater than 50 per cent. Though there are exceptions, for instance in the case of syndicated loans where its share has risen substantially, typically America's portion of the market has been very large, almost monopolistic, when a market is young, and is then eroded as the market develops and rivals appear, though normally not to the point where the United States loses its ascendancy. Japan has been a beneficiary of this process even to the point where in the Eurobond market its share now exceeds that of the United States.

This tendency for America's market shares to decline could easily be misinterpreted. Testimony presented later in this study suggests that the process is not necessarily a sign of declining competitiveness but a reflection of the country's successful exploitation of the life cycle which characterises an international capital market, its initiation with appropriate innovation, exploitation before rivals enter in numbers and the eventual emergence of overcapacity. The United States success in the older markets has been translated into success in the younger ones. It is also pertinent that in almost all these markets American institutions are in 'surplus' in the sense that their share tends to exceed the aggregate demand of United States customers.

The review of market developments suggests that historical factors have contributed substantially to America's dominance. Early United States regulatory restrictions on financial operations were such that American institutions were induced to develop new instruments which in effect, and for the most part, could only be traded in international markets. The original expertise which these firms in consequence acquired endowed them with a competitive edge which still endures.

The foregoing market histories suggest that United States financial institutions have also derived substantial competitive benefits from their domestic markets. Large-scale merger and acquisition activity which until recently has been a feature of the United States scene, the size of United States corporate demand for syndicated loans and the large and sophisticated domestic market for commercial paper have all contributed to the expertise and success of the country's financial institutions. Another factor which has promoted United States' shares in these markets as well as the profitability of the country's financial institutions is a tendency for their average unit values to be high.

At first blush, and against this background of United States dominance and superiority, the performance of the relevant British institutions appears to be commendable. The review suggests that the United Kingdom occupies second place, after the United States, in the foreign exchange, M&A and syndicated loans markets, and is effectively third, following the United States and Japan, in the international equity and commercial paper markets. Moreover in none of these markets has there been much indication of any significant long-term erosion of the United Kingdom's position.

Closer scrutiny suggests that this picture needs to be qualified in one or two significant respects. First there are signs that United Kingdom institutions tend to perform better in the older markets than in the younger ones. Our success in the foreign exchange market substantially reflects the play of historical factors, such as relatively extensive commercial bank networks inherited to some extent from a colonial past and expertise which derives from the dominant role which in earlier decades sterling played in international trade. Similarly the satisfactory performance of British banks in the market for syndicated loans and, more especially, M&A advice can be traced to institutional reputations of long standing and to skills gained as a consequence of a large-scale demand from domestic clients. In the case of the M&A market, independent British merchant banks (though perhaps not commercial banks) share with United States investment banks the inestimable competitive advantage associated with an absence of those conflicts of interest which hamper the operations in this activity of Continental universal banks.

Secondly, in contrast to the position of the United States, Japan and principal Continental competitors, the available evidence suggests that the United Kingdom may be in a 'deficit' position in the sense that the market shares held by the banks are less than the shares which British clients demand of most markets. This shortcoming could reflect the extent to which domestic British markets have been opened to foreign financial institutions and the degree to which in consequence British financial services are exposed to foreign competition. This openess has resulted for instance in American institutions acquiring a substantial share of the domestic British market for M&A advice, and in foreign financial institutions of a variety of nationalities penetrating the sterling segment of the Eurobond market.

Thirdly, there are indications that *vis-à-vis* the United States in particular the average value size of the financial units supplied by British banks to international capital markets may be relatively low. The negative impact of this on both the United Kingdom's market shares and the profitability of its financial institutions has been stressed. The extent to which this may be a general feature of British operations is considered again in the following chapter.

A special word needs to be said about the United Kingdom's performance in the Eurobond market where it has met with little success, securing as it does only a small and diminishing market share. In part this poor showing is due to the factors identified above, relatively low value issues, a 'deficit' between Britain's supply to and demand from this market, and the extent to which (in contrast to other currency sectors which are largely the preserve of the relevant national financial institutions) the sterling Eurobond network has been penetrated by foreign firms. In addition the evidence suggests that, compared with Japanese institutions for example, British banks have been relatively slow in exploiting the markets for new Eurobond variants, and compared with American firms that they are perhaps not sufficiently innovative. Nor have British institutions enjoyed to the same extent the competitive advantage which accrues to Continental banks from the joint experience of underwriting securities and, for placement purposes, retail banking.

A more pleasing note is struck when Britain's comparative performance is related to the experience of these Continental rivals in other markets. Not only are the shares of Germany, France and Switzerland usually smaller than the United Kingdom's but the evidence suggests that taken all round their shares declined substantially during the 1980s.

4

AN ANALYSIS OF COUNTRY SHARES IN SELECTED FINANCIAL MARKETS: 1989

INTRODUCTION

In the previous chapter country performances in selected international financial markets, as measured by market shares obtained by their respective financial institutions, were traced on an historical basis. Using essentially the same approach this chapter focuses, in greater detail, on country and institutional performances in 1989.

The market coverage is broadly the same as that adopted in the historical section, the principal variations being the exclusion of the foreign exchange market where statistical deficiencies preclude the kind of treatment essayed in this chapter,[1] a broadening of the market for Eurocommercial paper to include Eurocertificates of deposit, and a consideration of the market for international bonds inclusive of foreign bonds as well as Eurobonds.

Another distinction relates to the degree of market coverage. In the previous section data limitations meant that for historical consistency the relevant league tables were somewhat restricted in terms of the numbers of firms included. When attention is directed to 1989 it is possible to broaden the institutional coverage in the following manner: for worldwide M&A, the top 40 firms; cross-border M&A, 25 firms; syndicated loans, 50 firms; international bonds, 50 firms; Eurobonds, 50 firms; international equities, 20 firms; Euro-CP and CD, 50 firms; and Euro medium-term notes, 25 firms. As previously noted such extensions of coverage normally do not greatly change the pattern of country shares which emerge though there is a tendency for the largest shares to contract and for smaller share countries to appear in the tables.[2]

A word needs to be said about the country allocation of financial institutions. In the great majority of cases identification of nationality on the basis of ownership and control of an institution or its parent poses few problems.[3] However, recent changes in international ownership patterns suggest that, in any future compilation of the kind of tables presented in this chapter, the country allocation of financial institutions would need to be modified. In particular whilst Credit Suisse First Boston (although frequently referred to as 'international') has been allocated to the United States, C. S. Holdings of Switzerland recently raised its CSFB stake from 44 to 60 per cent so that strictly, this institution might now be regarded as Swiss. Because the Deutsche Bank acquired Morgan Grenfell at the end of 1989, for the purposes of table 4.1 which relates to the full year 1989 this institution retains its British identity. Cross-nationality minority shareholdings such as Nomura's 29 per cent holding in the American security house Wasserstein–Perella have been ignored. In accordance with the methodological approach adopted in this study, described in Chapter 2, the location of an office (other than location of head office) which conducts business is irrelevant to identification of nationality so that, for example, Banque Paribas (Suisse) whilst located and operating in Switzerland is designated French.[4]

It should be remembered that values presented in table 4.1, from which the country shares are derived, in no way relate to the turnover or receipts of national financial institutions. In the case of M&A activity they comprise the value of the mergers and acquisitions for which a company has advised; for bonds, commercial paper, international equities and medium-term notes they relate to the value of these instruments issued by the various institutions; and in the case of syndicated loans, to the value of the loans arranged by each financial institution. The revenue received by an institution in connection with a specific activity is frequently expressed in the form of a percentage fee (though there may be some fixed costs too) which varies between the financial instruments and institutions in question; some use is made below of such margins. Also it should be understood that the shares relate to principal activities in each market, for instance as lead managers in the case of bond issues and arrangers in the case of syndicated loans. The secondary activities of these institutions in these markets, their participation as co-managers in the Eurobond market for instance, are not directly taken into account. Another qualification to the comprehensiveness of league tables is that some activities, deals which fail or private placement, may not be announced.

COUNTRY SHARES OF FINANCIAL MARKETS, 1989

Despite the statistical qualifications referred to above the patterns of country shares shown in tables 4.1 and 4.2 for the various selected markets broadly conform with the results derived from the historical analysis.[5] By focusing attention on a single year it is possible to consider the cross-market performance of individual countries as well as examining shares in individual markets.

Table 4.1 *Country shares of selected financial markets, 1989*

	M&A world wide	M&A cross-border	Syndicated loans	International bonds	Eurobonds	International equities	Euro CP & CD	Euro MTNs
United States	721.2	163.0	312.4	71.1	50.0	6.5	531.0	177.8
Japan	6.4	—	22.4	107.2	94.2	2.8	69.2	5.6
United Kingdom	192.4	85.0	74.8	14.2	11.9	1.6	135.3	22.7
Germany	—	—	4.5	19.2	18.3	0.3	5.4	1.4
France	45.0	3.8	14.5	16.9	15.1	0.4	21.8	—
Italy	—	—	3.2	2.4	2.3	—	—	—
The Netherlands	2.1	—	—	2.8	2.6	0.8	2.3	2.1
Belgium	—	—	—	1.1	0.7	0.4	—	—
Switzerland	8.5	5.8	7.4	13.9	4.7	0.3	111.5	20.2
Canada	37.8	22.7	16.3	2.4	2.4	—	15.1	—
Australia	—	—	5.7	—	—	—	22.7	1.7
The Nordic group	—	—	—	—	0.6	0.3	20.5	1.4
Other	—	—	10.4	0.7	0.6	—	3.0	—
Total	1013.3	280.3	471.7	252.0	203.5	13.3	937.9	232.9

Sources: For M&A advisors worldwide and cross-border, *Euromoney*, March 1990, p. 41 and February, pp. 45, *et seq*; for international bond lead managers and Eurobond bookrunners, Eurocommercial paper (CP), certificates of deposit (CD), medium-term note (MTN) dealers, and syndicated loan arrangers see *Euromoney*, March 1990, Supplement 'Markets into the 1990s', pp. 6 *et seq*; for international equity issues see *Euromoney*, May 1990, p. 69.

Percentages

Table 4.2 *Country shares of selected financial markets, 1989*

	M&A world wide	M&A cross-border	Syndicated loans	International bonds	Eurobonds	International equities	Euro CP & CD	Euro MTNs
United States	71.2	58.2	66.2	28.2	24.6	48.9	56.6	76.4
Japan	0.6	—	4.7	42.6	46.3	21.4	7.4	2.4
United Kingdom	19.0	30.3	15.9	5.6	5.8	12.0	14.4	9.7
Germany	—	—	1.0	7.6	9.0	2.0	0.6	0.6
France	4.4	1.3	3.1	6.7	7.4	3.3	2.3	—
Italy	—	—	0.7	0.9	1.2	—	—	—
The Netherlands	0.2	—	—	1.1	1.3	5.9	0.2	0.9
Belgium	—	—	—	0.4	0.3	2.5	—	—
Switzerland	0.8	2.1	1.6	5.5	2.3	2.0	11.9	8.7
Canada	3.7	8.1	3.5	1.0	1.2	—	1.6	—
Australia	—	—	1.2	—	—	—	2.4	0.7
The Nordic group	—	—	—	—	0.3	2.1	2.2	0.6
Other	—	—	2.2	0.3	0.3	—	0.3	—
Total	100.0	100.0	100.0	100.0	100.0	100.0	100.0	100.0

Source: table 4.1.

The patterns of country market shares which emerge from tables 4.1 and 4.2 essentially corroborate the findings of Chapter 3. It is hardly surprising therefore that the most striking feature is the domination of these markets by American institutions. Leaving aside the market for international bonds, where the United States still accounts for about a quarter of the total, its share of markets ranges from about a half to three quarters.

Whilst the United Kingdom commanded significant shares in all the markets examined, in none did these approach those held by the United States. Britain's performance ranged from second place (after the United States) in M&A, syndicated loans, commercial paper and medium-term note markets, to third place (after the United States and Japan) in the market for international equities, down to an also-ran position in international bonds and Eurobonds.

There follows a group of countries, Switzerland, France and Canada, which hold relatively small stakes, typically less than 5 per cent, in most markets. The Netherlands too has a toehold in most markets. By contrast there is a lack of consistency in Germany's performance with a substantial share of international bonds and little presence elsewhere. Other countries which feature in these international financial markets are Italy, Belgium and the Nordic group.

AN ANALYSIS OF SHARES BY MARKET, 1989

The factors which immediately determine a country's share of an individual financial market as measured in this analysis are the number of national financial institutions which participate in the specified market, the average number of units of output 'produced' by

Table 4.3 *An analysis of the global M&A market, 1989*

	Number of firms	Units per firm	Value per unit US$ mn	Value per firm US$ mn	Country value US$ bn	Country share %
United States	17	84.5	501.9	42,411	721	71.2
Japan	3	33.7	63.5	2,140	6	0.6
United Kingdom	13	70.7	209.4	14,800	192	19.0
France	2	62.5	360.0	22,498	45	4.4
The Netherlands	1	7.0	295.0	2,065	2	0.2
Switzerland	1	59.0	143.6	8,472	8	0.8
Canada	3	31.0	406.1	12,589	38	3.7
All	40	68.5	369.7	25,324	1,013	100.0

Source: See table 4.1.

Table 4.4 *An analysis of the cross-border M&A market, 1989*

	Number of firms	Units per firm	Value per unit US$ mn	Value per firm US$ mn	Country value US$ bn	Country share %
United States	12	28.2	482.3	13,601	163	58.2
United Kingdom	8	29.7	360.0	10,692	85	30.3
France	1	12.0	314.1	3,769	4	1.3
Switzerland	1	16.0	364.2	5,827	6	2.1
Canada	3	14.7	517.0	7,600	23	8.1
All	25	25.8	433.9	11,195	280	100.0

Source: See table 4.1.

Table 4.5 *An analysis of the market for syndicated loans, 1989*

	Number of firms	Units per firm	Value per unit US$ mn	Value per firm US$ mn	Country value US$ bn	Country share %
United States	15	76.0	274.0	20,824	312	66.2
Japan	9	37.2	66.8	2,485	22	4.7
United Kingdom	9	45.1	184.3	8,312	75	15.9
Germany	2	13.5	166.6	2,249	5	1.0
France	4	24.5	148.2	3,631	15	3.1
Italy	1	44.0	73.2	3,221	3	0.7
Switzerland	2	23.0	160.3	3,687	7	1.6
Canada	3	25.7	211.9	5,446	16	3.5
Australia	2	27.5	103.8	2,854	6	1.3
Other	3	11.0	316.5	3,482	10	2.2
All	50	45.2	208.6	9,429	472	100.0

Source: See table 4.1.

each of these firms; and the average value of each of these units. For example table 4.3 reveals that in 1989 seventeen American financial institutions participated[6] in the global market for M&A advice, each being involved on average in 84.5 deals with an average value of US$501.9 million per deal. This means that United States institutions accounted (as shown as tables 4.1 and 4.2) for US$721 billion, or 71 per cent, of a total market of US$1013 billion. The shares of the other countries which competed in this market are analysed in the same way in table 4.3.

The table shows that all three basic explanatory factors contributed to America's dominance of this market. There were seventeen United States firms out of a total of 40, each 'producing' 84 units compared with an international average of 68, at a value of US$502 million per

Table 4.6 *An analysis of the market for international bonds, 1989*

	Number of firms	Units per firm	Value per unit US$ mn	Value per firm US$ mn	Country value US$ bn	Country share %
United States	11	49.8	129.8	6,464	71	28.2
Japan	11	65.5	149.0	9,759	107	42.6
United Kingdom	7	19.1	106.0	2,025	14	5.6
Germany	5	28.2	136.0	3,835	19	7.6
France	6	33.2	85.1	2,823	17	6.7
Italy	2	9.5	123.7	1,175	2	0.9
The Netherlands	2	16.0	87.0	1,392	3	1.1
Belgium	1	49.0	21.9	1,073	1	0.4
Switzerland	2	76.5	91.0	6,961	14	5.5
Canada	2	13.0	93.9	1,220	2	1.0
Other	1	4.0	169.5	678	1	0.3
All	50	40.5	124.4	5,038	252	100.0

Source: See table 4.1.

Table 4.7 *An analysis of the market for Eurobonds, 1989*

	Number of firms	Units per firm	Value per unit US$ mn	Value per firm US$ mn	Country value US$ bn	Country share %
United States	10	33.6	148.9	5,003	50	24.6
Japan	11	50.9	168.1	8,556	94	46.3
United Kingdom	7	14.6	116.5	1,701	12	5.8
Germany	5	25.0	146.2	3,655	18	8.9
France	6	21.8	115.6	2,520	15	7.4
Italy	2	9.5	123.7	1,175	2	1.2
The Netherlands	2	14.5	89.7	1,301	3	1.3
Belgium	1	10.0	65.6	656	1	0.3
Switzerland	2	19.5	120.1	2,342	5	2.3
Canada	2	13.0	93.9	1,221	2	1.2
The Nordic group	1	11.0	60.2	662	1	0.3
Other	1	3.0	202.0	606	1	0.3
All	50	27.8	146.3	4,067	204	100.0

Source: See table 4.1.

unit as opposed to a market average of US$370 million. The table reveals that neither relatively large numbers of units per firm (71 compared with a market average of 68), nor high values per unit (US$209 million compared with US$370 million), were responsible for Britain's very substantial share of this market. Rather is the United Kingdom's position attributable to the fact that a comparatively large number of its institutions, thirteen out of the total of 40, were active in global M&A advisory activity.

Table 4.8 *An analysis of the market for international equities, 1989*

	Number of firms	Units per firm	Value per unit US$ mn	Value per firm US$ mn	Country value US$ bn	Country share %
United States	7	14.3	65.2	932	6.5	48.9
Japan	3	5.3	177.9	943	2.8	21.4
United Kingdom	2	12.0	66.4	797	1.6	12.0
Germany	1	7.0	37.4	262	0.3	2.0
France	2	5.5	39.5	217	0.4	3.3
The Netherlands	2	4.0	98.9	396	0.8	5.9
Belgium	1	4.0	83.7	335	0.4	2.5
Switzerland	1	7.0	37.4	262	0.3	2.0
The Nordic group	1	7.0	40.0	280	0.3	2.1
All	20	9.2	72.4	666	13.3	100.0

Source: See table 4.1.

Table 4.9 *An analysis of the market for Euro CP and CD, 1989*

	Number of firms	Units per firm	Value per unit US$ mn	Value per firm US$ mn	Country value US$ bn	Country share %
United States	15	107.7	328.6	35,390	531	56.6
Japan	9	23.4	327.8	7,671	31	7.4
United Kingdom	7	74.4	259.7	19,322	135	14.4
Germany	1	21.0	256.7	5,391	5	0.6
France	4	21.5	253.8	5,457	22	2.3
The Netherlands	1	12.0	187.6	2,251	2	0.2
Switzerland	2	183.0	304.8	55,778	112	11.9
Canada	2	26.5	285.6	7,568	15	1.6
Australia	3	42.0	180.5	7,581	23	2.5
The Nordic group	4	26.2	195.5	5,122	20	2.1
Other	2	14.0	108.6	1,520	3	0.3
All	50	62.9	298.2	18,757	938	100.0

Source: See table 4.1.

The same analysis is repeated in tables 4.4–4.10 for the following markets: M&A cross-border, syndicated loans, international bonds, Eurobonds, international equities, Euro CP and CD and Euro MTNs. One of the most significant facts to emerge from these tables is that not only does the United States have comparatively large numbers of firms in all these eight markets, being headed in this sense (by Japan) only in the Eurobond market, but also in every instance bar one the units per firm and average unit values which characterise its institutions' operations are greater than the market average.[7]

Table 4.10 *An analysis of the market for Euro MTNs, 1989*

	Number of firms	Units per firm	Value per unit US$ mn	Value per firm US$ mn	Country value US$ bn	Country share %
United States	12	23.2	637.4	14,788	178	76.4
Japan	3	3.0	622.2	1,867	6	2.4
United Kingdom	3	10.7	708.9	7,585	23	9.7
Germany	1	5.0	277.4	1,387	1	0.6
The Netherlands	2	5.0	214.0	1,070	2	0.9
Switzerland	2	21.5	469.1	10,086	20	8.7
Australia	1	4.0	412.5	1,650	2	0.7
The Nordic group	1	6.0	233.3	1,400	1	0.6
All	25	15.5	600.2	9,303	233	100.0

BRITAIN'S COMPARATIVE PERFORMANCE

To focus on the United Kingdom's comparative performance in these markets tables 4.11, 4.12 and 4.13, derived from tables 4.3–4.10, show the relative position in terms of these explanatory factors of Britain and all competitors, Britain and the United States, and Britain and other countries.

It is difficult to discern much of a pattern in the first of these tables where the United Kingdom's performance is shown relative to competitors. In some markets (global M&A, cross-border M&A, syndicated loans, international equities, and Euro CP and CD) the numbers of units per firm achieved by British institutions are equal to or above the competitors' average, whilst in others (international bonds, Eurobonds and Euro MTNs) they are less. However, Britain's average 'product' values are relatively high only in the case of Euro MTNs; in all other markets they are low. The outcome is that when compared with competitor countries as a group the average output value for British financial institutions is less than that registered by competitors in all markets except international equities and, marginally, Euro CP and CD. This in turn suggests that participation by relatively large numbers of British institutions does much to boost the country's market shares.

More clearcut pictures emerge when Britain's performance is compared first, in table 4.12, with that of the United States and secondly, in table 4.13, with that of competitor countries, excluding the United States.[8] The Anglo-American comparison in table 4.12 reveals that in addition to a substantially lower British firm participation rate in every market, in virtually all instances units per firm and

Table 4.11 *Britain's performance relative to all competitors, 1989*

	UK: All relative			
	Numbers of firms	Units per firm	Value per unit	Value per firm
Global M&A	0.32	1.03	0.57	0.58
Cross-border M&A	0.32	1.15	0.82	0.96
Syndicated loans	0.18	1.00	0.88	0.88
International bonds	0.14	0.47	0.85	0.41
Eurobonds	0.14	0.53	0.80	0.42
International equities	0.10	1.30	0.92	1.20
Euro CP & CD	0.14	1.18	0.87	1.03
Euro MTNs	0.12	0.69	1.18	0.82

Source: tables 4.3–4.10.

Table 4.12 *Britain's performance relative to the United States, 1989*

	UK: US relative			
	Numbers of firms	Units per firm	Value per unit	Value per firm
Global M&A	0.76	0.84	0.42	0.35
Cross-border M&A	0.67	1.05	0.75	0.79
Syndicated loans	0.60	0.59	0.67	0.40
International bonds	0.64	0.38	0.82	0.31
Eurobonds	0.70	0.43	0.78	0.34
International equities	0.29	0.85	1.02	0.85
Euro CP & CD	0.47	0.69	0.79	0.55
Euro MTNs	0.25	0.46	1.11	0.51

Source: tables 4.3–4.10.

average values are lower, often much lower, than those registered by American firms. Exceptions are to be found only in the markets for cross-border M&A and MTNs where average British values appear to be slightly in excess of America's. Consequently for all markets the output values per firm achieved by British institutions are substantially below those recorded by United States banks and security houses.

Equally illuminating, but in a contrasting fashion, is the picture which emerges in table 4.13 for Britain's performance relative to other competitor nations. Only in the case of the markets for international bonds and Eurobonds are the number of units per firm which typify the activities of British institutions below those registered by their (non-American) competitors. For other markets the number of output units per British firm are substantially above those achieved by competitors. The picture for average values is rather different. Only in

Table 4.13 *Britain's performance relative to other countries, 1989*

	UK: Other[a] relative			
	Numbers of firms	Units per firm	Value per unit	Value per firm
Global M&A	1.30	1.84	0.81	1.48
Cross-border M&A	1.60	2.06	0.80	1.64
Syndicated loans	0.35	1.64	1.55	2.56
International bonds	0.33	0.64	1.11	0.72
Eurobonds	0.32	0.82	0.97	0.78
International equities	0.18	2.20	0.77	1.69
Euro CP & CD	0.25	2.07	0.96	1.99
Euro MTNs	0.30	1.39	1.68	2.34

Source: tables 4.3–4.10.
[a] The United Kingdom compared with all countries excluding the United States, and with all countries excluding Japan as well as the United States in the case of international bonds and Eurobonds.

the case of medium-term notes and syndicated loans are British average values significantly greater than those of their competitors; in other markets they are about the same or lower. The net outcome is that in contrast to the performance of British institutions *vis-à-vis* the United States, 'output value' per British firm substantially exceeds that of our competitors in all markets other than international bonds and Eurobonds where the record of British institutions is poor. It is also apparent that the United Kingdom's performance is boosted by relatively high institutional participation rates *vis-à-vis* individual countries in this group, especially in the market for M&A activity where British banks outnumber the combined competitor total.

AGGREGATE MARKET SHARES

For a variety of reasons these country shares can be aggregated across markets only in a very approximate fashion. First the absence in tables 4.1 and 4.2 of a share for a given country in a specific market does not mean, for reasons already considered, that the country plays no role whatsoever, though its actual market share is unlikely to be substantial. Furthermore the appropriate weights for cross-market aggregation, which should be based on the revenues earned by each country in each market, are not systematically available.

In the event, to obtain a rough indication of each country's share of the overall market, as constituted by these financial instruments, two weighting systems have been adopted. First shares have been calculated using the gross values given in table 4.1: the implicit assumption

Table 4.14 *Country shares of aggregated financial markets,[a] 1989*

	Market share		GDP		Fee weighted share/GDP relative[b]
	Gross value weighted %	Fee weighted %	US$ bn	%	
United States	62.3	66.3	4,118	32.7	2.03
United Kingdom	15.1	17.0	843	6.7	2.53
Japan	7.3	5.1	2,818	22.4	0.23
Switzerland	5.5	2.1	175	1.4	1.50
France	3.4	4.2	948	7.5	0.56
Canada	2.4	3.2	543	4.3	0.74
Germany	1.1	0.8	1,202	9.6	0.08
Australia	1.0	0.3	283	2.2	0.14
The Nordic group	0.8	0.1	384	3.0	0.03
The Netherlands	0.3	0.3	224	1.8	0.17
Italy	0.2	0.2	886	7.0	0.03
Belgium	0.1	0.1	170	1.3	0.08
Other	0.5	0.3			
Total	100.0	100.0	12,594[c]	100.0	

Source: See text where reasons are cited to explain why the market shares presented in this table are subject to significant statistical qualifications.
[a] The markets included are: global M&A, syndicated loans, international bonds, international equities, Euro CD and CP and Euro medium-term notes.
[b] Fee weighted market share relative to GDP.
[c] Excluding 'other'.

underlying this 'gross value weighted series' is that income-margins are identical in all markets. Secondly a 'fee weighted' series has been derived applying the market margins provided by a major financial institution.[9] It should be stressed that such margins vary not only between markets but also between firms and over time so that, at best, they should be accepted as no more than 'typical'.

The overall market shares which emerge are set out in table 4.14, where countries are ranked on the basis of the gross value weighted shares. Since no absolute values are available for foreign exchange activities that market cannot be included in the weighted share series. To avoid double counting two of the markets covered by tables 4.1 and 4.2, cross-border M&A and Eurobonds, have been excluded since they are already included in, respectively, the worldwide M&A and international bond markets.

It is clear that the two measures yield very similar pictures of aggregate market shares.[10] It is also plain that the United States plays an undisputed dominant role accounting for about two thirds of the world market for these financial services. In second place some way behind comes Britain with 15–17 per cent of the market. Japan occupies third place possessing something of the order of a tenth of the market. Of the countries with smaller stakes Switzerland, France and Canada perform the best. It should not escape attention that this global financial market is effectively shared among a comparatively small number of developed economies and that these, in turn, are dominated by a single country, the United States.[11]

It is illuminating to compare national performances as measured by these aggregate market shares with country size as measured by GDP. Table 4.14 shows that, when aggregate fee weighted shares are standardised in this fashion, Britain occupies pole position, the United States coming second and Switzerland third. These performances contrast sharply with those of such major economies as Japan, Germany and France.

AN ANALYSIS OF AGGREGATE SHARES

Table 4.15 summarises for each country the pattern of institutional market participation in 1989. The data relate to 97 financial institutions with a total of 235 individual market participations: the full schedule of institutions and the markets in which they held significant shares is given in Appendix A at the end of this book.

Table 4.16 shows for each country its gross value weighted[12] share, the number of its participating financial institutions, the total number of market participations, a coefficient of diversification (the number of these markets in which on average a country's institutions participate) and the market share per institution participation.

Three of these statistics, the number of firms, the coefficient of diversification and the average share per market participation, between them account for the aggregate country shares shown in the first column of the table. For instance, where they participate in an individual financial market each United States institution on average acquires 0.81 per cent of that market. This percentage share is boosted for each firm by the fact that, typically, each American institution participates in 2.85 financial markets and the total United States market share benefits from the fact that the country has 27 such firms.[13] These three explanatory elements simply reflect the fact that the higher a firm's share of a market, the more markets in which it participates and the greater the number of such firms in a country, the larger will be that country's share of the global financial market.

The contents of table 4.16 show that there is a positive relationship between country shares and each of the three factors. A further inspection of the data suggests that the main determinant is the average share obtained by a given institution in a specific market. The

Table 4.15 *The country pattern of institutional market participation, 1989*

	Number of institutions in individual markets					
	M&A world wide	Syndi-cated loans	Inter-national bonds	Inter-national equities	Euro CP & CD	Euro MTNs
United States	17	15	11	7	15	12
Japan	3	9	11	3	9	3
United Kingdom	13	9	7	2	7	3
Germany	—	2	5	1	1	1
France	2	4	6	2	4	—
Italy	—	1	2	—	—	—
The Netherlands	1	—	2	2	1	2
Belgium	—	—	1	1	—	—
Switzerland	1	2	2	1	2	2
Canada	3	3	2	—	2	—
Australia	—	2	—	—	3	1
The Nordic group	—	—	—	1	4	1
Other	—	3	1	—	2	—
Total	40	50	50	20	50	25

Sources: See table 4.1.

Table 4.16 *An analysis of aggregate market shares, 1989*

	Market share %	Number of institutions	Number of market partici-pations	Coefficient of diversi-fication[a]	Market share per partici-pation[b]
United States	62.3	27	77	2.85	0.81
Japan	7.3	14	38	2.71	0.19
United Kingdom	15.1	16	41	2.56	0.37
Germany	1.1	5	10	2.00	0.11
France	3.4	7	18	2.57	0.19
Italy	0.2	3	3	1.00	0.07
The Netherlands	0.3	3	8	2.67	0.04
Belgium	0.1	2	2	1.00	0.05
Switzerland	5.5	2	10	5.00	0.55
Canada	2.4	6	10	1.66	0.24
Australia	1.0	3	6	2.00	0.17
The Nordic group	0.8	4	6	1.50	0.13
Other	0.5	5	6	1.20	0.08
Total	100.0	97	235	2.42	0.43

Source: tables 4.1, 4.14 and 4.15.
[a] Number of market participations per institution.
[b] Aggregate market share per market participation.

association with the number of national financial institutions is perhaps least strong.[14] This is aptly illustrated by, and largely owing to, the position of Switzerland, ranked fourth by country share, first by diversification, second by firm market share but at the bottom of the list in terms of number of participating financial institutions. The United States' dominant position is associated with top rank in both number of firms and average firm market share, and second place for diversification. Japan and the United Kingdom score relatively highly on all three criteria: in the latter case with second position for number of participating firms, third for diversification and a firm market share which is about average.

SUMMARY

This chapter corroborates major conclusions derived from Chapter 3: the overall dominance of the selected markets by the United States and the generally commendable performance of British institutions in occupying a series of second and third places in terms of market shares.

It has been demonstrated how country shares in individual markets can be explained by three factors: the number of its financial institutions which substantially participate in the market in question; the average number of units (deals advised on, issues handled, and so on) 'produced' per institution; and the average value of these 'products'. In terms of all three factors the United Kingdom suffers in comparison with the United States. Fewer British institutions operate in these markets and on average they produce a smaller number of units of relatively low value.

A different picture emerges when the United Kingdom performance is measured alongside that of other country rivals taken as a group. Here the analysis reveals a relatively high degree of United Kingdom firm participation, especially in the case of M&A activity where British institutions outnumber the rival group, and, except in the case of the international bond market, comparatively large numbers of items produced per British institution. In terms of average values the United Kingdom's position is more equivocal *vis-à-vis* this group of competitors: in two markets British average values are relatively high but in others they are lower or about the same as those achieved by competitors. Nevertheless the net outcome is that, the international bond market aside, output values per British firm are superior to those achieved by non-American competitors.

The United Kingdom's performance in individual markets is reflected in the estimated aggregate cross-market country shares which suggest that Britain occupies second place ahead of Japan and after the United States: however the dominance of the United States is evident from the respective estimated global shares of the two countries, 62–66 per cent and 15–17 per cent. When global market shares are related to the size of the economy as measured by GDP, Britain features in the top group along with the United States and Switzerland.

The large global market share secured by the United States can be traced to three factors: the top position which it occupies, relative to other countries, for both numbers of participating financial insitutions and individual market shares obtained by these firms, together with its second place in terms of degree of market diversification. The United Kingdom's performance reflects its occupancy of second place for firm participation, third place for market diversification together with an average performance in terms of individual market shares obtained by British financial institutions.

5

A STATISTICAL COMPARISON OF NATIONAL BANKING SECTORS: 1989

INTRODUCTION

The previous chapter revealed how selected international financial markets are shared between the institutions of different nationalities and examined some of the factors which have influenced the size of these shares. A by-product of the analysis was the identification of the principal banks and and security houses which operate in these markets. In this chapter attention is focused on these institutions, again grouped by country of ownership and control, in an effort to determine whether there exist specific national characteristics which may influence their performance in international markets.

Where relevant and practicable the opportunity is seized to examine contrasts in the characteristics of commercial banks on the one hand and investment banks, merchant banks and security houses on the other, since the study suggests that the structure of a country's banking industry, in terms of these forms, may have a significant impact on its performance in international markets.

THE DATA

Both *Euromoney* (June, 1990) and *The Banker* (July, 1990) annually publish a list of the largest banks worldwide together with certain quantifiable characteristics. In the case of *Euromoney*'s top 500 banks they are identified and ranked by size of shareholders' equity: other features which are recorded for each bank are equity growth, net income, net income growth, total assets and assets growth. *The Banker*'s top 1,000 are also chosen and ranked by size of capital: other characteristics include capital growth, asset size, asset growth, capital–assets ratio, profits, profits growth, return on capital and return on assets.

These two sources suffer from certain major deficiencies for the purposes of this study. First in terms of institutional coverage they fall short of our needs by excluding security houses which, along with banks, play a major role in the markets that have been selected. Secondly, the measured characteristics exclude some variables which are of special interest when comparing inter-institutional and inter-country contrasts in competitive performance. In particular these sources contain no information relating to the listed banks for gross income and its components, expenses and their major elements or employment levels.[1]

To focus attention on performance in the chosen markets the data presented in the following tables are in principle restricted to the financial institutions which have been shown to be substantially active in the relevant markets and listed in Appendix A: *Schedule of Institutional Market Participation: 1989*. Furthermore, to base the analysis on as wide a range of institutional characteristics as possible the relevant data have been extracted from the firms' annual reports and accounts for the nearest financial year to 1989.

Whilst this *Schedule* constituted the basic list of firms to be included in the analysis it is subject to two significant qualifications. First some institutions were excluded from the analysis because their annual reports and accounts were unavailable or were in some significant respects inadequate. Secondly, since considerable attention is directed in this study to the role and performance of British merchant banks of both the independent and integrated variety, coverage has been extended beyond the basic list in the case of this category of financial institution. 71 institutions were eventually included in the analysis.

When culling the information from annual reports and accounts every effort has been made to process and present the data on as comparable a basis as possible.[2] To facilitate inter-country comparisons, values have been standardised in US$. Also an attempt has been made to single out, and present separately, provisions for bad debts in the single chosen year in order to avoid any short-term distortion in financial performance which might otherwise be present.

Certain data deficiencies persist. In particular the results presented for most institutions, the commercial and universal banks, are dominated by their retail activities, not those international capital market operations on which this study focuses. Secondly, not all the specified variables are available for all the covered institutions. This deficiency is pronounced, unfortunately, in the case of British merchant banks of both the independent and integrated variety. Thirdly, complete comparability cannot be achieved: for instance some employment data is available only on a full-time equivalent basis, other data relates to numbers of employees.

The basic data for each of the covered financial institutions are presented in Appendix B: *Basic Banking Data: 1989*. The selected statistics comprise, where feasible, the institution's total income apportioned between net interest and other income, total expenses apportioned between personnel costs and other expenses, net income, debt pro-

Table 5.1 *Banking sectors by firm size, 1989*

Country and type of financial institution	No.	Averages Employment '000	Assets US$bn	Income US$m
United States:				
Banks	13	31.2	74.2	3,968
Investment banks	5	13.1	57.7	2,726
Japan:				
Banks	9	11.8	298.4	4,780
Security houses	4	10.3	35.8	4,599
United Kingdom:				
Banks	5	77.1	125.1	6,053
Independent merchant banks	7	2.5	10.6	...
Integrated merchant banks	3	2.4	20.8	...
All merchant banks	10	2.5	13.7	...
Germany:				
Banks	3	14.1	122.0	2,722
France:				
Banks	3	55.9	206.0	5,799
Investment banks	2	21.4	97.0	...
All banks	5	42.1	162.4	...
Italy:				
Banks	3	18.4	86.8	2,541
The Netherlands:				
Banks	3	26.1	89.3	2,537
Switzerland:				
Banks	2	19.8	109.9	2,893
Canada:				
Banks	5	35.6	74.8	3,171
Australia:				
Banks	3	44.8	68.4	3,086

Source: Appendix B.

vision and net income after debt provisions, total assets and employment. Where relevant and practicable the results for a given country
are presented separately, on the one hand for commercial banks and on
the other for investment banks, merchant banks and security houses.

INSTITUTIONAL SIZE

Derived from Appendix B, *Basic Banking Data*: 1989, table 5.1 shows
for each country the average size of its relevant financial institutions

in terms of employment, assets and total income, which may be regarded as proximate measures of labour and capital inputs and of output. In those countries where the comparison is appropriate and practicable table 5.1 confirms that commercial banks operate on an appreciably larger scale than do investment banks, merchant banks and security houses. The contrast is most pronounced in the case of the United Kingdom where, measured by labour force, a merchant bank is on average no more than a thirtieth of the size of a commercial bank and, in terms of assets, about a tenth. Whilst for independent and integrated merchant banks average employment levels are about the same, the latter are about twice the size of the former when measured by assets.

In the United States too commercial banks are larger than investment banks on all three size criteria, assets, income and employment, but the size differentials are much smaller than in Britain. In Japan also the bank–security house size differential is not very large when measured by labour force and income differentials, but the average asset disparity is marked. In France the average labour force and asset size of Indosuez and Paribas is rather less than half of the corresponding size of BNP, Credit Lyonnais and Société Générale.

More pertinent are cross-nationality size differences. In the case of commercial banks the comparisons are best approached by considering first the case of Japan. Whilst the banks of this country employ on average no more than about 12,000 employees (the lowest figure for the ten countries shown in table 5.1), they are endowed with assets of about US$300 billion, much in excess of those held by the institutions of any other country. Average bank income in Japan is also high. Otherwise the table reveals that average commercial bank size among this group of countries is largest in the United Kingdom and France. British banks rank top in terms of labour force size (with 77,000 employees some way ahead of France with 56,000), and are also first in average income and third in average asset size. France holds second place on all three measures. American commercial banks occupy a middle position in the size scale. The average bank ranks fourth in terms of income, fifth for labour force size and no higher than ninth by assets.

Swiss and German banks are characterised by fairly high asset levels but are not very large when measured by employment or income. In contrast the Australian banks have fairly large employment levels but relatively low assets and incomes. Taken all round the Dutch and Italian banks operate on the smallest scale.

Whilst British commercial banks find themselves virtually at the top of the size league the opposite applies when British merchant banks are compared with their counterparts in other countries. Average assets of Indosuez and Paribas are no less than US$97 billion though in the case of the latter bank especially asset levels may be boosted by substantial commercial banking operations. These institutions are followed in second place by American investment banks with, on average, approximately US$60 billion assets apiece and then by Japanese security houses with US$36 billion. By contrast, on this criterion, British merchant banks are quite puny with, overall, some US$14 billion assets each, reflecting levels of US$11 billion and US$21 billion held by, respectively, independent and integrated merchant banks.

A similar pattern emerges when attention is directed to labour force size.[3] Again France heads the size list with an average of 21,000 employees in its two banks followed by Japan and the United States with labour forces of 10–13,000. Britain lags way behind with some 2,500 employees per merchant bank.

FACTOR RATIOS

There is no common accepted practice to apply when constructing factor ratios for banking analyses. One which is sometimes used focuses attention upon variations between banks in returns to equity. It is based on the relationship

$$R/E = R/A \times A/E$$

where R is profit, A assets and E equity capital. Thus variations between financial institutions in their returns to capital are seen to be determined, in the first instance, by contrasts in returns to assets and in degrees of leverage. This type of analysis suffers, in the present context, from a failure to take any account of labour inputs.

The approach adopted below is one which has a closer affinity with standard production functions in that it takes account of labour as well as capital inputs. It is founded on three ratios: gross income per employee, O/L, which can be regarded as a proxy for labour productivity; income per unit of assets, O/A; and assets per employee, A/L, an indication of capital intensity. It is instructive to consider inter-country contrasts in these three banking features in terms of the relationship

$$O/L = O/A \times A/L$$

where the proxy for labour productivity is a function of the capital coefficient and capital intensity.

Table 5.2 *Banking sectors by factor ratios, 1989*

Country and type of financial institution	No.	Income/ Employment US$'000	Income/ Assets %	Assets/ Employment US$000
United States:				
Banks	13	127.1	5.35	2,373
Investment banks	5	208.4	4.72	4,414
Japan:				
Banks	9	405.5	1.60	25,308
Security houses	4	444.4	12.86	3,458
United Kingdom:				
Banks	5	78.5	4.84	1,623
Independent merchant banks	7	...	...	4,183
Integrated merchant banks	3	...	...	8,733
All merchant banks	10	...	...	5,489
Germany:				
Banks	3	192.6	2.23	8,641
France:				
Banks	3	103.7	2.82	3,683
Investment banks	2	...	...	4,535
All banks	5	...	...	3,856
Italy:				
Banks	3	138.4	2.95	4,727
The Netherlands:				
Banks	3	97.1	2.84	3,415
Switzerland:				
Banks	2	146.2	2.63	5,558
Canada:				
Banks	5	89.0	4.24	2,101
Australia:				
Banks	3	68.9	4.51	1,528

Source: Appendix B.

Before reviewing the results obtained from this analysis a few words need to be said about the measures themselves. First net income, rather than the gross concept used, would constitute a superior output measure since by excluding 'other expenses', payments to suppliers and so on, it approximates more closely value added. Unfortunately data deficiencies are such that adoption of this income concept would lead to an exclusion from the analysis of both British and French investment bank sectors together with all Japanese banks. Nevertheless, this conceptual distinction was thought to be significant enough to justify a test being made on those eleven sectors (banks in the

United States, United Kingdom, Germany, France, Italy, the Netherlands, Switzerland, Canada and Australia, together with American
investment banks and Japanese security houses) for which both gross
and net income data are available. In the event, the ranking of these
sectors by gross income per employee is identical with their ranking
by net income per employee.

Secondly, capital inputs have been measured by total assets, real
and financial. Traditionally, when making comparisons of industrial
performance, only real assets, buildings, plant, machinery, vehicles
and so on, are taken into account. This approach is quite inappro-
priate for banking where real, as opposed to financial assets, comprise
a relatively small proportion of the total. This capital concept, total
assets, needs to be distinguished from 'capital' as measured by an
institution's equity. As will become apparent in Chapter 6, both these,
quite distinct, capital concepts are relevant to a financial institution's
performance, though in different ways: total assets being associated
with a bank's 'muscle' and the status of its equity base with its
reputation.

Thirdly, an earlier warning about the data on which this analysis is
based bears repetition: that variations in a given ratio between
countries and individual institutions will reflect in some measure
differences in product mix, especially contrasts in the scales of retail
and wholesale banking activities.

Table 5.2 displays the three relevant ratios. It reveals that among
commercial banks Japan records by far the highest level of average
gross income per employee, US$405,000. Above average results are
also registered by banks in Germany, Switzerland, Italy and the
United States. Relatively low gross income levels per employee are
features of the other countries in the table. The British banks achieved
no more than US$78,000 per capita, a performance which only
Australia with US$69,000 failed to match.

An above average level of gross income per employee may be
associated with a high return of gross income per unit of capital, high
capital intensity or a combination of both features. It emerges that the
Japanese banks' productivity superiority is due entirely to a very high
degree of capital intensity: in no other country do assets per employee
approach the level of US$25 million recorded by Japanese banks.
Their achievement is in no way associated with a high level of gross
income per unit of assets since in the case of this feature the level
recorded by Japan, 1.6 per cent, is the lowest of all the ten countries,
probably reflecting the low levels of interest paid and charged by the
country's banks.

Whether or not Japan is included it emerges very clearly that country differences in gross income per employee are shaped almost in their entirety by differentials in capital intensity, average levels of assets per employee: indeed contrasts in gross income per unit of assets appear to play a negative role. The rank correlation coefficient between labour productivity so measured and capital intensity, inclusive and exclusive of Japan are, respectively, +0.96 and +0.95. The rank correlation coefficients between labour productivity and gross income per unit of assets inclusive and exclusive of Japan are −0.73 and −0.63. Insofar as they are due to high rates of interest paid and charged by banks, high rates of gross income to assets will reflect a competitive disadvantage for the institutions of the relevant countries. For the United States a middling 'labour productivity' performance is associated with a middling capital intensity and the highest ratio of gross income to assets.

In accordance with these results Britain's poor performance in terms of gross income per employee is directly associated with an unduly low degree of capital intensity; only Australian banks, at US$1.5 million per employee, register a figure below the US$1.6 million per employee which typifies British banks. By contrast the 4.84 per cent gross income return to British bank assets does little to boost income per employee; and insofar as it reflects relatively high British interest rates, it curtails the British banks' abilities to compete on price in international capital markets.

Data deficiencies severely restrict the conclusions which can be drawn about the performance, in terms of these ratios, of merchant banks, investment banks and security houses, either cross-country or in comparison with commercial banks of the same nationality. American and Japanese data presented in table 5.2 suggest that gross income per employee tends to be higher in this type of banking institution than in commercial banks of the same nationality. However, whilst for United States investment banks this superior performance is associated again with relatively high capital intensity (in investment banks the ratio is almost twice as large as in commercial banks), in the case of Japanese security houses, against the otherwise almost universal principle, it is derived from low capital intensity but a very high ratio of gross income to capital.

The limited data available for the United Kingdom and France suggest that such financial institutions in these countries follow the American model where capital intensity is higher than in commercial banks. The disparity is rather more pronounced in the United Kingdom than in the United States. Taking the capital intensity of British commercial banks as unity the ratio of assets

Table 5.3 *Banking sectors by type of income, 1989*

Country and type of financial institution	No.	Total income US$mn	Net interest income US$mn	%	Other income US$mn	%
United States:						
Banks	13	51,579	29,311	56.8	22,268	43.2
Investment banks	6	19,888	812	4.1	19,076	95.9
Japan:						
Banks	9	43,020	18,261	42.4	24,759	57.6
Security houses	4	18,398	2,208	12.0	16,198	88.0
United Kingdom:						
Banks	5	30,266	18,735	61.9	11,531	38.1
Merchant banks	1	1,162	423	36.4	739	63.6
Germany:						
Banks	3	8,165	2,613	32.0	5,552	68.0
France:						
Banks	2	11,594	8,655	74.7	2,939	25.3
Italy:						
Banks	3	7,624	5,410	71.0	2,214	29.0
The Netherlands:						
Banks	3	7,610	5,149	67.7	2,461	32.3
Switzerland:						
Banks	2	5,785	1,997	34.5	3,788	65.5
Canada:						
Banks	5	15,854	11,161	70.4	4,693	29.6
Australia:						
Banks	3	9,258	5,943	64.2	3,315	35.8

Source: Appendix B.

to employees in independent British merchant banks is 2.6, in integrated merchant banks it is 5.4 and in all the covered merchant banks 3.4.

The same data deficiencies mean that investment/merchant banks can be compared across countries again only in terms of assets per employee. Table 5.2 suggests that at least for independent investment banking sectors international differences in capital intensity are not very pronounced, the levels for United States investment banks, independent British merchant banks, French investment banks and Japanese security houses being, respectively, US$4.4, 4.2, 3.9 and 3.5 million. In contrast capital intensity in integrated British merchant banks is as high as US$8.7 million.

Table 5.4 *Income and costs in national banking sectors, 1989*

		Average per institution: US $ million			
Country and type of financial institution	No.	Total income	Total expenses	Personnel costs	Other expenses	Net income

Country and type of financial institution	No.	Total income	Total expenses	Personnel costs	Other expenses	Net income
United States:						
Banks	13	3,968	2,702	1,343	1,359	1,265
All investment banks	6	3,315	2,945	1,718	1,226	370
Japan:						
Banks	2	4,782	3,195	946	2,248	1,587
Banks	9	4,780	3,145	...	...	1,635
Security houses	4	4,599	2,089	743	1,346	2,510
United Kingdom:						
Banks	5	6,053	4,000	2,342	1,658	2,053
Germany:						
Banks	3	2,722	1,949	1,151	798	773
France:						
Banks	3	5,799	3,996	2,382	1,614	1,803
Italy:						
Banks	3	2,541	1,641	1,059	582	900
The Netherlands:						
Banks	3	2,537	1,707	968	739	830
Switzerland:						
Banks	2	2,893	1,670	1,094	577	1,222
Canada:						
Banks	5	3,171	1,857	1,069	788	1,314
Australia:						
Banks	3	3,086	1,956	1,029	927	1,131

Source: Appendix B.

THE STRUCTURE OF BANKING INCOME

Table 5.3 shows how the structure of gross income, its split between net interest income and other forms of income such as fees and so on, varies between different types of banks and between countries. It confirms that in the case of investment banks and security houses non-interest income constitutes the largest slice of earnings. For six American investment banks such income accounts for no less than 96 per cent of the total, for the big four Japanese security houses 88 per cent and for the single British merchant bank for which data are available, Midland Montagu, 64 per cent.

Table 5.3 also reveals that perhaps contrary to expectations net

Table 5.5 *Patterns of income appropriation in national banking sectors: 1989*

Country and type of financial institution	No.	Percentages			
		Total income	Personnel costs	Other expenses	Net income
United States:					
Banks	13	100.0	33.9	34.3	31.9
All investment banks	6	100.0	51.8	37.0	11.2
Japan:					
Banks	2	100.0	19.8	47.0	33.2
Banks	9	100.0	65.8		34.2
Security houses	4	100.0	16.1	29.3	54.6
United Kingdom:					
Banks	5	100.0	38.7	27.4	33.9
Germany:					
Banks	3	100.0	42.3	29.3	28.4
France:					
Banks	3	100.0	41.1	27.8	31.1
Italy:					
Banks	3	100.0	41.7	22.9	35.4
The Netherlands:					
Banks	3	100.0	38.1	29.1	32.7
Switzerland:					
Banks	2	100.0	37.8	20.0	42.2
Canada:					
Banks	5	100.0	33.7	24.9	41.4
Australia:					
Banks	3	100.0	33.3	30.0	36.6

Source: table 5.4.

interest income by no means predominates in the earnings of commercial banks in the case of all countries. There is relatively little difference in the contribution of net interest income to the earnings of American, British, French, Canadian, Australian, Dutch and Italian banks, where the proportions range from 57 to 75 per cent. In contrast the net interest proportions in Japanese, Swiss and German banks are as low as 42 per cent, 34 per cent, and 32 per cent. In the latter two countries this reflects the domination of universal banks and the extent to which they play roles which in other countries are undertaken by investment banks and security houses.

COSTS AND INCOME APPROPRIATION

Table 5.4 sets out for each country the average recorded by financial institutions for total income (net of interest costs), total expenses, broken down into personnel and other costs, and net income, that is total income (net of interest) less total expenses.[4] On this basis it is possible, as shown in table 5.5, to determine how gross income is appropriated by three elements, personnel costs, other expenses and net income.

An outstanding feature of these two tables is the relatively high degree of international uniformity which they reveal in the profit margins of the commercial banks. Margins vary from 28 per cent registered, on average, by German banks, up to 42 per cent obtained by Swiss banks, but the average margins recorded for as many as seven of the countries, including the United Kingdom, lie within the relatively narrow range of 31–37 per cent.

The results obtained for six United States investment banks and four Japanese security houses are, to say the least, enigmatic. In the former case the margin, at 11 per cent, is very narrow and way below any of those recorded by the commercial banks in the ten countries. In sharp contrast the 55 per cent net income obtained by the big four Japanese security houses is substantially in excess of any country's commercial bank margin.

Apart from Japanese institutions where, for banks providing the relevant data, non-labour costs greatly exceed labour costs,[5] the latter kind of expense tends to exceed the former. As with profit margins there is much inter-country uniformity in the labour cost element: six countries, the United Kingdom, France, Germany, the Netherlands, Switzerland and Italy, fall within the narrow range of 38–42 per cent. For the first four of these countries non-labour costs are also virtually identical at about 27–29 per cent of total income; non-labour costs in Switzerland and Italy at about a fifth of total income are substantially less. In the United States, Australia and Canada, labour cost elements are almost identical at about a third of total income whilst in all three countries the non-labour cost element is similar to, or less than, this fraction.

There are sharp contrasts in income appropriation between American investment banks and Japanese security houses. In the former, as in most commercial banks, the labour cost element exceeds non-labour costs: at 52 per cent United States investment bank labour costs also exceed those recorded by the commercial banking sectors of any of these countries. At the opposite end of the spectrum labour costs in Japanese security houses account for no more than 16 per cent

Table 5.6 *Average personnel costs in national banking sectors, 1989*

Country and type of financial institution	No.	Personnel costs US$mn	Employment '000	Average personnel costs US$
United States				
Banks	13	17,463	405.9	43,027
Investment banks	5	7,290	65.4	111,468
Japan				
Banks	2	1,893	30.9	61,217
Security houses	4	2,971	41.4	71,789
United Kingdom:				
Banks	5	11,710	385.5	30,378
Independent merchant banks	7	976	17.8	54,915
Germany:				
Banks	3	3,452	42.4	81,500
France:				
Banks	3	7,146	167.8	42,586
Investment banks	2	2,144	42.8	50,069
Italy:				
Banks	3	3,178	55.1	57,702
The Netherlands:				
Banks	3	2,903	78.4	37,025
Switzerland:				
Banks	2	2,187	39.6	55,284
Canada:				
Banks	5	5,344	178.1	30,006
Australia:				
Banks	3	3,086	134.4	22,961

Source: Appendix B.

of total income,[6] much below the 29 per cent absorbed by non-labour expenses.

PERSONNEL COSTS

The analysis of labour costs can be carried further by comparing inter-institutional and inter-country differentials in average personnel costs, in which international differences in banking salaries will play the predominant role. Table 5.6 confirms that investment bankers are better rewarded than commercial bankers though this salary differential varies substantially between countries. The contrast is especially marked in Anglo-Saxon institutions. In the United States the average remuneration of commercial bankers is no more than 39 per cent of that enjoyed by investment bankers: in the United Kingdom it is 55 per cent. By contrast the proportion in France and Japan is 85 per cent.

An inter-country comparison of average remuneration in commercial banks shows the countries in table 5.6 falling into three broad groups. Among the highest payers are Germany, Japan, Italy and Switzerland with remuneration packages of, respectively, US$81,000, US$62,000, US$58,000 and US$55,000. Among the poorer payers are the United Kingdom and Canada with US$30,000 and Australia with US$23,000. Between these two groups lie the United States and France where employees receive on average US$43,000.

In the four countries where it is relevant the average remuneration for employees of investment and merchant banks, and of security houses are, in descending order, United States, US$111,000, Japan US$72,000, United Kingdom US$55,000 and France US$50,000.

SUMMARY

A statistical comparison of national banking sectors confirms that investment banking and security house activities are conducted on a smaller scale than commercial and universal banking operations. It reveals that in the United Kingdom this structural contrast in the scale of operations is especially marked, reflecting two features of the British banking scene. First United Kingdom commercial banks operate on a scale rarely matched by other countries. Secondly, and in sharp contrast, when compared with the size of rival foreign investment banks and security houses, whether measured by assets or employment, British merchant banks, especially the independents, are quite small.

Despite their relatively large size British commercial banks emerge badly when international performance is judged on the basis of gross income per employee. This reflects the fact that the capital intensity of their operations, total assets per employee, is to be found towards the bottom of the international list. Moreover the high ratio of gross income to assets, in as much as it stems from high domestic rates of interest, may constitute a competitive impediment in international financial markets.

Data limitations effectively preclude an assessment of the performance of British merchant banks in terms of gross income per employee. However it seems clear that in common with their position in other countries the capital intensity of such banks is substantially higher than that to be found in British commercial banks. More pertinently the data suggests there is little difference between the capital intensity of the operations of independent British merchant banks and foreign competitor investment banks and security houses, but that integrated British merchant banks are endowed with assets per employee significantly higher than the international average.

In the case of most of the other features which have been analysed in this chapter British commercial banks seem to differ little from the bulk of their competitors. For instance they are to be found in the main pack of countries when assessed by the proportion of non-interest income, net income margins, labour costs and other expenses. To illustrate this conformity the relevant percentages for these four features in the case of the United Kingdom and the other country average are respectively 62 and 57 per cent, 34 and 35 per cent, 36 and 36 per cent, and 27 and 33 per cent.

The British banking industry also conforms with the banking sectors of other countries by remunerating investment bankers at a higher level than commercial bankers, though as in the United States this differential is especially marked in Britain. There also exist sharp contrasts between average national remuneration levels, and British commercial and merchant bankers alike find themselves towards the bottom of the international scales.

6

EXPLANATIONS OF RELATIVE
PERFORMANCE

This chapter is based largely, though not exclusively, on interviews conducted with senior executives of financial institutions, of British and other nationalities, which are substantively active in the financial markets on which the study focuses. The 'Schedule of Institutional Market Participation, 1989' presented as Appendix A provides the 'population' of firms which were approached for interview. In the event, 36 interviews were conducted in London, Paris, Geneva and Frankfurt with financial institutions of British, American, Japanese, German, French, Swiss, Canadian and Nordic nationalities. The purpose of the interviews was to identify those factors which the interviewees considered to be mainly responsible for the success or failure of individual institutions, and national banking sectors, in winning shares in the chosen financial markets.

These views have been marshalled in the following manner. First, there is a group of topics that relates essentially to the structure of the national financial service industries which supply the markets in question. These topics include the relevance of economies of scale and scope in the provision of these financial products together with the impact of cross-nationality takeovers. Secondly, attention is directed to the role of human resources in winning market shares, a separate section being devoted to product innovation, a process closely related to labour force quality. Thirdly, interest is focused on the role of capital: in both its financial form as measured by equity and assets and also, more specifically, in its manifestation as technology. Fourthly, the influence of domestic economic and market conditions on the performance of a country's financial institutions is singled out for attention. Finally, the differential impact of major regulatory factors on market shares is considered.

THE STRUCTURE OF NATIONAL BANKING SECTORS: ECONOMIES OF SCOPE

The significance of economies of scope and scale in the provision of international financial services attract no less attention than they do in the context of manufacturing: 'the economics of supplying financial services internationally is jointly subject to economies of scale and economies of scope. The existence of both types of economies have strategic implications for players in the industry. Economies of scale suggest an emphasis on deepening activities within a cell or across cells in a product dimension. Economies of scope suggest an emphasis on broadening activities across cells' (Walter, 1988). Though these two dimensions are closely interrelated they are analysed below in separate sub-sections.

In the case of economies of scope a financial institution seeking to broaden the range of the markets which it serves is faced by three, not mutually exclusive, options: to establish new departments (that is to grow organically) which will supply these new products, to merge with or take over a national institution which provides such services, or to acquire a foreign institution with the requisite market coverage. This usually means, in the latter two contexts, a commercial bank buying a local or foreign security house, investment or merchant bank.

A financial institution, British or otherwise, seeking to expand the scale of its operations also has three options: to grow organically, take over or merge with a like national institution or with a similar kind of foreign institution. The study of such expansion within product lines and industry sub-sectors is best evaluated separately for, on the one hand, investment banks, merchant banks and security houses and, on the other, commercial banks which serve the international capital markets in question.

It is clear that, when considering the relevance of national contrasts in the scope and scale of operations in financial institutions, international differences in the structure of banking sectors (the relative mix of commercial banking, investment banking, integrated operations and cross-border institutional ownership) will occupy centre stage. It is also apparent that in the realisation of both economies of scope and scale the role of mergers between, and acquisition of, financial institutions, domestic and cross-border, has a potentially major role to play: the record suggests that this potential has been amply fulfilled. It is relevant therefore to consider, as a highly significant background factor, the degree of concentration which currently characterises the industry and the manner in which it is expected to change.

It is not at all uncommon at the national level for those financial services which are the subject of this study to be regarded as highly concentrated. As a random illustration: in the United States the top seven investment banks are responsible for advising on 80 per cent of M&A deals, only 1 per cent of United States banks have overseas branches and affiliates and 90 per cent of all American overseas banking assets are held by no more than twenty banks (Bellanger, 1988 and Gart, 1989). The high degree of concentration in the domestic commercial banking sectors of Britain and other countries is well documented.

Such a picture is quite misleading if extended to the kind of international financial markets which are the concern of this study. League tables which list even as many as the top fifty institutions sharing in a given market do not include all market participants. This simply reflects the fact that the markets in question are essentially international and open and therefore attract the attention and participation of financial institutions, with greater or lesser shares, from a range of countries.

It is widely anticipated that the next decade will witness a significant rise in the degree of concentration in these markets and a diminution in the number of financial institutions which dominate them. 'The merger movement among banks is under way. There are several reasons. One is the attempt to reach the 'critical mass' to compete in international markets. It is generally recognised that there is likely to be room for only a score or so of players able to claim a comprehensive worldwide coverage. They will certainly include several Japanese, a few from Europe and some Americans. But some of the present contestants will be weeded out' (*The Banker*, July 1990).

Apart from any autonomous long-term trend towards greater concentration, certain specific factors are likely to contribute to such a development. The prospect of continued weakness, during the immediate future, in capital markets is likely to have some impact: there are too many banks chasing static or shrinking markets and it is thought that the time has arrived when the number will be reduced essentially by mergers (*The Financial Times*, 20 November 1990). Looking somewhat further ahead deregulation in the United States and Japan will reinforce this trend: 'it is only a matter of time before Glass–Steagall crumbles in the United States. Right on its heels will be its equivalent, Article 65, in Japan . . . In fact, it is likely that within the next several years some fifteen institutions will control most of international banking and securities business on a global scale. They will not specialise in one area . . . they will each do it all'.[1] It is against this structural background that the future role and relative performance of British financial institutions needs to be considered.

There follow three sub-sections devoted respectively to economies of scope, economies of scale and the special relevance to comparative performance of cross-nationality acquisitions of financial institutions.

Economies of scope will be considered at two levels. The first of these is concerned with the relative merits in terms of operating efficiency and market capture of two forms of industrial structure in the financial services, the provision of the full range of capital market services by single financial entities which in effect combine the activities of commercial and investment banks, and the provision of the same services on a specialist and separate basis by commercial banks and investment banks respectively. The second focuses, rather more narrowly, on the economies of scope associated with market diversification within investment banks and security houses.

Universal banking

The theoretical advantages of banks providing a full range of all types of banking services are well known. First such a structure is frequently supported simply, and usually in rather general terms, on grounds of size. Walter, summarising a US Treasury study, writes: 'besides [advocating for American banks] additional capitalization, the Treasury paper pointed to greater earnings stability attributable to geographic and activity based diversification, improved safety and soundness due to a broader funding base and improved capitalization, and greater cost and marketing efficiencies due to economies of scale and scope' (Walter, 1988). Secondly, emphasis is placed on the commercial security which may be associated with full range banking. This is epitomised in a recent statement by the chairman of Credit Lyonnais, 'the charm of the universal bank is that you are present in all compartments of banking and financial activity. Events that are damaging in one compartment are often compensated in another' (*The Financial Times*, 5 October 1990). On the one hand the movement of commercial banks into capital market activities is seen as a hedge against long-term saturation of, and stagnation in, retail banking activities. On the other hand, and in principle, the relative stability of retail banking activities should help to dampen the effect of cycles to which capital markets tend to be prone.

Thirdly, an operational argument frequently put forward is that a combination of the financial 'muscle' associated with larger commercial banking assets and the know-how possessed by protagonists in capital markets provides an unbeatable competitive combination. Less specifically wide product coverage is thought in theory to yield, as a by-product, a supply of diverse market information and the availability of such data is said to be a vital ingredient in the institution's competitiveness.

In countries where commercial and investment banking have been undertaken by separate sub-sectors of the financial services industry such arguments have been adduced in favour of changing the industry structure in the direction of a Continental-style universal banking system. In recent years a structural change of this kind has proceeded in the United Kingdom and Canada through the medium of takeovers by the major commercial banks of some merchant banks, investment banks and security houses (Bellanger, 1988).

Whilst regulations, respectively the Glass–Steagall Act and Section 65, forbid the joint performance of banking and security operations in the domestic markets of the United States and Japan, this dichotomy is being gradually eroded[2] and is expected to disappear completely in the near future. The current American administration is planning legislation to allow banks to conduct all types of security business and in both the United States and Japan it appears that the major commercial banks intend to enter these markets. In sharp contrast to their position in domestic markets American and Japanese commercial banks can and do operate in a range of capital markets beyond the jurisdiction of their national regulations. Frequently this is achieved through the acquisition of foreign investment banks or security houses.[3]

A major finding of this study is that in sharp contradiction to these theoretically anticipated gains, and the structural changes which have characterised the banking scenes of different countries, the interviewees were virtually unanimous in their condemnation of the efficacy of commercial bank–investment bank mergers: the consensus is that, 'they do not work'. For example, a senior executive of a major British commercial bank was content to say that the institution's merchant banking activities were 'not very successful'. More trenchantly the managing director of a merchant bank integrated with a large British commercial bank averred that 'no commercial bank had successfully run an investment bank business'. Such views are echoed internationally. The senior executive of a Japanese bank asserted that 'the best commercial and investment banking systems are separate'.

There is just as much agreement about the primary reason why the integration of commercial and investment bank activities fail to work. It is due to the cultural contrasts between the two types of operation and, more precisely, to the lack of a common ethos which might bind commercial and investment bankers. Given a commercial bank's basic responsibility to its retail depositors it must necessarily operate in a relatively cautious fashion. It is essentially risk averse (its staff tend to be conservative, inflexible and inward-looking) as opposed to the risk-orientated nature of investment banks. Interviewees stressed that in contrast to commercial bankers investment bankers need to be 'nimble', 'predatory', 'aggressive', 'free wheeling', 'opportunistic', must work in an atmosphere of 'creative tension' and are driven by 'massive egos'.

Interviewees drew attention to a series of problems experienced as a consequence of this cultural clash. One of the most serious is that associated with remuneration: the need to reconcile commercial bank payment systems founded on basic salaries with the significantly higher payments, derived substantially from bonuses and commissions, which Chapter 5 revealed investment bankers receive. Secondly the 'strains' of such a commercial bank–investment bank 'mismatch', to use the words of a Canadian commercial banker, are frequently reflected in the development of uncooperative attitudes between the two banking wings. The same executive said that despite sharing a common building the group's commercial and investment bankers would not know each other in the lift.

Thirdly, interviewees believed that the acquisition of investment and merchant banks led to the management of commercial banks being overstretched, with a subsequent lack of control that lies at the root of operational problems that have arisen in integrated banking groups: the management problem is 'to keep the operations separate but to keep control'. Where exceptionally serious difficulties have arisen because of this management problem two kinds of solution have been tried, to sell the investment banking arm or to bring it under tighter control.

Fourthly, in some cases conflicts of interest have arisen as a result of the integration of commercial and investment bank activities. This problem can be acute for M&A advisory activities and especially for Continental banks given their extensive corporate holdings. Indeed it is believed that independent American and British advisors have gained business at the expense of Continental rivals largely by avoiding such conflicts.

Interviewees also revealed how such problems had a detrimental impact on the performance of integrated investment banks. The senior executive of an integrated British group claimed that to avoid the obvious pitfalls a deliberately unambitious strategy was adopted for the merchant bank subsidiary. Similarly, and for the same reasons, an American commercial bank severely restricted the nature and scale of the activities permitted to its investment banking arm. In general it is felt that once acquired, and protected, by the much larger asset base and earnings of the 'mother' commercial bank, an investment or merchant bank slips into a slothful operational mode, quite the reverse of what is required in the markets which it serves.

It is instructive to assess whether the available empirical evidence supports, on the one hand, the theoretical arguments in favour of the integration of commercial and investment banking or, on the other, the antipathy to this structural form voiced by the interviewees. In fact the evidence suggests, quite strongly, that a separation of commercial and investment banking activities, the system from which Britain has to some extent moved in recent years, generally provides a more competitive structure than a national set-up in which a full range of banking services is provided by individual financial institutions.

First British experience, even allowing for the current depressed state of virtually all relevant markets, has hardly proved a glowing testimony to the 'universal' system and has revealed serious flaws in the arguments which favour this structure. In contrast to the theory underpinning mergers of commercial and investment banks the frequency with which Charterhouse, a subsidiary of the Royal Bank of Scotland, has drawn on its parent's balance sheet 'is rare, having happened only a couple of times in 1988'. Similarly in the case of BZW there has been reference to 'the problems that arise when the parent puts up capital to support occasional capital intensive business at the subsidiary' (*The Financial Times*, 9 July 1989 and 30 November 1990) though it is generally accepted that BZW has experienced fewer problems and has performed rather better than other integrated merchant banks.

Problems have also arisen as a result of conflicts of interest. Both Samuel Montagu, the merchant bank subsidiary of the Midland Bank, and Charterhouse have provided advice to companies which launched hostile bids on their clearing bank parents' clients as a result of which these clients severed relations with the banks. Neither Lloyds Merchant Bank nor Charterhouse have made much impact on the markets with which this study is concerned; the initial impact of the merger between Hill Samuel, formerly regarded as a dynamic merchant bank, has been described as 'not auspicious',[4] and National Westminster has suffered a range of serious financial and management-related problems with County Natwest.

The experience of investment banks and security houses which have been acquired by larger American financial institutions is no more encouraging. Security Pacific, currently incurring along with most United States banks high loan loss provisions, is in the process of selling off its wholly-owned investment bank subsidiary, Hoare Govett (employing 8,000 worldwide), to the bank's managers in order to return to 'core' activities: 'security businesses do not work well when 100 per cent owned by a bank: it is a people business' (*The Financial Times*, 15 October and 11/12 December 1990). Citibank and its investment banking subsidiary, Scrimgeour, have experienced similar problems. American Express (as a non-bank allowed to own such a subsidiary) was obliged to shore up its 'beleaguered' investment banking arm, Shearson Lehman. The Prudential, America's largest insurance company, was obliged to inject new equity into investment banking subsidiary Pru-Bache to offset 1990 losses of US$250 million. Employment in the latter institution is being cut by two thirds marking the end of an 'ill-starred' attempt to build the company into an all-service bank (*The Financial Times*, 21 December 1990).

Credit Suisse First Boston (CSFB), the first large United States investment bank to be owned either by a foreign company or indeed by a commercial bank, has experienced such serious financial problems that one of its parents, CS Holdings (the holding company also of Credit Suisse), has been obliged to assume a majority stake. CSFB's difficulties derive largely from debt problems incurred by its United States affiliate bank, First Boston, but also it found itself competing with its associates, Credit Suisse and First Boston (*The Financial Times*, 12 and 28 December 1990).

A defence that such situations are simply attributable to the current depression in world capital markets coupled with excess banking capacity holds little water. The evidence suggests that whilst in the United States and other countries independent investment banks have suffered in terms of lower revenues, falling profits and staff cuts it is the investment banks and security houses integrated with commercial banks which have, in general, been most vulnerable. Such vulnerability also reflects the existence of interrelationships between financial markets which mean that the much vaunted 'muscle' of commercial banks can be weakened, as a result especially of high levels of bad debts, just at the time when their investment bank subsidiaries require it most.

The above examples taken from Britain, the United States and Switzerland can be bolstered by comparable experiences culled from Germany, France, Canada and Japan. Doubts were expressed in the interviews about the long-term success of the recent acquisition of Morgan Grenfell by the Deutsche Bank. Three major French banks, Banque Nationale de Paris, Société Générale and Credit Lyonnais, all made losses on their London security operations in 1989. In the case of Canada a 'strong performance' by the Canadian Imperial Bank of Commerce was marred by C$87 million losses incurred by Wood Gundy, its investment bank subsidiary, in 1989/90. Guinness Mahon, the Bank of Yokohama's investment bank subsidiary, has reported a loss in its latest financial year.[5]

Empirical evidence derived from the market performance of the major financial institutions supports the superiority of a banking structure based on a separation of commercial and investment banking activities. Those international markets examined in this study have been dominated throughout the 1980s by the United States and, in some cases in recent years, by Japan. In both countries these performances are associated, essentially, with the separation of, if not necessarily commercial and investment banking activities, then of commercial and investment banking institutions. Typically United States investment and security houses have competed in international markets without the support of commercial banks. Because they are not shackled by domestic American regulations in these markets they have also to some extent entered the foreign exchange and syndicated loan markets, traditionally the preserve of commercial banks. Correspondingly United States commercial banks, on the international scene, have entered security markets which domestically have hitherto been the preserve of investment banks. The same generalisations about operations on domestic and international markets can be made respectively about Japanese banks and security houses. Nor does the experience and performance of Continental universal banks lend much support to the efficacy of integrated commercial and investment banking systems. Countries which are characterised by such systems tend to claim smaller global market shares than the United States, Britain and Japan. In general their performance was not highly regarded by interviewees: 'they are not best in any markets but survive overall'.

It is tempting to draw a distinction between integrated universal banking systems which exist *ab initio* and those which have recently developed in Britain and Canada through the medium of commercial and investment bank acquisitions and mergers. It is possible that the cultural clash is less in evidence in the former than in the latter where it is highlighted and aggravated by the merger process. However the interviews revealed that, for example, remuneration problems associated with the joint provision of commercial and investment bank services are by no means absent in Continental banks especially where they have, as in most cases, a capital markets operation in London. Moreover conflicts of interest encountered in the provision of M&A advice are especially acute for universal banks. To the extent that national, commercial banking personnel are asked to staff their capital markets operations they are seen to be especially disadvantaged compared with 'Anglo-Saxon' rivals. Perhaps significantly, independent Continental investment banks are capable of good market performances. In 1989 Banque Paribas occupied 16th place in the international equity league, 11th in Eurobonds and dominated the

Ecubond market. In Italy there is a movement away from universal towards specialist banking. At present commercial banks are largely responsible for stock market operations but first stage parliamentary approval has now been given for the creation of specialist security houses (SIMs: Societa di Intermediazione Mobiliare) which will focus on security operations, bond issues and underwriting, about half of them being independent of banks (*The Financial Times*, 7 December 1990).

The foregoing paragraphs suggest that the single institution provision of a full range of banking services which results from the merger of commercial and investment banks may not be conducive to competitiveness: that, at this level, economies of scope are a mirage and that a degree of separation of commercial and investment banking activities is preferable. In practice some theoretical arguments in favour of an integrated range of activities do not hold and serious problems emerge.

Nonetheless it seems clear from the interviews that when they are allowed to do so both United States and Japanese commercial banks intend to enter the domain which at present is reserved domestically for investment banks and security houses. Whilst in view of the accumulated experience they seem reluctant to accomplish this through the acquisition of investment banks and security houses they appear to have every intention of developing their own capability. When pressed, American commercial bank directors agree that their intention to enter security activities is motivated simply by a sense that 'the grass is greener . . .', rather than by any economic logic. In any event market entry by organic development, as opposed to institutional acquisition, will substantially enlarge capacity without generating market growth.

Market diversification in investment banks and security houses

It would be impossible to consider market diversification and economies of scope within commercial banks without examining the role, normally a dominant one, of retail banking activities. Since the latter are excluded from this study this sub-section focuses on market diversification and economies of scope within the operations of investment banks and security houses.

In Chapter 4 it was demonstrated that large aggregate country shares in the selected financial markets are associated, *inter alia*, with high coefficients of market diversification which characterise their financial institutions. On the basis of both market share and diversification, the United States, United Kingdom and Switzerland rank relatively high. To a considerable extent this association merely reflects the fact that, other things being equal, the larger the number of markets in which, on average, a country's institutions participate the greater will be the national share of the global market.

Also, however, a general consensus amongst interviewees is that in the case of investment banks and security houses a wide spread of products, provided they are traded in profitable markets, has beneficial implications for performance and survivability. This belief is largely based on the supposition that a financial institution providing relatively few 'products' is more likely to suffer from market fluctuations than a more diversified institution. There is some evidence to support this view. Recently several independent French stockbrokers, lacking alternative investment banking roles, have failed following the deregulation of commission rates. As a result of the current slackening in global M&A activity Wasserstein Perella, the United States M&A boutique, may be facing difficult problems: 'unlike the big Wall Street firms, Wasserella is not a full service institution, so it does not have other businesses to compensate for the drop in M&A volumes' (*Euromoney*, October 1990). Referring to the latter situation the chief executive of the London-based subsidiary of a major United States investment bank asserted that, 'the significant advantage we have over Wasserstein Perella is that clients still want to talk to us. There are other things to talk about aside from M&A.'

It should be emphasised that product diversification by itself is not sufficient to shelter an investment bank from market vicissitudes. First, current conditions demonstrate that a broad spectrum of financial markets may be depressed, though to varying degrees, at the same time. This merely reflects the fact that, again to varying degrees, individual markets are subject to such common forces as the condition of stock markets and global levels of interest rates. For instance stock market falls are associated with contractions in stock turnover, new issues, M&A activity and also have knock-on effects on the Eurobond market.

Interviewees see product diversification *per se* to be less critical than the institution's ability to switch resources, rapidly and at short notice, between the markets it serves in response to actual, or even better, anticipated market developments. The need for such flexibility emerged from a recent survey of member firms of the International Stock Exchange (ISE) (ISE, 1990). This demonstrated that in the face of annual fluctuations as high as 40 per cent in equity trading member firms must have 'more flexible capital arrangements . . . if they are to avoid excess capacity in depressed times and to be able to cope with high levels of activity in more buoyant times'.

Such flexibility is aptly demonstrated by Salomon Brothers: in the face of weak markets the company discontinued its municipal bonds and commercial paper operations but now occupies a high position in the nascent MTN market (Salomon Bros, 1989 Annual Report). Again in anticipation of market developments 'major Euromarket houses [are] reorganising their operations to shift emphasis away from international debt securities to equity sales and trading'. Cited among this group of firms were CSFB, SBC, UBS and the Deutsche Bank though no British institutions were included (*Euromoney*, July 1989). The requirement for market diversification and flexibility is not restricted to principle products (M&A advice, international equities, Eurobonds, and so on) but also applies within these markets. In contrast to some slippage experienced in the Eurobond market in 1990 by most Japanese security houses Nomura managed to retain its top position thanks to the diversified nature of its business, by type of bond and currency, in this market, which in turn helped to shelter it from domestic Japanese stock market conditions (*The Financial Times*, 31 December, 1990).

The manner in which one market may grow out of, and supplant, another emerged from the survey of historical market developments in Chapter 3. This development process not only underscores the importance of market flexibility but also demonstrates the extent to which the various 'products' are relatively close substitutes. In this context interviewees stressed the operational efficiency which results from the extent to which a firm's experience in one market can enhance its performance in another. Another advantage which, it was emphasised, investment banks derive from a relatively high degree of market diversification is cross-fertilisation in the innovation process.

The need for flexibility and speed of response is demonstrated by current market developments: 'with most of their equity and bond operations in the doldrums, banks have been falling over one another chasing the fat fees supposedly on offer in this pan-European M&A business. Many will be disappointed' (*The Economist*, 20 January, 1990).

In brief, economies of scope tend to be significant within one kind of banking rather than across the commercial bank–investment bank divide. Those noted above for investment banking are matched by the comparative success of commercial banks in providing mortgages and life insurance alongside retail banking services.

Given the apparent advantages, subject to market flexibility, of product diversification, how does the British industry measure up in this respect compared with major competitors? The information assembled in Chapter 4 throws some light on this matter. Focusing attention on the market spread of independent investment banks and security houses, that is, leaving aside the activities in these markets of universal banks, commercial banks and their investment bank subsidiaries, reveals the following. Among such American institutions one, Merrill Lynch, functioned substantially in all six markets, M&A, syndicated loans, international bonds, international equities, Euro CP and CD and medium-term notes.[6] A further four, Goldman Sachs, Morgan Stanley, Salomon Brothers and Shearson Lehman, operated in five markets: in each case the missing market is that of syndicated loans, an activity typically requiring the larger asset base associated with major commercial banks.[7]

Market coverage by the Big Four Japanese houses is narrower and fairly uniform. Daiwa, Nomura and Yamaichi all hold significant shares in four markets: international bonds, international equities, Euro CP and CD and medium-term notes. Nikko operates on a substantial scale in the international bond market.

On average market participation by the principal British independents is less varied than is the case with the major American institutions. Outstandingly S.G. Warburg is substantially active in all six markets, followed by Kleinwort Benson in three (M&A, international bonds, Euro CP and CD), Barings in two (M&A and international bonds), Schroders in two (M&A and syndicated loans), and Hambros also in two (M&A and international bonds).

France is the only other country where independent investment banks play a significant role but again in a manner characterised by relatively low market diversification. Banque Indosuez and Banque Paribas operate in three markets and Lazard Frères in one.

THE STRUCTURE OF NATIONAL BANKING SECTORS: ECONOMIES OF SCALE

Much research has been directed towards measuring economies of scale in banking. A recent evaluation of the results suggests that the relevant economies may be reached at a relatively small size, less than $100 million of assets, after which there is little change. The variation in average costs between different sized banks, the standard measure of cost economies, is much smaller than the existing dispersion of average costs across banks in the same class (Humphrey, 1987). The relationship between scale and costs will plainly be quite different for commercial banks and investment banks.

Commercial banks

In commercial banks the relationship between costs and size will always be dominated by considerations relating to their retailing activities. Since such operations are outside the scope of this study most attention will be focused on security houses, investment and merchant banks. However it is instructive to identify certain aspects of mergers between commercial banks which do have implications in the present context.

There are obvious potential cost benefits and thus competitive advantages to be gained from domestic mergers between commercial banks. The principal one is the enhanced efficiency which stems from the rationalisation of, and the elimination of duplication in, their retail network. What is especially relevant for this study is that (a) the British banking system is relatively advanced in such restructuring but (b) other countries are seeking to catch up and reap the benefits already enjoyed by the British system. This process of domestic commercial bank mergers 'has already got under way in a number of smaller countries . . . the Netherlands, Denmark, and Norway – but it also applies to larger countries as well: Japan has produced two very large mergers and there is frequent speculation of a possible merger of leading New York banks' (*The Financial Times*, 20 November, 1990). Current takeovers of failed United States banks will reinforce this trend: 'the most powerful signs of these problems are in the commercial banking sector where failures are expected to rise and a wave of mergers is likely to slash operating expenses . . . All the top money centres (Citicorp, Chase, Chemical Bank, Manufacturers Hanover) have acknowledged the possibility of mergers' (*The Financial Times*, 28 December, 1990).

Italy is following other European countries with negotiations between the Banco di Roma and the Cassa di Risparmio di Roma and the fusion of interests between the Banca Commerciale Italiana, Credito Italiano, and Instituto Bancario di San Paulo di Torino. This 'reflects the growing concern . . . that the country's banks are too small, inefficient and domestically orientated to compete effectively with their big international rivals'. The Swiss banking system is far from immune to this trend towards domestic mergers: CS Holdings, the parent company of Credit Suisse, took control of Bank Leu early in 1990 (*The Financial Times*, 11 December, 1990). Several interviewees drew attention to the relatively large number of institutions which characterise the German banking scene.

It is difficult to speculate on the extent to which this 'catching up' process will improve the relative efficiency of Britain's competitors and even more so on the impact such domestic rationalisation will have on their operations in international capital markets. However, *ceteris paribus*, whatever its size it is logical to expect that the impact would be positive and, if only marginally, to the United Kingdom's detriment.

The rationale behind cross-border mergers and acquisitions of commercial banks is quite different from the motivations underlying domestic restructurings. The latter, as noted, are directed towards cost reductions and improvements in operating efficiency. Cross-border acquisitions, by contrast, are a means by which a bank extends its market and obtains a new chain of retail branches. In principle this form of expansion should have a beneficial indirect impact on any international capital market operations which a commercial bank undertakes as a consequence of the enlargement of its global network.[8]

Whilst cross-border commercial bank acquisitions have proceeded at a rapid pace it is difficult to discern much of a nationality pattern in terms of the countries from which these acquisitions have been made. However the flavour of the current European scene, especially relevant with the advent of 1992, may be conveyed by the following contemporary events. In 1989 Credit Lyonnais bought for 150 million effective control of Credito Bergamasco, an Italian bank. At the end of 1990 Barclays was seeking to purchase Européene de Banque, a French institution, to give it first position among foreign banks in France. As a result 'the 1992 banking stakes now have three clear leaders, including Barclays. The French entry is Credit Lyonnais . . . which has been setting up branches all round Europe. The German entry is Deutsche Bank which has expanded rapidly in the last three years'. The President of Credit Lyonnais claims the bank to be number one in Europe in terms of commercial bank branches and regards Barclays and the Deutsche Bank as Credit Lyonnais' main European competitors (*The Financial Times*, 15 and 24 May, 1989 and 13 December, 1990).

Investment banks and security houses

The statistical analysis of national banking sectors undertaken in Chapter 5 confirmed that the scale on which these kinds of financial institution operate, whether measured by employment, asset size or output, tends to be significantly below that which is typical of the average commercial bank. In part this is due to the absence, or relatively small size, of a retail network; in part it reflects the optimum scale of operations which, in the relevant markets, management can effectively oversee. For niche players within this sector of the financial service industry optimum size can be absolutely, as well as relatively, low.

Nevertheless some very pertinent questions can be posed about the implications of inter-country contrasts in the average size of investment banks, merchant banks and security houses for the relative performance of these national financial sectors. The matter is best considered against the background of the depressed markets which these institutions currently serve and the existence, generally recognised, of much surplus capacity on the international scene. The prevalence of these conditions has important implications for the degree of concentration which, at both the domestic and international level, characterises this segment of the financial services industry and for the role which mergers and failures may play in changing the industry's structure. The differential impact of these processes as between countries will do much to shape the relative competitiveness of their investment banks and security houses.

For some years now the banking scene has witnessed a great deal of merger activity both between commercial banks themselves, especially but not exclusively on the domestic market, and as shown above between commercial banks and investment banks both domestically and on a cross-nationality basis. This activity has been accompanied by much discussion about the advantages and disadvantages of both types of merger activity and, *inter alia*, about their implications for institutional efficiency and relative competitiveness. At some stage interviews with the executives of financial institutions automatically turned to this topic. In sharp contrast hardly any attention is paid to the role, and possible implications for the major global players, of mergers, either domestic or cross-border, between investment banks, merchant banks or security houses. Unless the topic was deliberately broached it would not be referred to. Yet given the current degree of surplus global capacity pressures undoubtedly exist to reduce, either by elimination or merger, the number of investment banks competing for the available business, a process that would raise the degree of concentration in this international financial service industry.

It would be wrong to suggest that horizontal mergers, either domestic or cross-border, never occur in this sub-sector. Such mergers were implemented between United States investment banks when fixed commissions were abandoned in the 1970s. Currently in the United States Shearson Lehman and Prudential Bache, two of Wall Street's largest security houses, are discussing the possible merger of their 'back office' operations. Wood Gundy, the investment banking arm of the Imperial Bank of Canada, has bought Merrill Lynch's retail business network in Canada. Following the recent abandonment in France of the fixed commission system a number of Paris brokers were acquired by foreign financial institutions, Warburg and BZW featuring among the purchasers.

This type of merger and acquisition is expected to continue. A recent survey by Moodys of American security houses and investment banks concludes that there could be more mergers, realignments and outright failures. Given that they are experiencing the worst trading conditions for more than twenty years, Japan's medium-sized brokerages 'may be hard put to keep their independence'. One of them, Sanyo, already has affiliations with Nomura though perhaps significantly it 'would turn to its bank (Daiwa Bank) for support in a crisis' (*The Financial Times*, 21 December, 1990).

Whilst the scale of horizontal mergers and acquisitions, domestic or cross-nationality, is really quite small when compared with the number of both horizontal commercial bank mergers and commercial bank/investment bank takeovers, some very significant economies could be reaped from an increase in the scale of activity which would result from mergers of investment banks. It is true that the substantial benefits which accrue from the rationalisation of domestic retail networks when commercial banks join forces do not for the most part apply when investment or merchant banks merge.[9] However, significant gains can accrue to those investment banks and security houses which play major roles in global capital markets from the removal of duplication which would accompany the merger and rationalisation of the firms' international networks. The global networks of independent investment banks and security houses are often more restricted than those operated by universal banks and those to which integrated investment banks have access thanks to the international operations of their parent commercial banks. In this respect at least independent investment banks may be at a competitive disadvantage compared with integrated investment banks.

In addition to the competitive gains which derive from the merger of global networks, improvements in efficiency also stem from the merger of the office operations. The possible merger of the back office operations of Shearson Lehman and Prudential–Bache is being considered because of the cost savings which would result and it 'could mark the start of a much larger rationalisation of back offices of many Wall St. Firms' (*The Financial Times*, 19 December, 1990).

Thirdly, the potential for larger-scale operations which the merger and acquisition of this kind of financial institution provides would facilitate a greater degree of market and product diversification. The relevance of such diversification to the efficiency and competitiveness of investment banks and security houses has already been identified. Its significance was emphasised by an interviewee who stressed that medium-sized banks and security houses tend to be at a competitive disadvantage *vis-à-vis*, on the one hand, niche players who focus on and have great expertise in one market and, on the other, the larger firms active in the full range of international capital markets.

Fourthly, it is generally accepted that a large investment bank or security house is better placed to handle the higher value deals or issues than a small or medium-sized firm. At several junctures in this study attention has been drawn to the extent to which this particular operational capability enhances the performance of financial institutions in terms of both market shares and profitability.

It is difficult to explain the sharp contrast between, on the one hand, the obvious operational gains to be derived from horizontal mergers between investment banks and, on the other hand, the minimal extent of such mergers and takeovers. No rational economic or operational explanation was forthcoming during the course of the interviews. Rather the consensus was that the comparative absence of such mergers reflected the special ethos and culture of investment bankers, their greatly developed sense of independence rendering such mergers and acquisitions improbable.

Yet such mergers or takeovers would seem to be especially appropriate for the independent segment of British merchant banking. Chapter 5 revealed that, of all the types of banking sector which were analysed of whatever nationality, British merchant banks are the smallest whether measured by average asset size or employment levels. It is highly likely that this has encumbered British independents when competing for large deals and issues and the success achieved by the much bigger United States investment banks and Japanese security houses suggests that there exist significant economies of scale to be reaped from a growth in the average size of British merchant banks.

Against this background it is revealing, and somewhat disheartening, to record the responses of senior executives of three British merchant banks when asked about the advantages to be obtained from, and prospects of, mergers or acquisitions within the industry. The first agreed that there was no fundamental reason why such mergers should not take place and that, in present market circumstances, they would make good economic and operational sense. He then added 'but we would never dream of it'. The second stated that a strong independent merchant bank would never wish to merge though it might indulge in surreptitious takeovers through the medium of team poaching. The third was also adamant that it would be nigh impossible to promote mergers between British merchant banks. He added, 'I would much prefer to see excess capacity removed by some of our number going bust'.

Such reactions, whilst they may echo the attitudes of investment bankers worldwide, are perhaps accentuated in the case of British firms by longstanding family associations and traditions. Whilst it is difficult not to admire the individuality and independence which such responses reflect they do not augur well for any improvement in the United Kingdom's international performance from a restructuring of this sector of British financial services.

MARKET SHARES AND CROSS-NATIONALITY TAKEOVERS

Structural factors associated with scale and scope of operations also have a direct impact on performance because the most immediate way in which a country's share of a market may be raised is for one of its financial institutions to acquire a foreign bank or security house already in possession of a market share. For example the British merchant bank Morgan Grenfell was acquired in 1989 by the German Deutsche Bank so that in accordance with the measurement method adopted in this study any future market shares acquired by Morgan Grenfell should be credited to Germany not the United Kingdom. This process of cross-border acquisition constitutes an important qualification to the relationship between the size of a country's market share and the competitiveness of its financial institutions. Whilst such an acquisition directly improves the *performance* of the acquiring country's banking sector as measured by market penetration this in no way reflects the innate competitiveness of the national banking sector in question and it may or may not improve the operational efficiency of the acquiring country's financial institutions.

Two major objectives, or a combination of them, induce financial firms to undertake cross-border takeovers.[10] One prime motivation is to acquire expertise and performance in markets or products where the buying institution is comparatively weak. The Deutsche Bank's purchase of Morgan Grenfell was prompted by a desire to gain access to the latter's experience in M&A operations. Secondly, such takeovers represent a method by which foreign banks believe they will more easily penetrate the domestic market of the purchased institution: thus Guinness–Mahon was acquired by the Bank of Yokohama 'to provide clients with services in the UK' (*The Financial Times*, 27 November, 1990).

Whilst its quantification would be difficult and complex it seems likely that a balance sheet of such inter-country acquisitions in recent years would show the United Kingdom to be in deficit in the sense that the number (and probably size) of United Kingdom financial institutions taken over by foreign banks would exceed the number of foreign institutions acquired by British firms. A spate of such foreign acquisitions (of United Kingdom merchant banks, brokers and jobbers) was associated with the Big Bang; more recently the anticipation of the freeing of the Community's financial markets in 1992 may have played a role. Random illustrations of this foreign incursion into the British financial service industry are the Deutsche Bank and Morgan Grenfell, UBS and Phillips & Drew, the Bank of Yokohama and Guinness–Mahon, Credit Lyonnais and Alexanders, Laing and Cruickshank and the Hong Kong and Shanghai Banking Corporation and James Capel.

The traffic is by no means one way, as the operation of Warburg Soditic in Switzerland and the Midland Bank's acquisition of Germany's Trinkaus and Burkhardt demonstrates. Nevertheless there can be little doubt that the pattern of cross-nationality takeovers has been such as to have had a negative impact on the United Kingdom's performance as measured by the market shares obtained by British-owned and controlled financial institutions.

Whether they have detrimentally affected the relative efficiency of the British financial services industry is another matter. Indeed there are reasons for supposing that the international competitiveness of those foreign institutions acquiring United Kingdom banks and security operations, if anything, may be weakened relative to the efficiency of the remaining British industry.

First, *a priori*, it seems plausible that the more efficient British institutions will be resistant to foreign takeovers. Secondly, there was a majority view among interviewees that foreign penetration of domestic markets may not be most effectively achieved by institutional acquisitions. It was stressed in particular that the purchase of goodwill which this strategy necessitates has in practice proved to be excessively expensive: the Deutsche Bank's acquisition of Morgan Grenfell cost almost £1 billion. The preference appears to be for staffing a newly-established overseas subsidiary or branch office with local personnel who possess the appropriate expertise and local contacts.

However, the principal reason why the performance of these cross-nationality acquisitions must be questioned resides in the fact that for the most part they seek to combine commercial and investment bank activities. Evidence presented above suggests that the mixture of these two operations, especially in the case of newly merged financial institutions, has not been very successful. Cited among the major reasons for this is the culture clash which exists between commercial and investment bankers, even of the same nationality. In the case of the cross-border acquisitions of this kind the problems associated with this type of culture clash are compounded by those which stem from cultural contrasts between management teams of different nationalities. In these circumstances, whilst such cross-nationality takeovers may provide an immediate boost to the performance of the acquiring country's financial service industry as measured by market shares, there must be misgivings about the impact on its inherent efficiency and international competitiveness. Many interviewees expressed the opinion that, for example, the operations which resulted from foreign takeovers of British institutions associated with the Big Bang have not proved very successful, especially when exposed to market conditions of the kind currently experienced.

HUMAN RESOURCES

The weight which should be attached to the labour force factor in determining the competitiveness of a financial institution is widely emphasised. Walter states, 'in today's evolving competitive environment human capital can be viewed as a financial institution's most important asset, and many of the critical capabilities for exploiting competitive opportunities depend directly upon the quality of human resources within the organisation' (Walter, 1988). This view is endorsed by Sherman, 'Like restaurants and Broadway shows, financial institutions are mainly the product of the people who work them: the human capital. In the past, balance sheet capital and regulatory position advantages may have obscured this fact. The successful financial institutions of the 1990s however . . . will find and hold the best people for the job' (Sherman, 1988). In a recent speech focused on the financial service industry Sir Leon Brittan claimed that 'the quality of the workforce and not that of the software will be the test of companies' success in the 1990s'. After suggesting that technological factors tend to be relatively uniform between financial institutions he continued 'controlling costs will always be necessary for success but only the provision of quality will guarantee it and that quality can only be determined by the workforce' (*The Financial Times*, 8 December, 1990).

There is further agreement that the human factor, and inter-firm labour force contrasts, are especially significant in the case of investment banks and security houses. Dyche writes, 'the one factor that outweighs any other in the determination of success in investment banking, however, goes back to the quality of the professional staff' (Dyche, 1988). Chu dwells on the matter at greater length, 'investment bankers, by the nature of their work and the structure of their remuneration, must be entrepreneurial . . . In this kind of organizational and economic environment, individual professionals not only represent the raw material of the business but are indisputably the business's most important asset. Of course, financial institutions such as commercial banks, insurance companies and pension funds have the same mandate to invest and reinvest available funds: however their most important assets are the financial assets themselves, and individuals are relegated to more passive roles as asset managers' (Chu, 1988). This difference in the role of human resources in commercial and investment banking is closely associated with the cultural contrasts already noted, which exist between the two banking forms.

The interviews fully reinforce this appreciation of the paramount importance of labour force quality in determining an institution's fate in the financial markets on which this study has focused. The comment of one interviewee, a British managing director of the London-based investment banking arm of a large American commercial bank, can stand for virtually all other comments, 'nothing is more important than human resources, not even technology'. At the same time it was stressed that the significance of the labour factor varied substantially between markets and products: it would seem that human resource quality requirements are higher in certain foreign exchange operations and M&A advisory activities than they are, for example, in the organisation of some syndicated loans.

Whilst it emerged from the interviews that inter-firm contrasts in labour force capabilities and their development have played and will continue to play an important role in shaping relative institutional efficiency, it is initially somewhat surprising, against the above background, that in the event national labour force characteristics (innate abilities, occupational proclivities, educational standards and training methods) have a relatively muted impact on the competitiveness of countries' financial service industries in the markets which concern us. The reasons for this are considered under three headings: firms' staffing, recruitment and training policies; labour force mobility; and common labour pools.

The staffing and recruitment policies of the type of financial institution considered in this study are greatly influenced by a fundamental characteristic of their activities, the need to maintain, and operate through the medium of, an international network. A consequence is that on grounds of both cost minimisation and operational efficiency their overseas operations, whether branches or subsidiaries, are largely staffed by locally recruited workers. It is the universal practice that lower staff grades and computer-related employees are taken on locally. Local recruitment however does not cease here. It is the common practice for senior management and other executives to be hired from the domestic labour market partly as a means of minimising costs but more significantly as a way of penetrating domestic markets. Typically at the senior staff level a three-way nationality split applies with the executives comprising expatriates from the firm's national headquarters, senior management recruited in the host country and staff with third country nationality in the process of being circulated around the firm's network.

The cost incentive for local recruitment is obvious especially in the case of lower-paid staff grades. It is cheaper to recruit locally than to pay relocation and accommodation expenses to expatriate staff. The operational inducement for the employment of local staff is perhaps even more important. Whilst the nature of global networks was found to differ substantially and somewhat haphazardly between the various financial institutions (some favour the acquisition of appropriate local institutions, banks or security houses, together with their employees, others prefer to set up branches and 'buy local people' to staff them) the underlying motivation is common: to obtain locally-based senior people with knowledge of the domestic markets and culture, and in possession of local business contacts. The net effect is that these financial institutions (in the case of commercial banks, the relevant operations and divisions) are staffed by a labour force which comprises a high proportion of non-nationals. Time and again interviewees stated that, apart from the cost and operational considerations referred to above, nationality is essentially 'irrelevant' in the recruitment process. The extent to which this makes for a degree of uniformity in these financial institutions' labour forces is reinforced by a commonality in the recruitment policies which are pursued to obtain potential local senior managers. Interviews revealed that in the great majority of cases the financial institutions in question annually sought a number of locals with MBAs or good university degrees and English as a working language. The only significant limitation to these cross-nationality recruitment policies appears to be associated with obtaining work permits. This restriction is significant, for example, in Switzerland and for non-Community staff in London also.

A nationality breakdown of operating group directors provided in S.G. Warburg's Annual Report for 1989/90 aptly illustrates the cosmopolitan, international, nature of these kinds of financial institution. In a total of 218 directors 35 were nationalities other than British. The United States accounted for nine, Germany and Japan four each, the Netherlands, Canada and France three each, Denmark, Switzerland and Australia two each, and Spain, Italy and New Zealand one apiece (S.G. Warburg, 1989 Annual Report and Accounts). Another independent British merchant bank claimed that a fifth of its London executives were non-British and a United States investment bank that 17 of its top 24 posts in London were held by non-American citizens. Of the 36 interviews which have been conducted exactly a half were with people having a nationality different from that of the financial institution which they represented. There is an impression that senior management positions, and board membership, in Japanese, German and Swiss institutions are less open to foreign penetration than is the case, for instance, in American and British banks.

Training methods also contribute to a degree of uniformity in labour force standards. Whilst it is general practice for lower staff grades throughout the network to be instructed and to gain experience locally, 'on the job', the tendency towards cross-nationality uniformity within the firm's labour force is promoted by the practice of providing common, headquarters based, training courses for senior and potentially senior staff grades. The training arrangement of the Japanese bank Sumitomo aptly illustrates this practice: 'in fiscal 1989 Sumitomo Bank opened an employee training facility within its London computer centre . . . The new facility began training programmes for employees of all the Bank's European operations in February 1990' (Sumitomo Bank 1990 Annual Report). Uniform labour force standards are further enhanced by the policy of rotating trainees and senior management around the global network. Nor are training programmes restricted to promoting common cross-nationality standards within each company: some are provided on a uniform industry-wide basis. The Association of International Bond Dealers, the organisation of dealers in the Eurobond market, provides at Montreux and through the University of Reading, common training courses for the employees of its members' firms regardless of nationality.

Another, associated, reason why national labour force characteristics are not stamped on the performance of these financial institutions is labour force mobility. The manpower which supplies the financial products of interest to us is highly mobile especially in the case of investment banks and security houses. Although the pace of such moves has recently slackened the financial press was earlier replete with cases where individuals and, not unusually, whole teams of employees have been poached from one financial establishment by another. Team poaching is linked closely with product innovation and attempts on the part of financial institutions to break into new markets by acquiring the requisite know-how from rival firms. Originally the practice was confined to American institutions and

indeed they still appear to participate in this activity to a disproportionate extent. In 1980 a team comprising no less than thirteen people
was induced by CSFB to move from Kidder Peabody. Ten years later
the same investment bank 'stole a whole team of one of the most
highly regarded derivatives groups . . . from Bankers Trust' shortly
after poaching a Salomon Brothers bond trading team (*Euromoney*,
November 1990 and *The Financial Times*, 28 December, 1990). In turn
Salomon Brothers recently 'lured away' a Merrill Lynch team
responsible for the development of the highly profitable variable rate
note and these two United States institutions now dominate the
market for this instrument. In order to form an LDC debt unit
Morgan Stanley acquired a team of six specialising in this market
from Dillon Reed (*The Financial Times*, 13 July and 21 September,
1990).

Whilst much of this mobility takes place among American institutions it is evident from the interviews that cross-nationality poaching
is a widespread practice, in effect contributing to the formation of a
common international labour pool from which financial institutions
draw irrespective of their nationality. Almost all interviewees could
cite cases in which their own institution had acted as a poacher or had
been poached. For example, in order to set up a capital markets
operation in London a major French bank recruited an American
team from a United States investment bank, a Japanese bank hired a
former senior executive of First Boston to establish an M&A boutique
and a contraction in the operations of an integrated British merchant
bank followed the loss of a sales team to a rival group. The British
manager of a London-based French bank operation summarised the
situation by saying, 'poaching is endemic, cross-nationality and
ruthless'.

The special position of the City of London as the major centre from
which the kind of capital markets surveyed in this study are served
has also contributed to a degree of uniformity in the human resources
employed by rival firms of different nationalities. Moreover there
appears to be general agreement among London-based financial
institutions, of whatever nationality, that perhaps in contrast to many
other segments of the British labour market, the requisite skills are
available and currently in ample supply given the present over-
capacity in these financial services. Interviewees contrasted the City's
youthful, computer-skilled labour force with the 'quill-pen clerks' of
two decades ago.

Whilst for these reasons there is potential for much uniformity in
the quality of the human resources employed by these financial
institutions the interviews also revealed a series of labour force factors

which favour some, especially American, firms at the expense of others. First United States institutions have access to a substantial pool of domestically provided MBAs who are widely regarded as comprising, at least in the initial training stages, a superior 'raw material' to the kind of graduates available for recruitment in Britain and on the Continent. Until recently at any rate possession of an MBA was a 'must' for consideration by a major American investment bank in the United States. With this single qualification British graduates are regarded as second to none.

Secondly interviewees, regardless of nationality, were agreed that training programmes and human resource development in American institutions are superior to those found in firms of other nationalities. The Australian manager of the London-based operation of a United States commercial bank went so far as to say that in this field American institutions are 'light years ahead' and characterised their training programmes as 'thorough, continuous and provided on a life-time basis'. The German manager of another American operation claimed that United States firms 'provide the best training at all levels'. Emphasis was placed on the extent to which labour force flexibility was achieved by initial training in a variety of financial markets and product lines, the relatively high degree of centralised, as opposed to local, training and the extent to which staff are rotated between jobs and locations.

Whilst the training provisions of British banks are not in general regarded as as rigorous or intensive as those which, on the whole, are implemented by United States financial institutions, they are nevertheless thought to be at least as good as, and in some ways perhaps superior to, those offered by Continental and Japanese rivals. Training provided by the latter group is regarded in some quarters as rather conservative.

Thirdly, cross-nationality labour mobility occurs only as a result of the substantial (and until recently very substantial) financial inducements which personnel are offered. Whilst there is in effect a common pool of skilled labour from which all the relevant financial institutions can draw it seems inevitable that those which can pay the most are in a position to get the best. The impression gained from interviews is that this has favoured United States firms (though for cultural reasons not so much Japanese) which started bidding up salaries in the 1980s, rather than, say, British institutions. It was revealed in Chapter 5 that the average remuneration levels paid by United States investment banks are the highest in the world, whilst those paid by British banks are among the lowest. As a result it is difficult to avoid the conclusion that British financial institutions have been net losers from cross-nationality labour mobility though interviewees agreed that foreign banks in London need to pay a premium to obtain British labour of a given calibre. On the other hand British financial institutions should have gained from having on their doorstep, as a result of the external economies associated with the concentration of these international financial services in London, probably the largest pool of skilled financial service workers in the world. This is seen by the interviewees to be reflected, especially, in the 'openness', the international orientation, of the City labour force. It is contrasted with the inward-looking, unduly conventional attitudes, to be found among banking executives in Continental centres and in Tokyo, which pose recruitment problems for foreign banks.

Given the current slackness in the City's labour market there is some preference for staff at all levels to prefer employment with British institutions which are regarded as relatively secure compared with foreign institutions based in London. However a more typical, longer-term, City labour market situation would be one in which there is substantial competition for experienced staff. In these circumstances, and despite enjoying access to a local pool of skilled labour, to some extent British institutions could lose out in recruitment to certain foreign companies, American, Japanese and perhaps Continental, which are in a position to offer more attractive remuneration packages.

INNOVATION

Quotations from interviews underscore the great, almost overwhelming, significance for success in the selected markets of the innovative process: 'innovation is the single most important factor in winning initial market shares'; 'innovation is the lifeblood of capital markets'; 'innovation is fundamental to success'; and 'the whole point of investment banking is to be innovative'.

These universally held views confirm what other observers have already concluded. Chu writes, 'In recent decades the first or second firm that enters a new market segment and can attain market dominance has been able to achieve profitability and visibility in that market segment that far exceed the competition. For example, in such areas as high-yield bonds, mergers and acquisitions, and mortgage-backed securities, the leaders in the business were among the first entrants who have been able to maintain market dominance' (Chu, 1988). Hamilton, referring to the role of 'ideas banks' in the early Eurobond market, points out that 'in the fierce competition that developed to gain a share in the action of the world's fastest-growing market there was constant pressure to produce new ideas that would persuade borrowers to issue notes' (Hamilton, 1986). Given the almost paramount importance of this element in the competitive process it should be stressed that innovative success depends fundamentally on the nature and quality of an institution's human resources (frequently in conjunction with appropriate technology) and relatively little on a bank's capital resources. It also emerged from interviews that whilst its overall importance was not in doubt the role of innovation varies significantly between different markets. It is thought to play a comparatively smaller role in the case of syndicated loans and foreign exchange (with the important exception of foreign exchange derivatives), a more important part in M&A advice, and was claimed to be a vital ingredient in securitisation. It follows that, whilst innovation is of crucial significance to investment banks, its contribution in the capital markets served to a disproportionate extent by commercial and universal banks, though important, is not as substantial.

A clear and consistent picture emerged from the interviews of the cycle which capital market innovations and their exploitation follow. Because a financial institution has no legal proprietorial interest in a new product, the sequence which ensues after its launch can be summarised as the initial domination of the market by the bank in question, associated with high profit margins, a subsequent influx of competitors with identical or close substitute products, a narrowing of margins and the emergence of overcapacity. One interviewee likened the process to that of a nomadic tribe wandering from one pasture to another. More succinctly the chief executive of an American investment bank claimed that 'the key to success in these markets is to identify a growth area as a consequence of the firm's innovative capability, step in quickly, exploit the market and leave before excess capacity develops as a consequence of rivals' reactions'. The consensus is that the pace of this product/market cycle accelerated during the late 1980s.

Such short-term aspects should not, however, be overemphasised. Providing an institution can ensure a continuous stream of innovations it may retain its market share on a longer-term basis. Moreover it was stressed by a number of respondents that simply possessing a *reputation* for innovative ability is sufficient to ensure a substantial longer-term market share. Again these views confirm earlier observations about the innovative process in capital markets. Walter writes, 'it is important for an institution to maintain a continuous stream of innovations' and 'some institutions are consistently more innovative than others' (Walter, 1988). Gart comments, 'if the corporation being approached likes the [new] idea, the investment banker making the proposal usually gets the deal, regardless of the previous relationship that existed with another investment bank. There is no monopoly on successful ideas: other investment banking firms will copy them or offer improved versions. It is important to note that new investment products come on line monthly; their number and variety are limited only by the human imagination' (Gart, 1989).

Interviewees stressed that much innovation consists of little more than relatively minor product differentiation, the repackaging of ideas in a slightly different form. If carried to extremes this can be counter-productive in that each product, say a Eurobond issue, is in some respect unique, a feature which may restrict its marketability and attractiveness to lenders.

In the course of the interviews an attempt was made to identify the processes by which product innovation in these markets normally occurs. If it is essentially a random event there is little point in searching for national patterns in the innovative process. It emerged that innovation is far from a haphazard business and of the two forms which the process may assume the one which is based on a systematic response to clients' needs is more effective than that which relies on the autonomous generation of new ideas by some kind of 'think tank'. There was a general consensus that the transmission of clients' specific, and hitherto unmet requirements, via selling and trading staff to a small team of skilled, and appropriately equipped, personnel charged with providing a solution is the most effective framework for product innovation. In contrast the activities of a relatively isolated research group charged specifically with the task of producing new products in a vacuum rarely yields acceptable results, the products which emerge being frequently too complex for the client's purpose.

It appears that the effectiveness of the innovative process is greatly enhanced when the financial institution can draw upon expertise in different markets. The senior executive of a major United States investment bank claimed that 'much innovation combines features and elements of different products so that it helps to be in several markets to yield the requisite degree of cross-fertilisation'.

The unanimous opinion is that, taken as a group, American financial institutions have been, and continue to be, superior at product innovation to those of any other nationality. The relevant quotations range from 'United States banks are best' to 'the United States is streets ahead'. The banks, for the most part investment banks, which are most frequently cited for their innovative achievement are CSFB, Goldman Sachs, Morgan Stanley and Salomon

Brothers and, in the case of foreign exchange derivatives for instance, Bankers Trust, Chase Manhattan and J. P. Morgan are often named.

Illustrations of the paramount position of United States banks are to be found in a 1987 Eurobond survey which identified four new products: the first listing of capital currency units (for a London-based consortium of five Nordic banks) on the London Stock Exchange; the first multi currency (four tranches – Deutschmarks, Swiss francs, the US dollar and pound sterling) convertible bond; the first 'naked gold warrant'; and the first international equity notes. In the latter three cases the innovating institutions were all American, respectively CSFB, Citicorp Investment Bank and CSFB; a then British merchant bank, Morgan Grenfell, was responsible for the first (*Euromoney*, September, 1987). Similarly, in 1990 five United States banks (Citicorp, J. P. Morgan, Bankers Trust, CSFB, and Chase Manhattan) occupied the top position in a list of the most innovative firms in the Euronote market and four American banks (CSFB, Bankers Trust, Morgan Stanley, J. P. Morgan) occupied four of the top five places among the most innovative institutions in the Eurobond market. Again the fifth institution was a British merchant bank, Warburg (*Euromoney*, September 1990).

In the summer of 1990 'the Gulf crisis hit the Eurobond market hard. To make up for the lack of new issues, syndicate teams at the top London houses have been working overtime to come up with new instruments that appeal to investors in the changed climate'. Out of six banks especially active in this way four were American (Shearson Lehman, Bankers Trust, Morgan Stanley and Merrill Lynch), one was British (Samuel Montagu) and one French (Société Générale) (*Euromoney*, September, 1990). More recent instances of American innovation are the first issue of asset-backed securities in the German market by Citibank, the first French franc Eurobond issue following French Treasury permission to allow non-French banks to issue such bonds, by J. P. Morgan, and the first kind of 'war insurance' in the form of oil-indexed warrants offered by Goldman Sachs (*The Financial Times*, 30 November and 17/18 December, 1990).

There was a fairly general consensus that, again taken as a group, British banks occupy second place in innovative capability. Indeed Continental bankers referred on occasion to innovative strength as being an 'Anglo-Saxon' feature, drawing attention to the high degree of mobility of capital markets staff between American and British banks. The British banks most frequently cited for such qualities were Warburgs, Hambros and Midland Montagu. Some interviewees expressed the opinion that British innovation was stronger, though essentially learned from the United States, in M&A techniques rather than in security market operations.

Continental banks were thought to occupy third place. Among them French banks (Paribas was frequently said to have a commitment to innovation) were regarded as being generally more innovative than Swiss or German institutions.

Japanese banks have long been criticised for their lack of creativity, a verdict fully endorsed by the interviewees: 'while [Japanese institutions] may excel at taking what others create and offering it at lower prices, they seem unable to create new instruments and mechanisms' (Bellanger, 1987b). A possible explanation of this weakness which emerged from the interviews is the tendency for Japanese banks to favour the less successful approach to the innovative process: the 'think tank'. The 'Financial Engineering Departments' which feature so prominently in the annual reports of Japanese financial institutions are widely regarded as little more than shop window dressing designed to impress clients. This contrasts sharply with concrete examples of actual product innovation which the annual reports of United States banks frequently contain.[11] To mitigate the competitive disadvantages which stem from this deficiency there has been a tendency for Japanese banks to obtain innovative expertise by acquiring relevant American institutions.

Not only is it conceded that, as a group, American banks are by some way the most innovative but also, in the words of a British merchant banker, this advantage 'is the major reason for the United States' domination of the markets'. It is instructive therefore to single out the causes of America's innovative and creative superiority.

Beneficial features of the American domestic scene were often cited as underlying explanations of United States banks' innovativeness. Allusions were made in this context not so much to the size and scale of domestic capital markets, though they too are relevant, but rather to the sophistication and demanding nature of the banks' American clients, both borrowers and lenders. By comparison domestic clients in other countries were thought to be conservative in their outlook, unwilling to experiment and less inclined to put pressure on their banks to come up with new products. British clients, whilst not in the American class, are regarded as more adventuresome than their Continental counterparts.

This strength is reinforced by the client-led innovation process adopted and refined by United States banks. Though not alone in employing this approach it appears to have been implemented especially effectively in the United States. Interviewees stressed, in particular, the extent to which this approach is supported by highly qualified, highly motivated, 'rocket scientists' remunerated largely on the basis of results. In the final analysis successful innovation depends on high quality human resources and the edge which American financial institutions have been shown to enjoy in this respect does much to account for their innovative superiority.

Thirdly, market diversification, which is a major characteristic of American banks, especially investment banks, is also conducive to effective innovation. The senior executive of a United States investment bank claimed that much innovation can be traced to personnel who find themselves operating in a depressed capital market, left with time on their hands and therefore much pressure to devise a new product.

There is also, apparently, a tendency for American banks operating in these markets to be 'transaction' rather than 'relationship' driven: they quit saturated markets as quickly as they can promote new ones. Whatever disadvantages such an approach may have it is one which accords very well with the innovative cycle and the 'nomadic' aspects of capital markets.

THE ROLE OF CAPITAL

The point has already been made that a minimum scale of activities must be achieved by financial institutions if they are to compete effectively in international markets. Interviewees also stressed that access to a minimum level of resources is pre-requisite for the 'credibility' which firms need if they are to be major players in these markets. A senior executive of a major British bank summarised this basic requirement, 'in the case of all markets financial institutions must have a minimum critical mass of resources since this gives the credibility which is so important in competitiveness and explains why small banks and other financial institutions do not fare well'.

Once this minimum resource qualification has been achieved it is believed that inter-firm differences in capital size play a relatively minor role in their relative performance. Chu writes, 'it is clear that beyond the threshold amount of capital necessary to underwrite or place sizeable financings, the other key success factors are the quality of senior line professionals . . . aggressiveness and innovation'.[12] The head of capital markets at an integrated British merchant bank went further, 'for capital markets asset size and capital is less important than staff quality'.

Indeed in the case of capital market operations unduly large commercial, universal and integrated banks may suffer competitive disadvantages associated with inflexibility, resistance to change, innovation lags and management problems. Interviewees noted that in certain markets, for example M&A advisory services, comparatively small institutions may be more successful than large groups. It is also recognised that the importance of the capital factor varies significantly between markets playing a greater role in syndicated loans and security underwriting than in M&A advice.

To analyse in more detail the role of capital in the competitive process it is helpful to consider separately first the operational significance of financial 'muscle' (and its cost) as measured essentially by asset size and secondly the role of reputation and creditworthiness as reflected by the capitalisation of financial institutions. The distinction between these two, quite different, 'capital' concepts is highlighted by contemporary developments. Many banks are no longer trying to increase their assets but rather to shrink them. At the same time, and in sharp contrast, these institutions would like, and are seeking, to expand their equity capital basis.

Asset size and capital costs

Very large financial institutions will normally be in a position to establish larger global networks than smaller ones for the penetration of the domestic markets of other countries and the provision of 'placing' and 'distribution' facilities for international capital market products. In this respect those major commercial and universal banks with global aspirations will generally enjoy an edge over independent investment banks and security houses and, among the latter, the larger institutions will have a competitive advantage over the smaller. The director of an independent British merchant bank was convinced that in this respect the larger Japanese and American institutions are competitively superior to their rivals.

It has been argued that serving a diversity of capital markets confers competitive benefits on the financial institution in question. Clearly the larger the asset base the greater the number of markets which can be supplied and it is relevant, as demonstrated in earlier chapters, that compared with major American institutions independent British merchant banks are characterised on average by both smaller asset bases and less market diversification.

Not only does capital intensity differ substantially between financial products but also it varies with the nature of an institution's participation in the market. In the case of merger and acquisition operations and syndicated loans, for instance, an institution may function, respectively, as an adviser or arranger with little or no commitment of its assets.

Both foreign and British interviewees expressed a feeling that because of their relatively restricted asset bases capital participation by independent British merchant banks in a variety of markets has been impaired.[13] It is thought that this weakness will eventually damage their credibility in such markets and thus their competitiveness: 'innovations in the securities underwriting business and merchant-banking transactions requiring extensive commitments of the firm's own capital have given players with large capital bases a significant competitive advantage' (Walter, 1988).

It emerged that the most significant way in which asset size influences operational success is the manner in which large assets are associated with the average value of the capital market products which it supplies. It is agreed in the industry that a larger asset base enables an institution to advise and participate in larger value M&A deals, high value syndicated loans and the major Eurobond, commercial paper, international equity and medium-term note issues. Almost always the high value products in any market are the most profitable, reflect and contribute to the firm's success and, by definition, help to reward it with a large market share.

The explanation of this feature of high value deals resides in the fact that, to all intents and purposes, in the case of most financial services a firm's costs vary with the number of products supplied whilst its revenue is a function of their value. In the words of the head of banking at Merrill Lynch, 'it takes just as many people to do a $50 million deal as it does to do a $500 million deal'.[14] The director of a major United States investment bank claimed that 'our large assets enable us to undertake big value Eurobond issues which is very important to profitability since costs are less than proportionate to issue value'. This was echoed by an official of a large Japanese bank who said 'costs are fixed not variable and so we have advantages in our large value deals'. The director of a British merchant bank, agreeing that a larger asset base would help acquire higher value deals, pointed out that 'costs are a function of number of deals'. He described how in the case of low value bond and M&A deals the bank was sometimes obliged to charge a fixed 'documentation fee' on top of any *ad valorem* charges to yield a profit.

This does not preclude the possibility that the larger value deals and issues carry relatively narrow margins since they typically involve large sovereign or corporate, low risk, clients with sophisticated approaches to capital markets. In any event a consensus emerged from the interviews that smaller operators, with restricted asset bases, cannot afford the risk exposure which the more lucrative high market share deals require. It is especially pertinent therefore that the group chief executive of a small independent merchant bank said 'only a few British merchant banks can tender for large deals'.

When attention was switched in the interviews from the impact of asset size on an institution's performance to the significance of capital costs the spotlight automatically focused on Japanese firms. It is universally accepted that, at least until very recently, the low cost of the resources which have been available to Japanese financial institutions has played a major role in their success in obtaining market shares. There emerged several reasons why both retail and wholesale funds placed with Japanese banks and security houses came very cheaply. First the strength of the Japanese economy during the 1980s and the associated monetary policy pursued by the authorities were conducive to low levels of interest rates. Secondly, this was buttressed by regulations which specifically influenced, and kept to a minimum, the interest rates paid and charged by financial institutions. Thirdly, and again until comparatively recently, buoyant Japanese stock markets coupled with equity warrant issuing techniques enabled Japanese banks to raise new capital at almost zero (or even, in conjunction with swap operations, negative) cost. Fourthly, previously untrammeled by capital adequacy requirements to the same extent as have been, for example, British banks, Japanese institutions operated with highly leveraged capital structures.

These factors combined to enable Japanese banks and security houses to compete in international markets at prices and margins which competitors found very difficult to match yet which yielded returns to capital as high as any. This strength has also manifested itself in the cross-subsidisation of financial markets (including between domestic Japanese and international markets), the development of loss leader products and thus the ability to 'buy' large shares of international markets and high, if not unduly profitable, places in the relevant 'league tables'. The sheer size of the funds which Japanese institutions have been able to commit to these markets has also been conducive to their acceptance of very narrow margins.

Japanese institutions enjoyed this capital cost advantage over both British banks and the financial institutions of other nationalities engaged in these markets. However the view was expressed that in this context British institutions were also at a competitive disadvantage *vis-à-vis* those of most other countries. Over the long term United Kingdom interest rates have been significantly above those found, for instance, in Switzerland and Germany. The head of corporate banking of a major British commercial bank claimed that, as a result of relatively high interest rates and inflation, in order to raise new capital a typical British bank needed to pay 18 per cent (post tax), significantly more than the cost faced by United States and German banks and much more than is paid by Japanese institutions.

Capital and reputation

The competitive advantages associated with asset size can be eroded if the reputation or creditworthiness of a financial institution is in some respect impaired. Reputation depends in part on financial 'muscle' as measured by asset size but mostly on the quality of the balance sheet, on the nature and security of the institution's assets, and on its capital adequacy ratios. The capitalisation of the financial institution as measured by its stock market valuation is a useful indicator of the firm's 'reputation'. A variety of factors which recently have had detrimental effects on commercial and investment banking activities worldwide have severely distorted correlations between asset size and market capitalisation. Currently 'large asset size is meaningless in judging a bank's value. US banks have seen their shares fall by as much as two thirds. The giant Japanese banks have fared only slightly better . . . down by 40–50 per cent'. Valuations of British banks have been less impaired though their share prices have fallen as indeed they have even for Continental banks 'where conditions are more robust' (*The Financial Times*, 31 December, 1990).

Aside from any non-quantifiable impact which such loss of valuation may have on a bank's reputation and thus competitiveness there are detrimental operational repercussions. The institution will have greater difficulty attracting the resources (wholesale or retail deposits, new capital) needed to fund its market operations and for those funds it does obtain it will need to pay above-average rates of interest, a major hindrance when competing in international markets.

These developments have been reflected in the credit ratings attached to the principal financial institutions of the major competing countries, ratings which significantly influence the terms on which they can obtain additional resources. Recently *Euromoney* compiled a list of the world's 100 best banks using criteria which *inter alia* included their credit ratings. When these banks are grouped and their credit ratings averaged by nationality the following country sequence emerges: Switzerland with an average rating of 10.00, United Kingdom 9.75, Germany 9.53, France 9.23,

Japan 9.18, the Netherlands 9.03, Canada 9.03, Australia 8.88, Italy 8.96 and the United States 8.44.[15]

The results of interviews and other evidence which has been assembled suggest first that expensive, sophisticated, electronic technology plays a role in financial institutions' 'production' processes which is perhaps more important than in any other major economic activity but secondly that levels of technology have a comparatively muted impact on the relative competitiveness of financial institutions in the markets which interest us. For purposes of exposition it is convenient to consider the role of technology in the operations of commercial banks, investment banks and security houses under two headings, market-specific and firm specific technologies.

Market-specific technologies may in turn be broken down into two sub-groups: common technologies which characterise certain international capital markets and those to be found in individual financial centres. Two important examples of the former kind are Euroclear and SWIFT. Euroclear is the system operated from Brussels which is owned and used as a common system by 125 banks for clearing transactions in the Eurobond and international equity market (Walmsley, 1988). SWIFT (the Society for World Interbank Financial Telecommunications) is the primary technology for international transfer of funds and 'was born out of common interest in the banking community'. There are now about 3,000 users in almost a hundred countries participating in an up-graded version of the system, SWIFT II (*The Financial Times*, 4 February, 1989 and *The Financial Times*, 1990). The relevant feature of this kind of technology is that it is accessible to all financial institutions on a common footing so that it endows no individual firm with a competitive edge.

This latter generalisation applies with almost equal force to the second type of market-specific technology, the systems which are to be found in individual financial centres. Although such technologies may be used to different extents by institutions they are again uniformly accessible and thus confer no competitive advantage on individual firms operating in these centres. Unlike international market technologies, however, they have an impact on the relative attractiveness of individual financial centres, an issue with which this study is not centrally concerned.

For instance a prime motive for the eventual adoption by the London market of Taurus, the new electronic clearance and settlement system in which share certificates will be replaced by computer entries, is to 'reinforce the City's claim to being Europe's largest financial trading centre'. Similarly a battle is developing between Frankfurt's new exchange, the Deutsche Terminborse and the London Financial Futures Exchange. This will be a contest between the old-style trading methods found in London's futures pits and Frankfurt's expensive integrated trading and clearing system. A third illustration is provided by the introduction of a Computer Assisted Trading System (CATS) on the Brussels stock exchange in an effort 'to make Brussels more competitive with other European financial centres in the run up to 1992'. In the United States there is concern that the New York Stock Exchange's floor-based continuous auction trading system 'may become an anachronism in the electronic age' (*The Financial Times*, 25 January 1989, 26 November and 10 December 1990 and 2 January 1991).

It can be argued that such common technology systems may exert an indirect impact on company competitiveness to the extent that the institutions of some nationalities will benefit when their activities are concentrated in domestic centres which enjoy superior systems. However such an effect is likely to be minimal. Whilst, for example, British financial institutions may benefit to the extent that their activities are concentrated in the City, foreign institutions are also located in London to an unprecedented extent. Secondly, 'generally speaking, the same equipment or systems are ultimately available in all competing locations' (*Bank of England Quarterly Bulletin*, November 1989). Thirdly inter-centre technology differentials are set to narrow. Great efforts are currently being made to devise, especially within the framework of the European Community, a common system for cross-border securities trading. At present 'every country has its own and idosyncratic local settlement procedure' which raises problems for the harmonisation and development of international equity trading: 'a long-term objective of the securities industry must be global instead of national electronic settlement' (*The Financial Times*, 1990, and 28 November, 1990).

Whilst the ability of firm-specific technology to influence the relative competitiveness of individual financial institutions is greater than in the case of market and location-specific systems, here too the pressures towards uniformity are strong. Before considering the reasons for this it must be emphasised that the role of technology in the 'production process' varies quite sharply between the various financial services.

As with manufacturing industry the scope for the application of modern technology is greatest, and its impact strongest, for those services which are homogeneous in nature and produced in large numbers by hitherto labour-intensive techniques. In the case of financial services this means that the earliest, most extensive and intensive application of new technologies was to be found in retail banking (de la Mothe, 1986). Now, however, sophisticated technology is an important ingredient in wholesale and investment banking activities though its role varies greatly between the various 'products' supplied. It emerged from the interviews that, in terms of the markets considered in this study, the technological requirements of the procedures associated with M&A activity and syndicated loans were substantially less demanding than those for activities in foreign exchange operations and security markets. In contrast to earlier applications of technology in retail banking, its use in these markets owes little to labour-intensive procedures but everything to the importance of speed and complexity of transactions, especially where derivate products, swaps, options, and so on, are concerned. It follows that the optimum technological requirements of the type of financial institution considered here will vary with the blend of its activities.

A major pressure towards uniformity between institutions in the use of firm-specific technology is that all the relevant financial institutions, regardless of nationality, have access to the same equipment and common suppliers. Sir Leon Brittan recently pointed out that 'already technical know how, while important, is no longer a guarantee of success. Almost every product, financial or technical, can be copied as the necessary technology becomes even more widely accessible' (*The Financial Times*, 8 December 1990). The hardware to be found in medium and small-sized banks especially is dominated by one supplier, IBM. A current illustration of the cross-nationality commonality of such technology is provided by the development and introduction of the Financial Information Systems Tool. FIST 'converts signals from any source into one format that the dealer's computer recognises. It is reckoned to beat conventional data routes by five minutes, a big lead for market traders'. Significantly it has already been adopted by three major financial institutions, each of a different nationality, the Sumitomo Bank, Credit Lyonnais and Kleinwort Benson (*Financial Times*, 1990).

The potential inter-firm uniformity of systems breaks down a little, but not substantially, when attention is focused on software. Whilst it was clear from the interviews that companies frequently buy in software from specialist suppliers, with its potential similarity between firms, much is also developed 'in house', a practice conducive to inter-firm systems differentials. Little pattern emerged during the interviews about the relative weight of these approaches nor of an association between their comparative usage and the nationality of the financial institutions in question. However there were indications that where 'in house' produced software was used the principal motivation was not to exploit any proprietorial competitive advantage that may be associated with it but rather to enjoy the benefits derived from having a system tailor-made to the firm's specific requirements.

The extent to which this potential for uniformity in technology between the major market participants is converted in actual commonality of operations depends greatly on the principal motivations underlying their introduction of technologies. Three possible motivations emerged: a desire to possess the latest, state of the art, technology as a means of presenting clients with a suitable image; an eagerness to keep abreast of the technologies adopted by rivals; and the firm's operational requirements relative to available technology.

The interviewees attached much weight to the latter objective, the institution's substantive operational requirements. In addition to the technological requirements of specific market activities, interviewees referred to wider benefits which stem from recent technologies, especially the extent to which they meet management's needs for information and risk control. Nevertheless it is also evident that essentially emulatory motives play a role in the introduction of technology in financial institutions. The interviews revealed that a combination of a desire to keep abreast of rivals, the rapid rate of change in the technologies used by the industry and the expensiveness of these changes[16] has caused problems. This process was variously characterised as: 'developing a momentum all of its own'; 'running fast just to stay in the same place'; 'a management nightmare'. One senior executive wistfully expressed a desire for an industry-wide moratorium on the introduction of new technology.

The impact of these motivations reinforces the other factors which have been found conducive to a high degree of uniformity in the technology, techniques and systems employed by these financial institutions. In the words of the director of a British merchant bank, the outcome is 'common standards based on best practice'. It should be appreciated that the financial institutions embraced in this study are for the most part large and that, therefore, the cost of investment in technology, whilst high and often irksome, is not likely to prove the constraint which it might do for the excluded medium-sized and smaller financial institutions.

In the face of the evidence and opinions about a high degree of inter-firm uniformity in levels of technology when pressed a number of interviewees admitted the possible existence of relatively marginal technological differentials which could even follow nationality lines. Some stated spontaneously that until a few years ago American institutions, taken as a group, enjoyed a competitive edge in this respect which, to a degree, may still endure. To the extent that a pecking order can be discerned from the interviews the United States is followed by the United Kingdom and, in turn, Japan and Continental countries.[17]

DOMESTIC CONDITIONS

As originally conceived, the list of topics which it was intended to broach during the course of the interviews failed to contain any reference to the relevance of domestic market conditions to competitive performance. In part this omission reflected what was anticipated to be the paramount importance in shaping the competitiveness of banks of such factors as quality of labour force, availability of capital, levels of technology and the role of innovation. In part it reflected an assumption that since the study focused on performance in international rather than domestic arenas then national economic and market conditions would play only a peripheral role. However from the very first interview it emerged spontaneously, and with much force, that features of both domestic financial markets and the domestic economy greatly influence the performance of British banks and our competitors in both domestic and global markets. Domestic conditions have a direct impact on both the inherent efficiency of a country's financial institutions and also on their performance as measured by the market shares which they obtain. Attention is directed below first to the influence of the size, nature and accessibility of domestic financial markets and secondly to the role of such macroeconomic features as interest rates, levels of savings and wealth and the international status of a country's currency.

The influence of domestic markets

Interviewees were in general agreement that, as with manufacturing industries, an extensive domestic demand for financial services is conducive to a good performance by a country's financial institutions, not only domestically but also in international arenas. Whilst the relevant causal link may lie in part through economies of scale the key factor most commonly identified was the importance of the expertise and experience which large domestic markets confer on a country's banks. Interviewees were of the opinion that, out of the main protagonists, American, Japanese and Swiss financial institutions draw most strength from this source.[18] Switzerland finds itself among this group on account of the enormous foreign-owned funds which it hosts.

It became commonplace to hear bankers of all types and nationalities stress the manner in which, throughout the postwar period, American firms have used their large, highly competitive and sophisticated domestic market to develop a variety of financial products, as a 'test bed' in one interviewee's words, prior to their export overseas. This advantage was frequently linked with their innovative strength to explain the degree to which United States banks have dominated international markets. Whilst this market factor extends, in the case of the United States, to virtually all products, it was thought to be especially relevant for M&A activity and security operations. In the case of the United Kingdom, reference to the beneficial effects of domestic market size was usually restricted to M&A advisory activity. Conversely the Japanese weakness in M&A markets is attributed to the comparatively small extent of M&A activity in Japan and the consequent lack of experience of Japanese institutions in this area, a contrast to conditions in other domestic Japanese markets.

Whilst the impact of regulatory factors *per se* is the subject of the following section they cannot be excluded from an examination of links which exist between domestic markets and performance in international capital markets. In particular, given the importance of the placement and distribution of financial products in winning market shares, the extent to which domestic retail banking remains protected restricts the incursions of foreign banks and thus exerts a powerful influence on the performance of the banks of different nationalities. The relative inaccessibility of the domestic markets of a given country to foreign financial institutions, other things being equal, will boost the national share of financial markets, though not necessarily or even probably the efficiency of the country's banks.

The British and United States markets are widely regarded as being the most open and, therefore, their institutions are in principle at a disadvantage in this respect. For the United Kingdom this impact is evident in the extent to which the domestic British M&A advisory market has been penetrated by foreign, mainly United States, banks and in the manner in which non-British institutions have penetrated the sterling Eurobond market. Some interviewees, mainly British, believed that insufficient attention has been paid to the balance between the economic gains which have stemmed from opening the City to foreign competition, as a consequence of the Big Bang and earlier developments, and the losses which may have ensued as a result of the penetration of domestic financial markets by foreign rivals. It is clear that for some time now British financial institutions have been exposed, on both domestic and international fronts, to large-scale competition from the very best, most efficient, financial institutions of virtually all the countries of the world. It is vitally important when evaluating the results of this study not to lose sight of this fundamental consideration, nor of the fact that in the face of such high-pressure competition the relevant British banking sectors have survived substantively undiminished and have managed to retain large shares of the markets in question.

Interviewees drew attention to the fact that regulations affecting domestic United States markets have done much to promote the overseas performance of United States' banks. Longstanding restrictions on interstate banking coupled with strict limitations on market diversification imposed by the Glass–Steagall rules in effect meant that the expansionary ambitions of the more competitive United States banks could be realised only by a diversion of their resources into international markets and also, as far as possible, into the domestic markets of other countries.

Regulatory features of the domestic markets of the other major competing countries have rendered them much less open than those of the United Kingdom and the United States. Such protection may help to boost the market shares obtained by the institutions of these countries but are thought to have had a detrimental impact on their efficiency. In particular given the importance of placement and distribution facilities in winning shares of capital markets, the extent to which retail banking is still protected in some countries restricts competition from foreign banks.

Contrasts in ease of access to domestic retail or capital markets which stem essentially from regulatory factors may be accentuated by a variety of informal barriers. These range from relatively systematic hindrances such as those which result from the existence of cartels, via less formalised 'club effects', through to cultural and language barriers. Both regulatory and less formal barriers combine not only to restrict the penetration of domestic markets by foreign banks but also to endow domestic financial institutions with high rents and excess profits on the basis of which they can seek through competitive pricing and low margins to capture shares of international markets.

Most of these features, and their consequences, are thought to apply most of all to the Japanese scene. Domestic Japanese financial markets are not only large but also protected by regulatory requirements. These restrictions are reinforced by a 'club effect' based on a system of company cross-holdings, cartelised house banks and the existence of close ties between bankers and civil servants, on top of which foreign banks face both cultural and language problems. The result has been not merely a low degree of overseas capture of domestic Japanese markets but, more signficant in the present context, the provision of a financial launch pad in the form of protected profits from which Japanese financial institutions have penetrated international markets by means of aggressive pricing, narrow margins and cross-product subsidisation. It is generally accepted that the profitability of Japanese institutions in the Euro-bond market in no way matches the size of the shares they have 'bought'.

Interviewees believed that many of these features are to be found, though perhaps in a less extreme form, in Germany where the domestic market is regarded as 'one of the most impregnable'. Again the role of cartelisation and the close links which exist between industrial groups and house banks were stressed by interviewees. Special emphasis was placed on the ability of domestic German banks to remove and appoint company chairmen and the effective monopoly which this confers in financial matters.[19] Not only do such arrangements fail to promote the efficiency of German financial services but also, it is agreed, they have produced a generation of bankers who are essentially conservative and 'inward looking'.

Though falling into the group of countries where domestic markets are regarded as substantially protected by formal and/or informal features, the general view is that French markets are rather more open than those of Germany or Switzerland. Cartelisation exists – but is perhaps less strong as a consequence of the independence of the investment banks Paribas and Indosuez – the 'club effect' persists and links with government are evident in the degree of bank national-isation.

Switzerland's special feature is a large 'domestic' market, consti-tuted mainly of foreign-owned funds, which effectively owes its existence to the desire of investors to hold money in a country which hitherto has enjoyed the special attractions of political and financial stability and banking secrecy. Possessing a captive international market on their doorstep the cartelised Swiss banks, with the help of entry barriers, have secured shares of international financial markets out of proportion to the economy's size. They have needed to make little effort when distributing the products in question, merely placing them with their private clients and, since the latter tend to be essentially quiescent investors, Swiss banks pay relatively little interest for their funds whilst levying high charges. Such conditions have provided the country's financial institutions with a large, protected, highly profitable 'domestic' market, a competitive strength which, as in the case of Japanese institutions, has stood them in good stead in their search for shares in international markets.

To round off this section a word needs to be said about the

importance of the 'club effect' in the performance of British financial institutions. However strong the role of informal links (through school, university, regiment or career) between British bankers, industrialists and civil servants may once have been in influencing the market shares of United Kingdom financial institutions *vis-à-vis* their domestic and overseas competitors, it is apparent from the interviews that, first, they have been substantially weakened over time and secondly that, the United States apart, they are probably less significant than in any of our major competitor countries. The reasons adduced by interviewees for this diminution in the British 'club effect' were the openness of the City and an almost predominant overseas presence, a consequent internationalisation of the financial services labour force with, *inter alia*, foreign banks employing many British personnel, and an absence of preferential treatment from British administrations of the kind found on the Continent and in Japan, reflecting the government's attitude that the City must stand alone. The extra degree of competition to which British financial services have in consequence been exposed may well have had a beneficial impact on their efficiency. For instance, it is generally believed in the banking community that Warburg's focus and success on international markets stems in a large measure from the fact that this relative newcomer to the United Kingdom scene was never admitted as a full member of the British 'club' and was therefore obliged at an early stage to direct much of its energies overseas.

Macroeconomic considerations

Three macroeconomic factors were regarded by interviewees as being especially important in influencing the performance of a country's financial institutions in the selected markets: levels of savings and wealth; rates of interest; and the international role of a country's currency.

Inter-country differences in the stock of savings available for investment in international capital markets, either directly or through financial institution intermediation, have a major impact on relative national performance. This is because the ability to distribute financial products is a key element in a bank's performance combined with the fact that the financial institutions of a given country will always have an edge in placing products in the domestic market.

The performance of United States and Swiss financial institutions has for many years received a boost from this factor, in the former case perhaps tempered by the comparative openness of domestic markets, in the latter case reflecting the 'captive' market of foreign-owned deposits placed with Swiss banks. The rapid increase in incomes and living standards in Japan is generally acknowledged to have contributed a great deal to the rising shares which the country's financial institutions have won in international markets, especially the Eurobond market. The availability of substantial investment funds could play a comparably important role in the performance of German banks. By contrast it can hardly be claimed that, taking the postwar period as a whole, British institutions have enjoyed a significant boost from this source.

Contrasts in rates of interest which financial firms must pay to obtain funds for reinvestment in international markets plainly have a direct impact on price competition, and thus shares, in these markets. Again the United Kingdom's comparative performance can hardly have been improved by this factor. Japanese and Swiss firms especially have benefited from the low cost of the funds at their disposal and the former have taken full advantage of this in their pricing policies.

Interviewees for the most part believed that the role and status of a currency has had a significant influence on the performance of a country's financial institutions in global markets. The early dominance of sterling was cited as a major cause of the large shares held by British banks in the foreign exchange markets. That the performance continues to be impressive is attributed to a legacy of capacity, capability and expertise which endures after the original *raison d'être* has been substantially eroded. The major role played in international trade and markets by the dollar for most of the postwar period and by the yen more recently is widely regarded as a principal ingredient in the long-standing success of United States banks and the enlarged market shares obtained by Japanese institutions. The strength of the Deutschmark offers substantial potential for the future performance of German banks.

REGULATORY FACTORS

The relative performance of financial institutions in domestic and global capital markets is influenced by a plethora of rules and regulations applied at the national and international level. From this range of regulatory influences attention is focused below on three areas which aroused most interest in the course of the interviews on account of their significant implications for international trade in financial services in general and for country shares of financial markets in particular: the implications of the adoption of uniform banking capital ratios; the possible disappearance of the statutory separation of commercial banking and security operations in the

United States and Japan; and the implementation in 1992 of the European Community's free market in financial services. A common feature of each of these areas is that they entail major changes, probably in the very near future, in the regulatory framework within which capital markets function and therefore have potentially important implications for developments in market shares held by the financial institutions of different countries.

Capital adequacy requirements

The differential regulation of financial institutions, as opposed and in addition to the national impact of market regulation, is seen to have had a significant impact on country shares of national markets. The example of such an impact most commonly cited is the competitive advantage which Japanese financial institutions have derived from this source. It was common for interviewees to highlight the contrast between the relatively lax control of banks and security houses exercised by the Japanese central bank and Ministry of Finance and the tight regulatory reins which the British authorities have imposed on financial institutions in recent years.

Japanese firms are said to have benefited especially from the low capital–asset ratios which have characterised their operations. The high degree of leverage which this implies has shaped the country's share of markets in two ways. First, a given amount of capital forms the basis of a relatively large volume of banking assets available for capturing market shares. Secondly, to obtain a given rate of return on the banks's capital, assets can be loaned at relatively low cost compared with the interest charges which less highly leveraged institutions must charge.

It is widely anticipated that the implementation in the near future of international minimum capital adequacy standards will go most of the way towards eliminating inter-country differences in competitive advantage which stem from this source: in this sense the playing field will become much more level. The principal instrument for achieving this will be the common standard established by the Bank for International Settlements, the Cooke Ratio. By March 1993 banks must hold capital equivalent to at least 8 per cent of their assets.[20] Capital is divided into two tiers, Tier I core capital based on normal equity definitions and Tier II for which a variety of near-capital instruments qualify, and different types of asset are weighted according to their degree of riskiness.

Whilst capital adequacy ratios currently vary between financial institutions within a country there was a consensus about their pattern and that significant inter-country differentials do exist. Taken overall the banking sectors of Switzerland, the United Kingdom and Germany are expected to have little difficulty in meeting the BIS requirements.[21] Those of the United States, France, Italy and, especially, Japan are expected to encounter difficulties: it has been estimated that seven of the world's ten largest banks, all of them Japanese, are short of the BIS capital requirements by as much, in total, as US$15 billion.

Efforts to achieve the minimum requirements may take the form of raising additional capital, contracting asset size or a combination of both. In practice, given the current condition of capital markets domestic and international, a curtailment of assets and asset growth in the immediate future is likely to be the most feasible option and such a strategy will inevitably have a negative impact on the shares of international markets captured by Japanese and United States financial institutions. The depressed state of capital markets means that raising additional Tier I equity capital is a difficult and expensive business. Indeed in the case of Japanese banks, which are allowed to treat 45 per cent of unrealised equity gains as capital, recent stock market collapses have been a major contributory factor in the deterioration of their capital–asset ratios.[22] Attempts by banks to ensure adequate Tier II capital by the issue of subordinated capital in the form, for example, of perpetual floating rate notes and variable rate notes, have also encountered difficulties in contemporary market conditions (*The Financial Times*, 6 December 1990). Certainly, in the case of Japanese banks, the current curtailment of their international expansion has been directly attributed to problems associated with their capital ratios (*The Financial Times*, 8 November 1990).

The statutory separation of financial operations

When the impact of regulatory factors on country shares of financial markets was broached during interviews, the statutory separation of financial operations aroused less interest than either of the other two topics considered in this section. Yet given the probable abandonment in the near future of the legislation which currently ensures the separation of commercial banking and security operations in the United States and Japan (respectively the Glass–Steagall Act and Article 65 of the Securities and Exchange Law), the implications of such deregulation for relative competitiveness and national market shares are likely to be very important.

In the past this kind of legislation has influenced country market shares by two distinct routes. First there is no doubt that the existence of such regulation in the United States and Japan, and until 1986 in Canada also, in effect ensured that their commercial banks could only participate in security operations offshore, in international capital markets and the domestic markets of other countries. This could not but bolster their market shares at the relative expense of Continental universal banks which have a longstanding history of participation in a full range of financial activities and of British banks where such practice is relatively recent.

Secondly, evidence presented in this study suggests that the domestic separation of and thus specialisation in commercial banking and investment banking is conducive to a comparatively high degree of operational efficiency especially in the case of investment bank and security house operations. On the one hand the empirical evidence shows how well these specialist United States and Japanese financial institutions have performed internationally as reflected in the market shares which they have captured, in the case of United States investment banks over long periods and in the case of Japanese security houses more recently. On the other we have the benefit, in recent years, of the British 'experiment' (and to a lesser extent Canadian experience) examined earlier which suggests that those merchant banks which have been integrated with commercial banks have performed less effectively than independent merchant banks.

If this should be the case then the consequences of the repeal of Glass–Steagall in the United States and of Article 65 in Japan could have major implications for the relative competitiveness of the financial institutions of these countries and thus, by implication, of the performance of British banks and those of other major competitors. Much will depend on the kind of structural adjustment which ensues in the United States and Japanese financial service industries. Executives of United States and Japanese commercial banks had little doubt that eventually they would move into securities operations though the institutional form which this intended incursion would take is less certain. On the one hand it was claimed that experience in offshore security activities has endowed American and Japanese banks with the required expertise so that they can organically develop their own operations: in effect they would adopt the Continental universal mode. All the evidence indicates that this mode is less effective than the specialism associated with the current United States and Japanese structures. On the other hand they could follow British practice and acquire investment banks or security houses. British experience suggests, again, that such a structure is less competitive than the current United States and Japanese systems.

The impact of 1992 EC deregulation

Two crucial aspects of the formal implementation of a free market in the European Community for financial services in 1992 are vital in the context of this study: the extent to which the relevant directives will in practice open the domestic markets of member countries to each other; and the degree to which the same markets will be accessible to the financial institutions of third countries, in particular to United States, Japanese and Swiss firms.

It is not mere cynicism which lies behind the almost universal opinion among interviewees that the formal opening of markets to member country financial institutions in 1992 will have little impact, at least in the short and medium term, on patterns of competition and country market shares. Specific reasons were cited to explain why in any but the longer term not much would change. First, continued restrictions on market access by non-national firms may arise as a consequence of interpretational problems associated with the relevant EC directives. It is feared that these difficulties may match those encountered with deregulation on the Japanese scene.

Secondly, it is generally believed that the cornerstone of free market access, the provision of a community-wide banking licence to any bank incorporated within a member state on the basis of home country control, may count for relatively little in the face of longstanding informal links, described above, which have been established between domestic clients and national financial institutions. Often the relevant informal barriers were ascribed to unspecified 'cultural differences' though those which persist between members of the Community will hardly be as wide as those, language and other, which separate Japan from Community members. More specifically interviewees referred to the kind of phenomena which are subsumed under what, in the previous section, has been termed the 'club effect': a myriad of close associations between the senior management of national financial institutions, clients, corporate and otherwise, and civil servants. Recent developments in Swiss markets were cited as confirmation of the strength of this factor. It is claimed that neither the relative ease with which it is now possible to obtain a Swiss banking licence nor the formal abandonment of the Swiss banking cartel has significantly improved, or is expected to improve in the immediate future, foreign banks' access to markets, domestic or otherwise, based in Switzerland.

Thirdly, it was emphasised that cross-border lending activities undertaken by the financial institutions of member countries would always be hindered, in comparison with domestic banking activities, until a common currency has been adopted. Fourthly, the penetration of domestic capital markets on a Community-wide basis hinges crucially on the establishment by member states' banks of retail branch networks, for placement purposes, in other member countries. Yet setting up overseas retail networks is known from past experience to be very difficult, with domestic banks retaining a persistent natural advantage, and even in the Community their development is expected 'to take decades'. In these circumstances it is hardly surprising that, in the capital markets surveyed here, the immediate marketing objectives were specified by a senior executive of an overseas arm of a United Kingdom merchant bank: 'we would not try to compete with German institutions in the German market but seek to sell German securities to the rest of the world'.

Taking account of such considerations, it was generally accepted among interviewees that following the 1992 deregulation the most open Community markets will be those of the United Kingdom, the Netherlands, Belgium and France. Markets in Italy, Germany and Spain are expected to be amongst the less accessible. The majority view was that British financial services in general, and the independent merchant banks in particular, thanks to the extent to which they are already exposed to international competition, are well placed in the relevant markets compared with Community competitors. This view was qualified in certain respects. It was questioned whether British commercial banks are committed to establishing Continental networks on the scale which appears to be the objective of, in particular, the highly European-oriented Deutsche Bank. The view was also expressed that French investment banks may take advantage of the gap in domestic German markets which arises from a virtual absence of indigenous specialist investment banking.

Interviewees accepted that the net outcome of deliberations and regulations affecting the access of non-member countries to the financial markets of member countries after 1992 will be that the financial institutions of such third countries will not be placed at any significant disadvantage. It is anticipated that 'national' treatment of third countries will triumph over reciprocity. The financial institutions of third countries are likely to be treated in the Community on the same footing as the institutions of member countries and not, on a reciprocal basis, in the same manner as member country banks are treated in the third countries in question. In return, however, it is expected that third country financial regulations will not discriminate, in their treatment of foreign institutions, against Community banks. Accepting this anticipated regulatory background and the fact that third country institutions will encounter, alongside member country banks, the same informal, cultural barriers in individual domestic Community markets, it is expected that they will experience neither significant advantages nor disadvantages compared with member country firms.

Consequently, abstracting from certain operational weaknesses to which they may currently be subject, United States institutions are likely to retain their underlying, long-term, competitive strengths *vis-à-vis* both British and Continental EC member country banks. However in the case of the other two major non-member competitors, Japan and Switzerland, the general view is that their competitive prospects in the markets of the community are not good.

Japanese financial institutions like those of the United States and for similar reasons are currently experiencing operational difficulties in international capital markets. Unlike United States institutions, however, they are seen as suffering from longer-term disabilities in their operations in the financial markets of the European Community. In particular the cultural gap which exists between potential Community clients (those in the important German and French markets were commonly cited in this context) and Japanese financial institutions are claimed to be especially large. Also attention was drawn to an innate lack of flexibility and rapidity of reaction (major disabilities in capital markets) that is thought to characterise Japanese firms and which is associated with the overcentralisation of management and a need to refer most decisions back to Tokyo.

The formal opening of Community financial markets in 1992 could have negative implications of a very special nature for Switzerland. The country's financial services are already experiencing fundamental changes as a consequence of deregulation, domestic macroeconomic conditions and external political developments. The establishment of foreign banks in Switzerland is now comparatively easy and formally the Swiss banking cartel has been disbanded, though as yet neither development has had much discernible impact on competitive patterns. A rise in domestic interest rates has lessened the capital cost advantage which Swiss financial institutions enjoyed whilst higher inflation rates have weakened the attraction of the Swiss franc for non-resident depositors. Improved European political stability has also had a detrimental impact on the attraction of Switzerland as a haven for funds.

The advantage enjoyed by Swiss financial institutions which remains largely unscathed is banking secrecy. Should Switzerland join or affiliate with the European Community (as is now being discussed under the umbrella of a European Economic Area) it is difficult to see how Swiss banking secrecy rules could survive unchanged. Their erosion would mean that the basic competitive power base of Swiss banks (low cost access to vast investor funds) would be greatly weakened. This would imply not only a curb on any Swiss threat to the domestic markets of Community member countries but also vulnerability of the Swiss market itself to incursions by foreign financial institutions.

SUMMARY

The factors which have been identified in this chapter, largely on the basis of views expressed by practitioners in international capital markets, as explanations of differences in institutional and country performance, can be considered under three headings. First are a series of factors associated with industry structure, and especially the way in which inter-country contrasts in the composition of the banking industry as between independent investment banks and commercial banks, integrated banking forms and universal bank systems influence market performance through their implications for economies of scope and scale. Secondly, attention has been directed to the roles of labour and capital. In the case of the former special emphasis has been placed on the innovative process and for the latter on the impact of technology on performance. Thirdly, a series of special factors associated with domestic economic and market circumstances and with regulatory regimes has been scrutinised.

Inter-country differences in economies and diseconomies of scope associated with contrasts in the national structures of financial services play a more important role than economies of scale or indeed many other relevant factors in shaping a country's performance in the selected markets. The general view supported by a considerable body of evidence is that, in contrast to expectations, attempts to merge commercial and investment banking activities are attended by substantial diseconomies of scope and a loss of operational efficiency and performance. These losses stem from commercial–investment banks culture clashes, associated management and remuneration problems and the conflicts of interest which the merging of these activities bring.

In addition to anecdotal evidence about the difficulties which have attended such mergers the empirical record reveals how superior has been the performance of the United States and to a lesser extent Japan, countries where there exists a domestic separation between commercial banking and investment banking/security house activities, compared with the achievements of the universal banking systems of continental Europe. The implications of this for the efficiency of Britain's banking structure are plain and unwelcome. Takeovers of merchant banks by commercial banks have been accompanied by acute operational difficulties and a deterioration in the performance of integrated compared with independent merchant banks.

In contrast the economies of scope which accompany market diversification within investment banking activities are widely believed to be positive and substantial. They derive from a spread of market risks, given sufficient operational flexibility, mutual market support, and cross-market innovative fertilisation and promote the acquisition of large shares in the global capital market.

In all probability British commercial banks have now reached a size beyond which further economies of scale cannot be reaped. Such economies, associated largely with retailing activities, bring only indirect benefits to capital market operations, by enlarging the size of international networks. To the extent that rival countries are now catching up with the United Kingdom through the medium of commercial bank mergers the performance of their institutions in the selected markets may be marginally enhanced.

In contrast to the scale on which commercial bank mergers and commercial bank takeovers of investment or merchant banks have occurred, horizontal mergers between investment or merchant banks, either domestic or cross-nationality, are almost non-existent. Yet the potential economies which can be reaped are substantial. They include improved performance stemming from the amalgamation of back office operations, the merging of international networks, increased market diversity and, above all, the ability to undertake high value deals and issues. The latter capability is an especially important ingredient in an investment bank's performance and profitability, though it is one in which it is generally believed that independent British merchant banks are at a competitive disadvantage compared with their rivals. Had recent years witnessed horizontal mergers between British merchant banks on the scale of merchant bank takeovers by commercial banks there is every likelihood that the British banking industry would be significantly more competitive than it is.

Cross-border takeovers by financial institutions have probably had a detrimental impact on British market shares since it is likely that there has been a resulting net 'loss' of British institutions. This outcome does not necessarily imply a negative impact on relative British efficiency. Where such acquisitions comprise foreign commercial banks taking over merchant banks a nationality cultural gap is added to the ethos contrast which exists between commercial and investment bankers.

The quality of human resources is universally regarded as of paramount importance to institutions' performance in the markets on which this study has focused. It is somewhat surprising therefore that the evidence suggests that contrasts in national labour force characteristics do not necessarily play a dominant role in the determination of country market shares. This reflects the operation of a series of factors which promote a high degree of uniformity in the labour forces of these financial institutions including the multi-national nature of the firms' manpower, cross-nationality team poaching and the role of the City as a provider of a common labour pool.

To the extent that firm and nationality contrasts in human resource capabilities persist it is accepted that United States institutions emerge with the upper hand as a result of their access to a large number of MBAs, their superior training methods and more effective remuneration systems.

Human resource quality is closely associated with product innovation, a process which is universally seen as the key to performance in international capital markets. The acquisition and retention of large market shares depends on successfully exploiting the life cycle of each financial product. American banks are regarded as being far ahead of their rivals in innovation followed at some distance by British, Continental and Japanese institutions. The reasons cited for America's lead are the sophistication of their domestic clients' needs, an innovative system which relies on responding to those needs rather than on autonomous product generation, market diversification and cross-product fertilisation and a degree of superiority in the human resources of the country's financial institutions.

The relationship between capital and performance comprises three elements, the significance of asset size and capital costs to operational requirements, the association between the equity capital base and reputation and the role of technology.

It is accepted that, other things being equal, a large asset base enhances performance through its promotion of an extensive international network, market diversification and large value deals and issues. The financial institutions embraced by this study appear to possess adequate asset bases judged by these criteria though, as noted above, the ability of independent British merchant banks to undertake sufficiently large value deals was questioned on the grounds of their restricted asset levels. The general consensus is that, for a variety of reasons, the costs of Japanese institutions' funds are below those paid by their rivals and that much of the success recently enjoyed by Japan in these markets is due to this factor.

The relevance of an institution's reputation to its competitiveness and ability to attract custom in the selected markets was frequently emphasised. If stock market valuation and credit rating are taken as indicators of this factor then, currently, Continental and British institutions are in a somewhat stronger position than their Japanese and, especially, United States rivals.

Much of the technology associated with the provision of financial services is market or centre specific and, therefore, to all intents and purposes common to the operations of all financial institutions. The interviews suggested that inter-country differences in firm-specific technology may also not be pronounced and so have only a muted effect on inter-country competitiveness and performance. Since the relevant hardware is available to all, and because we are dealing essentially with major financial institutions motivated by common operational requirements, technology standards tend to be relatively uniform based on current best practice. There is scope for variation inasmuch as software is developed in-house rather than being bought in from common external sources. To the extent that national contrasts in technological capabilities do exist, it is accepted that the United States institutions retain some of their original lead.

Influences on performance deriving from domestic conditions can be sub-divided into those associated with domestic capital markets and those deriving from national economic conditions. It is widely agreed that much of the success achieved in capital markets by United States institutions can be traced to the country's large sophisticated domestic market which has been used as a 'test bed' before financial products are launched internationally. This beneficial factor has operated despite the 'openness' of American markets. The institutions of Japan, especially, Switzerland, Germany and France have enjoyed a similar advantage because their domestic markets benefit from a degree of protection by formal and informal barriers. In contrast Britain's domestic markets are relatively small compared with some of those of their rivals' and are also among the most open in the world.

Nor do British institutions indirectly derive much competitive advantage from the country's national economic features. Domestic funds available for investment are not available on the scale which is to be found in the United States, Switzerland or Japan. Capital costs as dictated by interest levels have been consistently higher in the United Kingdom than in Japan, Switzerland and Germany and the international role of sterling has declined relative to that of the dollar, yen and Deutschmark.

The United Kingdom, along with Switzerland and Germany, features among those countries where the competitiveness of financial institutions should emerge largely unscathed as a consequence of the implementation of the common BIS capital adequacy ratios. In contrast the relative competitiveness of many Japanese, American, French and Italian banks may suffer because of higher capital costs or a retrenchment in asset expansion which will need to be undertaken for compliance with the BIS ratios.

The abandonment or erosion of Glass–Steagall and Article 65 provisions may paradoxically have a detrimental impact on the performance of United States and Japanese institutions. As related above, the track record for mergers between commercial banks and investment banks and security houses which could result from such regulatory changes has been far from good.

Interviewees were sceptical about any significant impact, in anything but the medium to long term, from the opening of the Community's financial markets. In support of this view they cited the strength and persistence of informal barriers to market entry. However in the long term British institutions, having already experienced and essentially survived exposure to foreign competition in domestic markets, should enjoy an advantage over their protected, still somewhat inward looking, Community competitors. It is anticipated that third countries will eventually compete in Europe on substantially equal terms with the financial institutions of member countries. Whilst, as in the past, United States firms should perform well, Japanese institutions and Swiss banks may find themselves at a disadvantage.

7

BRITAIN'S PERFORMANCE

It is plain from this study that the capital markets which have occupied centre stage (foreign exchange, merger and acquisition advice, syndicated loans, Eurobonds, international equities, Euro-commercial paper and medium-term notes) are dominated by the United States. In all but one of them (Eurobonds) the country's financial institutions account for the bulk of output. The United Kingdom occupies at some distance second place with British institutions achieving a series of second and third largest market shares.

An approximate measure of national shares in the global market, based on this sample of activities, suggests that American institutions account for no less than some two thirds of the aggregate with British firms taking a further 17 per cent. In no way can the United States' performance be attributed simply to the country's size and this factor is even less relevant in the case of the United Kingdom. In terms of global market share relative to GDP, Britain's performance is second to none, our nearest rivals being the United States and Switzerland.

Joint Anglo-Saxon market domination to the tune of more than four fifths of the total is surely remarkable. It is difficult to dissociate such success from two features which the two countries' systems share in common: basically open, unprotected, domestic financial markets and a consequent exposure of national financial institutions to untrammelled international competition; and the essential separation of commercial and investment banking activities, to a greater extent in the United States than in the United Kingdom.

None of the rest of the pack (Japan, France, Switzerland, Canada, Germany, Australia, the Nordic group, the Netherlands, Italy and Belgium) won shares in excess of 10 per cent. It is significant however that financial systems in Japan and France, the two countries in this list which performed best, are also characterised by a degree of separation of commercial and investment banking operations.

Performance as measured by market shares is influenced by a series of factors which range beyond the efficiency, narrowly defined, of a country's financial institutions, although by biasing the market selection towards international arenas it is intended that, as much as possible, national contrasts in innate competitiveness substantially influence the results. Some of the factors which, it emerged, have the strongest influence on market shares are those such as the nature of domestic markets, national economic features, regulatory regimes and industrial structures, that reflect the ambience in which a country's financial institutions function rather than factors which have a more narrow and immediate impact on their operational efficiency. Some which fall in the latter category, human resources, capital inputs, technology, whilst absolutely very important in the production of these financial services, appear to have a relatively muted impact on inter-country performance. Since the study suggests that Britain's commendable results in these capital markets have been achieved largely in the absence of the special background features which have favoured the operations of major rivals, it is very probable that the outcome reflects a relatively high degree of efficiency and competitiveness among these British institutions.

The research unearthed a whole series of factors which are responsible for the United States domination of these markets: regulatory factors that triggered an early entry into international capital markets; a resulting expertise which was reflected in an ability to innovate and exploit the life cycles of capital market products; access to human resources and technologies that were in some measure superior to those available to rivals; and a scale of operations characterised by high institutional participation, large volumes and high value products and a high degree of market diversification.

Two further background factors have had major impacts on the American performance. First, all the evidence suggests that separate structures for commercial and investment banking, legally enforced in the domestic markets of the United States, provide a superior competitive basis to 'universal' banking for operations in international capital markets. Secondly the existence of a large, sophisticated but 'open' domestic market for financial services endowed American financial institutions with a test bed for new products and promoted their efficiency as a result of unfettered competition from national and foreign companies.

Japanese institutions too have enjoyed a competitive advantage as a consequence of their access to a large domestic market which has also provided a source of inexpensive funds. In their case however the existence of a domestic springboard is in part due to formal and informal barriers to foreign entry, a factor inimicable to operational efficiency. As in the United States, Japanese institutions gain from the domestic separation of commercial banking and security operations.

For the most part Britain's major Continental rivals find themselves at a disadvantage insofar as their operations in the selected markets are conducted by the less suitable universal banking structures. They also lack the efficiency boost associated with open domestic markets. However, formal and less formal market protection and, in the case of Switzerland the availability of large expatriate funds, provide relatively secure 'domestic' bases from which forays can be made into international markets. In the case of Switzerland and Germany especially, this has been accompanied by the competitive advantages which stem from appropriate domestic conditions, strong currencies and relatively low interest rates.

In contrast British financial institutions, *inter alia*, have derived little competitive benefit from these latter influences though the earlier international role of sterling helps to explain why the United Kingdom is strong in some older markets. Nor, compared with the United States, Japan or even Switzerland, can British institutions be regarded as gaining from access to a large domestic market. Capital costs, as dictated by national interest-rate levels, can hardly have worked to their advantage. On the other hand the market analysis revealed a relatively large number of British institutions active in these markets, producing comparatively large numbers of service units. However, their record in terms of unit values, especially compared with the United States but also in some instances relative to other competitors, is less good.

This latter operational failing is associated with a structural weakness revealed by the study, the small size of independent British merchant banks. The evidence strongly suggests that had recent changes in the structure of British banking taken the form of mergers between merchant banks rather than acquisitions of merchant banks by commercial banks the British industry would be even more competitive in international markets.

Given, on the one hand, the degree of success which the United Kingdom has enjoyed in these markets and, on the other, the disabilities from which, relative to competitors, the country's financial institutions have suffered, it is difficult to avoid the impression that their performance is substantially attributable to inherent efficiency, even though this concept is difficult to identify and quantify directly. In turn it is hard not to attribute much of this efficiency to the exposure in recent years of British institutions to essentially unrestricted competition in domestic and international markets from the best financial institutions in the world. This honing of the competitive capabilities of the British industry has not been without cost. Rivals, especially American institutions, have won substantial shares in British markets to the point where in some cases the United Kingdom experiences a deficit in supply. Also British market shares have been lost when, in order to enter the relevant markets, foreign banks have bought British institutions.

Operational and financial problems associated with recession, collapses in property and security markets, and sharp increases in bad debt provisions have recently harmed the banking sectors of all countries. Nevertheless the extent of these detrimental impacts is not uniform across countries and, in the short to medium term, will influence relative market performance. The evidence indicates that whilst British financial institutions, taken as a group, may not be as healthy as those of, say, Switzerland, they are better placed in these respects than their American and Japanese rivals.

Future shifts in relative performance are likely to be strongly influenced by regulatory factors. Whilst it is widely recognised that the introduction of BIS capital adequacy ratios will circumscribe the activities of American and Japanese banks, the United Kingdom finds itself amongst those countries where compliance will be relatively easy. Similarly, any flirtation on the part of American and Japanese commercial banks with investment bank or security house takeovers consequent on the abandonment of their statutory separation could well be accompanied by a loss of performance. Given its recent experience of this form of structural change it seems unlikely that Britain will go any further down the same path.

Whilst there is no denying the underlying competitive strength of America's institutions, and in the longer term perhaps those of Japan too, the circumstances identified above will not afford them the best basis for entry into continental Community markets following the latters' liberalisation in 1992. This should make room for an improvement in the performance of British institutions in the markets of co-member states. It is irrelevant whether the comparatively poor international performance of Continental countries in these markets reflects their dependence on the universal banking system or the degree of protection which their domestic markets enjoy. In the longer term, although subject to delay as a result of the persistence of informal restrictions, the opportunities exist for substantial British gains. This study suggests that if one measure were to be singled out for improving Britain's performance in international capital markets it would be a restructuring of the British banking industry from which should emerge fewer, larger, stronger independent investment banks.

APPENDIX A

SCHEDULE OF INSTITUTIONAL MARKET PARTICIPATION, 1989

	M&A world-wide	M&A cross-border	Syndi-cated loans	Inter-national bonds	Euro-bonds	Inter-national equities	Euro CP & CD	Euro MTNs
United States								
Bank of America			✓				✓	
Bank of Boston			✓					
Bankers Trust	✓		✓	✓	✓		✓	✓
Bear Stearns	✓	✓						
Chase Investment			✓		✓		✓	✓
Chemical Bank	✓		✓				✓	
Citicorp	✓		✓	✓			✓	✓
Continental Illinois			✓				✓	
CSFB[a]	✓	✓	✓	✓	✓	✓	✓	✓
Dillon Read	✓							
Drexell, Burnham, Lambert	✓	✓		✓				
First Interstate							✓	✓
First National Chicago			✓				✓	✓
Goldman Sachs	✓	✓		✓	✓	✓	✓	✓
Kidder Peabody	✓			✓	✓			
Manufacturers Hanover			✓				✓	
Mellon Bank			✓					
Merrill Lynch	✓	✓	✓	✓	✓	✓	✓	✓
JP Morgan	✓	✓	✓	✓	✓		✓	✓
Morgan Stanley	✓	✓		✓	✓	✓	✓	✓
Bank of New York			✓					
Prudential Bache						✓		
Paine Webber	✓	✓						
Salomon	✓	✓		✓	✓	✓		✓
Security Pacific	✓	✓	✓					
Shearson Lehman	✓	✓		✓	✓	✓	✓	✓
Wasserstein Perella	✓	✓						
Japan								
Dai Ichi Kangyo Bank			✓				✓	

	M&A world-wide	M&A cross-border	Syndi-cated loans	Inter-national bonds	Euro-bonds	Inter-national equities	Euro CP & CD	Euro MTNs
Daiwa				✓	✓	✓	✓	✓
Fuji Bank			✓					
IBJ	✓			✓	✓	✓	✓	
Long Term Credit Bank	✓			✓	✓	✓		
Mitsui Bank				✓		✓	✓	
Mitsubishi Bank				✓	✓	✓		
Nikko					✓	✓		
Nippon Credit Bank					✓	✓		
Nomura				✓	✓	✓	✓	✓
Sanwa Bank	✓		✓	✓			✓	
Sumitomo Bank			✓	✓	✓		✓	
Bank of Tokyo			✓	✓	✓		✓	
Yamaichi				✓	✓	✓	✓	✓
United Kingdom								
Barclays	✓	✓	✓	✓	✓		✓	✓
Barings	✓	✓		✓	✓			
Charterhouse	✓							
Hambros	✓			✓	✓			
Hill Samuel	✓							
Kleinwort Benson	✓	✓		✓	✓		✓	
Laing & Cruickshank[a]	✓							
Morgan Grenfell	✓	✓	✓				✓	
National Westminster				✓	✓	✓	✓	✓
Lloyds Bank				✓			✓	
Robert Fleming	✓					✓		
NM Rothschild	✓	✓	✓					
Midland Montagu	✓	✓	✓	✓	✓		✓	
Schroders	✓	✓	✓					
S G Warburg	✓	✓	✓	✓	✓	✓	✓	✓
Standard Chartered			✓					
Germany								
Commerzbank				✓	✓	✓		
Deutsche Bank				✓	✓	✓	✓	✓
Dresdner Bank				✓	✓			
Westdeutsche Bank				✓	✓			
Trinkaus & Burkhardt[a]				✓	✓			
France								
Credit Commercial	✓			✓	✓			
Credit Lyonnais			✓	✓	✓		✓	
Lazard Frères	✓	✓						
Banque Indosuez				✓	✓	✓	✓	
Banque Nationale de Paris			✓	✓	✓		✓	
Banque Paribas			✓	✓	✓	✓		
Société Générale			✓	✓	✓		✓	

	M&A world-wide	M&A cross-border	Syndi-cated loans	Inter-national bonds	Euro-bonds	Inter-national equities	Euro CP & CD	Euro MTNs
Italy								
Banca Commerciale Italiana			✓					
IB San Paolo di Torino				✓	✓			
Banco di Roma				✓	✓			
The Netherlands								
Algemene Bank				✓	✓			✓
Amro	✓			✓	✓	✓	✓	✓
Nederlandsche Middenstandbank						✓		
Belgium								
Kredietbank				✓	✓			
Général Bank						✓		
Switzerland								
SBC			✓	✓	✓	✓	✓	✓
UBS	✓	✓	✓	✓	✓		✓	✓
Canada								
Bank of Montreal			✓					
Nesbitt Thomson	✓	✓						
RBC (Dominion Securities)	✓	✓	✓				✓	
Scotia McLeod				✓	✓			
Toronto Dominion			✓					
Canadian Imperial/ Wood Gundy	✓	✓		✓	✓		✓	
Australia								
ANZ			✓				✓	
Commonwealth Bank of Australia							✓	✓
Westpac			✓				✓	
The Nordic Group								
Enskilda						✓	✓	✓
Kansallis Bank Group							✓	
Svenska Bank Group					✓		✓	
Den Norske							✓	

Sources: See text.
[a] Nationality classification is affected by ownership changes.

APPENDIX B

BASIC BANKING DATA, 1989

All figures other than employment data are in US$ million

	Net interest	Other income	Total income	Personnel costs	Other expenses	Total expenses
US Banks						
Bank America Corp	4,023	1,830	5,853	1,966	1,769	3,735
Bank of Boston	1,154	894	2,048	608	599	1,206
Bankers Trust	859	1,953	2,813	1,100	658	1,758
Chase Manhattan	3,025	1,945	4,970	1,829	1,873	3,702
Chemical Banking Corp	2,017	1,404	3,421	1,356	1,384	2,740
Citicorp	7,358	6,394	13,752	4,457	5,241	9,698
Continental Bank Corp	540	452	992	364	287	652
First Chicago Corp	1,250	1,136	2,386	677	756	1,433
First Interstate	2,422	1,159	3,581	1,220	1,326	2,546
Manufacturers Hanover	1,634	1,532	3,166	1,038	1,086	2,124
Mellon Bank Corp	819	785	1,604	535	568	1,103
Bank of New York	1,253	920	2,172	701	624	1,325
Security Pacific Corp	2,957	1,865	4,821	1,613	1,496	3,109
US Investment Banks and Securities Houses						
Bear Stearns	167	1,002	1,169	608	368	976
Merrill Lynch	415	5,846	6,261	3,021	2,929	5,949
Morgan Stanley	140	2,312	2,453	1,138	577	1,714
Paine Webber	212	1,515	1,727	1,038	607	1,645
Salomon Inc	(335)	3,241	2,906	1,343	823	2,166
Shearson Lehman Hutton	213	5,160	5,373	3,163	2,054	5,217
Japanese Banks						
Dai-Ichi Kangyo	2,723	3,561	6,285	1,153	2,961	4,115
Fuji Bank	2,545	3,404	5,949	...	...	3,679
IBJ	2,864	2,559	5,423	...	...	4,175
Long-Term Credit Bank	911	1,757	2,668	...	...	1,720
Mitsui Bank	1,456	1,822	3,279	739	1,535	2,275
Nippon Credit Bank	984	1,524	2,508	...	...	2,004

All figures other than employment data are in US$ million

	Net interest	Other income	Total income	Personnel costs	Other expenses	Total expenses
Sanwa Bank	2,485	3,596	6,080	...	...	3,725
Sumitomo Bank	2,954	3,727	6,681	...	...	4,037
Bank of Tokyo	1,338	2,809	4,148	...	...	2,574
Japanese Security Houses						
Daiwa Securities	559	3,868	4,427	671	1,173	1,844
Nikko Securities	464	3,331	3,795	678	1,151	1,829
Nomura Securities	791	5,789	6,581	943	1,910	2,852
Yamaichi Securities	394	3,201	3,595	680	1,151	1,831
UK Banks						
Barclays	5,506	3,424	8,931	3,323	2,392	5,716
Lloyds	3,550	2,281	5,831	2,175	1,530	3,705
Midland	2,979	2,145	5,123	2,112	1,596	3,708
National Westminster	5,637	2,985	8,622	3,487	2,256	5,743
Standard Chartered	1,063	696	1,759	613	518	1,131
UK Merchant Banks						
Integrated						
Charterhouse	...	...	...	...	...	...
BZW	...	...	...	...	...	...
Midland Montagu	423	739	1,162	...	...	979
Independents						
Barings	...	...	...	151	...	...
Robert Fleming	...	...	...	106	...	...
Hambros	...	...	...	173	...	...
Kleinwort Benson	...	...	...	154	...	...
Morgan Grenfell	...	...	...	79	...	...
NM Rotschild	...	...	...	33	...	...
S G Warburg	...	...	...	280	...	...
German Banks						
Commerzbank	1,019	1,615	2,634	1,231	827	2,058
Dresdner Bank	1,484	2,128	3,612	1,663	869	2,532
Westdeutsche LB	110	1,809	1,919	558	699	1,257
French Banks						
BNP	4,611	1,417	6,028	2,519	1,564	4,083
Credit Lyonnais			5,804	2,472	1,629	4,101
Société Générale	4,044	1,522	5,566	2,155	1,650	3,805
Banque Indosuez	630	...	...	686	...	...
Banque Paribas	...	...	...	1,458	...	...
Italian Banks						
BCI	1,840	802	2,642	1,166	627	1,793
Banco di Roma	1,022	657	1,679	814	349	1,163
IB San Paolo di Torino	2,548	755	3,303	1,198	770	1,968

All figures other than employment data are in US$ million

	Net interest	Other income	Total income	Personnel costs	Other expenses	Total expenses
Dutch Banks						
ABN	1,636	1,032	2,669	1,171	688	1,859
AMRO	1,378	795	2,173	825	539	1,364
NMB Postbank	2,134	634	2,768	907	991	1,898
Swiss Banks						
SBC	882	1,834	2,716	1,030	585	1,615
UBS	1,115	1,955	3,069	1,157	568	1,726
Canadian Banks						
Canadian Imperial	2,510	1,028	3,538	1,225	880	2,105
Bank of Montreal	2,123	957	3,080	1,103	889	1,992
RBC	3,098	1,314	4,412	1,458	1,050	2,508
Scotiabank	1,771	727	2,498	837	583	1,420
Toronto Dominion	1,659	668	2,326	720	539	1,259
Australian Banks						
ANZ	1,862	1,325	3,187	1,003	1,027	2,030
Commonwealth Bank	1,801	756	2,557	911	725	1,636
Westpac	2,280	1,234	3,514	1,172	1,029	2,201

All figures other than employment data are in US$ million

	Net income	Debt provisions	Net income after debt provisions	Assets	Employment
US Banks					
Bank America Corp	2,118	770	1,348	98,764	54,779
Bank of Boston	842	722	120	39,178	18,800
Bankers Trust	1,055	1,877	(822)	55,658	13,230
Chase Manhattan	1,268	1,737	(469)	107,369	41,610
Chemical Banking Corp	681	1,135	(454)	71,513	29,139
Citicorp	4,054	2,521	1,533	230,643	92,000
Continental Bank Corp	341	44	297	29,549	9,624
First Chicago Corp	954	482	472	47,907	18,158
First Interstate	1,035	1,204	(169)	59,051	36,027
Manufacturers Hanover	1,042	1,404	(362)	60,479	20,034
Mellon Bank Corp	501	297	204	31,467	16,700
Bank of New York	848	783	65	48,856	14,883
Security Pacific Corp	1,712	548	1,165	83,943	40,882
US Investment Banks and Securities Houses					
Bear Stearns	193	...	193	31,547	5,000
Merrill Lynch	312	...	312	63,942	...
Morgan Stanley	738	...	738	53,276	6,640
Paine Webber	83	...	83	22,096	12,900
Salomon Inc	740	...	740	118,250	8,900
Shearson Lehman Hutton	156	...	156	63,548	32,000
Japanese Banks					
Dai-Ichi Kangyo	2,170	259	1,911	435,222	18,466
Fuji Bank	2,269	305	1,964	403,265	15,377
IBJ	1,248	193	1,055	284,834	7,500
Long-Term Credit Bank	948	191	757	201,445	3,593
Mitsui Bank	1,004	182	822	221,045	10,565
Nippon Credit Bank	504	62	442	117,539	2,530
Sanwa Bank	2,356	324	2,031	387,011	14,497
Sumitomo Bank	2,644	287	2,357	406,642	16,479
Bank of Tokyo	1,573	481	1,092	228,183	17,081
Japanese Security Houses					
Daiwa Securities	2,583	...	2,583	44,924	11,790
Nikko Securities	1,966	...	1,966	29,674	9,596
Nomura Securities	3,728	...	3,728	38,989	10,899
Yamaichi Securities	1,764	...	1,764	29,547	9,100
UK Banks					
Barclays	3,215	2,249	966	205,462	116,500
Lloyds	2,127	3,394	(1,267)	92,643	84,000
Midland	1,415	1,906	(491)	100,591	60,237
National Westminster	2,879	2,310	569	187,064	96,000
Standard Chartered	628	958	(330)	39,715	28,741
UK Merchant Banks					
Integrated					
Charterhouse	66	...	66	3,189	957

All figures other than employment data are in US$ million

	Net income	Debt provisions	Net income after debt provisions	Assets	Employment
BZW	87	...	87	10,715	1,200
Midland Montagu	184	85	98	48,622	5,000
Independents					
Barings	106	...	106	6,568	1,749
Robert Fleming	...	...	...	5,104	2,278
Hambros	121	...	121	8,221	6,120
Kleinwort Benson	134	...	134	15,177	2,615
Morgan Grenfell	119	...	119	10,651	1,512
NM Rothschild	...	...	...	7,043	586
S G Warburg	302	...	302	21,583	2,913
German Banks					
Commerzbank	577	39	538	113,346	16,350
Dresdner Bank	1,080	345	735	147,680	21,833
Westdeutsche LB	662	416	246	104,990	4,173
French Banks					
BNP	1,945	1,102	843	231,463	60,333
Credit Lyonnais	1,704	1,085	619	210,727	61,508
Société Générale	1,761	833	928	175,787	45,950
Banque Indosuez	414	223	191	55,316	16,347
Banque Paribas	1,433	615	818	138,668	26,474
Italian Banks					
BCI	849	219	630	88,594	20,942
Banco di Roma	515	349	166	64,472	13,727
IB San Paolo di Torino	1,335	349	986	107,403	20,407
Dutch Banks					
ABN	809	297	513	90,199	31,994
AMRO	810	313	497	93,604	23,718
NMB Postbank	870	417	454	83,997	22,697
Swiss Banks					
SBC	1,101	451	650	105,534	18,349
UBS	1,343	557	787	114,334	21,210
Canadian Banks					
Canadian Imperial	1,433	833	600	85,652	36,466
Bank of Montreal	1,088	1,010	78	67,454	33,666
RBC	1,904	1,179	724	98,000	54,469
Scotiabank	1,077	765	312	69,232	29,618
Toronto Dominion	1,067	197	870	53,905	23,881
Australian Banks					
ANZ	1,158	420	738	67,235	47,009
Commonwealth Bank	921	349	572	51,863	39,871
Westpac	1,313	459	854	86,205	47,525

United States
Banks
The financial year for all US banks is the calendar year. Provisions for bad debts include loan losses, credit losses and possible credit losses. Employment data for Bank America comprise full-time equivalent number of staff in December 1989; for Manufacturers Hanover they relate to the number of full-time equivalent employees at year end; and for Security Pacific, First Interstate and Mellon Bank to the average full-time equivalent number of employees for the year. For all other US banks employment is the total number of employees at year end.

Investment banks and security houses
The financial year for Bear Stearns is to 30 June 1990 and for the remaining United States securities houses it is the calendar year. For Bear Stearns, Morgan Stanley, Salomon Bros and Shearson Lehman Hutton, interest income comprises interest and dividend income.

Employment data for Morgan Stanley, Paine Webber and Salomon relate to the number of employees at year end. Employment figures for Bear Stearns and Shearson Lehman were obtained directly.

Japan

The financial year for all Japanese institutions runs to 31 March 1990. The exchange rate used is 158 Yen to US$1, the rate prevailing on 31 March 1990.

Banks
Employment relates to the number of employees as at 31 March for Dai-Ichi Kangyo, Fuji, Mitsui, and Sumitomo Banks, as at 30 June for the Long Term Credit Bank, and as at 1 August for The Bank of Tokyo. For IBJ an employment figure was obtained directly and for Nippon Credit Bank and Sanwa Bank it was derived from alternative Japanese statistical sources.

Securities houses
Interest income refers to interest and dividend income. Employment in the case of Nomura comprises the number of employees in the parent company only, for Daiwa it is the number of employees as of

30 June 1990, and for Nikko and Yamaichi it is the number of employees as of 31 March 1990.

United Kingdom

The financial year for most British institutions is the calendar year. For Robert Fleming, Hambros, N. M. Rothschild and S. G. Warburg it is the year to 31 March 1990 and for Charterhouse the year to 30 September 1989. The exchange rate used is 0.62 to US$1, the rate prevailing on 31 December 1989.

Banks

Employment data comprise: for Barclays, Lloyds and Standard Chartered the number of employees at 31 December 1989; for Midland the full-time equivalent number of employees at 31 December 1989; and for National Westminster the average number of persons employed each week excluding those who work mainly outside the United Kingdom.

Integrated merchant banks

Profit before tax is the only income figure reported by most of these banks and this is identified with net income. Midland Montagu reports a full set of income and expenditure statistics including provisions for bad debts. Employment figures for BZW, Charterhouse and Midland Montagu were obtained directly.

Independent merchant banks

The only income figure widely reported is profit before tax, which has been equated to net income. Robert Fleming and N. M. Rothschild report only profit after tax. None of these merchant banks report provisions for bad debts. Employment refers to the average number of people employed mainly in the United Kingdom during the financial year. Personnel costs are the remuneration of these employees.

Germany

The financial year for all these banks is the calendar year. The exchange rate used is DM1.69 to US$1, the rate prevailing on 31 December 1989.

   Net interest income comprises interest and similar income less interest and similar expenses for Dresdner and Commerzbank and relates to net interest income and other fees for West LB. Net interest income also includes interest in the mortgage bank business for Dresdner Bank. Other income includes commissions and other service charges received together with current income from investments and securities for Dresdner Bank, and additionally income from leased equipment in the case of Commerzbank. For the West LB Group other income consists of currrent income on securities and equity capital participations, commissions and other fees on services offered by the bank.

Other expenses consist of commissions and similar service charges paid, personnel costs, other operating expenses, and depreciation for Dresdner Bank and Commerzbank. For West LB other expenses consist of commissions and other fees paid on services, staff expenses, operating expenses for banking business and for non-bank group services and depreciation.

Employment data relate to the number of employees at year end for Dresdner Bank and Commerzbank Group and average number of employees in the reporting year for West LB.

France

The financial year for all French institutions is the calendar year. The exchange rate used is 5.788 French francs to US$1, the rate prevailing on 31 December 1989.

Income and expenses are not broken down into interest and other components for Paribas where the only useful income measure is net income. Indosuez quotes a figure for net interest income, but does not break down net other income into income and expenses so again only net income is available, consisting of net operating income minus depreciation and amortisation. For Credit Lyonnais a figure is available for total income, but not separately for net interest income. BNP and Société Générale provide an income breakdown compatible with our requirements.

Employment for all banks relates to the number of employees as at the calendar year end.

Italy

The financial year for the Italian banks is the calendar year. The exchange rate used is 1270.5 lira to US$1 the rate prevailing on 31 December 1989.

Other income for Banco di Roma consists only of non-interest income and other expenses comprise operating expenses, depreciation and revaluation deficits on securities and investments. Other income for San Paolo di Torino consists of other operating income, gains on the contribution of the public works section to Crediop, and other income, net. Other expenses include operating expenses, losses on investments and securities relating to valuation adjustments, depreciation and amortisation.

Employment data comprise for BCI the average number of personnel in 1989, and for Banco di Roma and San Paolo di Torino the number of employees at year end.

The Netherlands

The financial year for all the Dutch banks is the calendar year. The exchange rate used is 1.92 guilders to US$1 the rate prevailing on 31 December 1989. Employment is the number of employees at year end for ABN and AMRO and the average full-time equivalent number of employees for NMB Postbank. ABN and AMRO merged in 1990.

Switzerland

The financial year for the two Swiss banks is the calendar year. The exchange rate employed is 1.54 Swiss francs to US$1 the rate prevailing on 31 December 1989. Employment data comprise the number of employees for SBC and UBS but exclude personnel of UBS subsidiaries.

Canada

The financial year for Canadian banks is the year to 31 October 1989. The exchange rate used is Canadian $1.17 to US$1, the rate prevailing on 31 October 1989. Employment is the number of employees for Scotiabank, Bank of Montreal, RBC and CIBC, and full-time equivalent number of employees for Toronto Dominion, all at 31 October 1989.

Australia

The financial year for Westpac and ANZ runs to 30 September 1989 and for the Commonwealth Bank to 30 June 1990. The exchange rate used is Australian $1.26 to US$1 the rate prevailing on 30 June 1990. Employment figures measure the number of employees at year end.

NOTES

2 Assessing the Comparative Performance of Financial Services

1 National Economic Development Council (1988). The sectoral value added data used in this analysis are taken from EEC (1988) and the purchasing power parities are those compiled for financial services by the OECD.

2 EEC (1988). By focusing from the outset on comparative sectoral productivity levels within a country, rather than on a comparison of absolute productivity levels between countries, the following approach has more affinity with international trade theory.

3 The 1986 results were derived from *Euromoney*, June, 1987 and the 1987 results from *The Banker*, July, 1988. Because for some years profits in the banking sector can be negative (as was the case for Denmark in 1986 and for the United States and Norway in 1987) it is impracticable to use this variable for assessing international competitiveness.

4 Though the Saudi International Bank, Moscow Narodny Bank and the Scandinavian Bank Group feature in 1986 at the foot of the list of eighteen banks in the United Kingdom.

5 In the case of the United Kingdom, for instance, the list includes not only the four major retail banks characterised by an average per capita asset level of $1.1 million, but also five merchant banks (Kleinwort Benson, Morgan Grenfell, Warburg, Schroders and Hill Samuel) with average per capita assets of $3 million.

6 These price comparisons are subject to further qualifications. In the case of banking services the 'prices' relate to charges relative to general money market rates and so do not represent cost to the consumer. The insurance 'prices' also seem to reflect, in part, inter-country differences in construction costs in the case of home and fire insurance and differences in mortality rates in the case of life insurance.

7 A footnote to table 3.6 of the balance of payments accounts reads, 'financial and consultancy services provided by overseas residents to other UK institutions are included indistinguishably within [the separate category of] debits' (CSO, 1988).

8 Financed by the City and undertaken by the London Business School.

9 'Euro is increasingly becoming a misnomer for the global market place which raises funds around the world and lends them to countries and companies in currencies outside the country of issue. Although many Euromarket transactions are arranged in London, there is not a single national regulatory agency supervising this market, nor is it considered any bank's home market' (Bellanger, S., 1987).

3 Changes in Country Shares of Selected Financial Markets

1 Since this information is published in May of each year it is assumed that it relates to the financial year ending in April.

2 KPMG data presented in *The Financial Times*, 16 October 1990.

3 *The Economist*, 20 January, 1990 and *The Financial Times*, 24 September, 1990, which also points out: 'Merger mania may have run its course in the US and Britain but is far from over in Continental Europe . . . Unlike purely national mergers the overwhelming motivation [is] to gain access to new markets'.

4 'International mergers and acquisitions', *The Financial Times Survey*, 18 October, 1990, pp. 36 and 37. The American performance may also receive a boost as a result of the extent to which United States commercial banks have started 'to chip away at the monopoly' in this market of British and American merchant and investment banks (*Euromoney*, February, 1990, p. 45).

5 *The Financial Times*, 26 July, 1990, 26 July, 1989, 18 July, 1990 and 7 September, 1990.

6 Between 1980 and September 1989: see *Euromoney*, December, 1989, Supplement, 'Financing Corporate America', p. 23.

7 It is distinctive from a foreign bond which is issued by a foreign borrower in the domestic market of a particular country and denominated in that country's currency.

8 Formed in 1969 as a self-regulatory organisation of dealers in Eurobonds and centred in Zurich.

9 American commercial banks were prevented by law from underwriting securities in the United States and, as demonstrated above, were slow to undertake this activity overseas (Hamilton, 1986).

10 Coverage of the top ten lead managers (top eight in the case of the French franc) embraces the bulk of each currency sector, ranging from 74 to 100 per cent.

11 Percentages for nationality of borrowers are based on data relating to international bonds, 1989, provided by the Bank of England.

12 The data in this table differ from those presented for international equities in Chapter 4 partly because the latter embraces the top twenty, rather than ten, institutions, partly as a result of some definitional differences. However, the patterns of country shares which emerge for 1989 are broadly similar.

13 Since the method used to allocate share issue values between lead and co-lead managers in a syndicate involves some double counting the resulting absolute values have little meaning in themselves and only the percentage country shares derived therefrom are presented in table 3.25.

14 Based on data presented in table 3.25 and in *Euromoney*, May, 1990, pp. 57–62.

15 The importance, and interaction, of these features was exemplified in a recent four tranche international equity issue coordinated for the National Australian Bank by Merrill Lynch (*Euromoney*, January, 1989, Supplement, 'Funding techniques', pp. 22–5).

16 This latter instrument has been referred to by a variety of names including note purchase facility, revolving underwriting facility, Euronote issuance facility, Euronote purchase agreement.

17 In this case the historical series based on data supplied by the Bank of England do not relate to a uniform number of arrangers.

18 The exceptions being the Eurobond market recently and the international equity market in 1985.

4 An Analysis of Country Shares in Selected Financial Markets: 1989

1 An absence of foreign exchange values as opposed to estimated percentage market shares.

2 There are a few other definitional differences between the historical series and those analysed in this chapter. For instance the historical data for medium-term notes were derived from league tables of 'arrangers', those analysed here relate to 'dealers'. The difference between the two parallels that between Eurobond lead managers and co-managers: arrangers of medium-term note programmes are responsible for syndication among a small number of dealers. The main feature of both series is the dominant role which American institutions play in this market.

3 Compared with industrial organisations there are remarkably few financial institutions which can be regarded as truly 'multinational'. To some extent Credit Suisse First Boston and the London, New York and Paris arms of Lazard Brothers may be regarded as falling in this category.

4 Ownership by the Midland Bank of Trinkaus & Burkhardt means that its country classification would also need to be changed.

5 Presented, respectively by market, in tables 3.4, 3.6, 3.11, 3.15, 3.23, 3.26 and 3.29.

6 To be precise, held a significant market share.

7 The exception being the market for international equities where the American value per unit US$65 million is a little below the market average of US$72 million.

8 In the case of the markets for international bonds and Eurobonds, with all competitor countries excluding Japan as well as the United States.

9 It was requested that these margins be treated confidentially.

10 The rank correlation between the two series is +0.91.

11 In the case of both Japan and Switzerland the 'fee weighted' shares are held down by the relatively small role which each country's financial institutions play in the M&A advisory market to which a relatively high fee margin is attached.

12 The following analysis is more conveniently applied to this aggregate series.

13 That is arithmetically: 0.81 per cent × 2.85 × 27 = 62.3 per cent.

14 The rank correlation coefficients between country market shares and firm shares, market diversification and number of firms are, respectively, + 0.94, + 0.78 and + 0.69.

5 A Statistical Comparison of National Banking Sectors: 1989

1 Some of these coverage deficiencies are rectified in tables for 'The world's 100 best banks' in *Euromoney*, December, 1990, pp. 22ff. However, not only are certain significant characteristics (for example employment levels) still not embraced but also, by restricting the list to 100 banks, many of those institutions listed in the Schedule of Institutional Market Participation, 1989 (Appendix A) are excluded.

2 The nature of the information is described in Appendix B.

3 For this type of bank data deficiencies effectively preclude any cross-country comparisons based on average income.

4 Thus net income is equivalent to profits before any allowance is made for bad debts.

5 This substantially reflects the high income/employment ratios which are a feature of Japanese banks.

6 This is associated with high labour productivity in these institutions as measured by gross income per employee.

6 Explanations of Relative Performance

1 Garten (1988). Garten concludes that eventually there will be little difference in

nature of activities between Citibank, Merrill Lynch, Nomura and Deutsche Bank. No British institution features in this illustrative list.

2 Certain security operations now performed by American commercial banks are identified in Dyche (1988).

3 By way of illustration Security Pacific acquired Hoare Govett and Sumitomo bought Swiss Banco del Gottardo.

4 One interviewee described this relationship as 'too cosy' drawing attention to the loss of dynamism in a merchant bank when it becomes attached to, and can depend on, a much larger financial institution. Typically investment banking arms contribute relatively small revenues and profits to the group. Problems at Hill Samuel have culminated in management shake-ups.

5 Significantly the Bank of Yokohama is set to 'tighten management control' (*The Financial Times*, 28 April, 1991).

6 CSFB also had a share of all six markets but has not been regarded as independent for the purpose of this analysis because of its CS Holdings parentage. Shearson Lehman, owned by a non-bank, American Express, is included.

7 Investment banks may undertake foreign exchange operations though normally they are intended to serve purely internal functions and none feature among the top major international players in this market which is dominated by commercial banks.

8 However, it is necessary to offset against such indirect benefits to capital market operations any direct losses suffered by the commercial banks on their 'bread and butter' operations in the process of breaking into a new market. The financial press is currently replete with instances of retrenchment by banks of their international networks.

9 This qualification applies with less force to the United States and Japan where some security houses operate substantial retail networks.

10 We are not here concerned with the cross-border acquisition of minority stakes in financial organisations even though such moves may portend takeovers in the long term.

11 For instance the 1989 Annual Report of Salomon Brothers includes a whole section which is devoted to the firm's latest innovations.

12 Chu (1988). He also writes, 'the size and capital do not ensure long-term market leadership . . . If capital alone was the answer, firms that have cash laden parents . . . should all dominate the market'.

13 This contrasts, for example, with the position of Japanese institutions in the market for syndicated loans where Japanese banks tend to be weak on syndication but, because of the assets at their disposal, strong on capital participation.

14 *Euromoney*, October, 1990. See also Smith (1989), 'In the case of mortgages for example the output associated with writing £500,000 in a deed is . . . little different from that inscribing £50,000'.

15 *Euromoney*, December, 1990, pp. 23–6. These measures were based on averages of numerical ratings assigned to the credit assessments of Moody's, Standard and Poor's and IBCA.

16 Proportions of 15–20 per cent were quoted as typical of the share of information technology in total expenses.

17 That inter-country differences in technology levels persist to some extent is suggested by the contents of the Annual Report 1990 of Nikko Securities, 'until five years ago information technology based asset management was virtually unheard of in Japan though it had long played a major role in portfolio investment in the United States'. Nikko has now developed its own technology with the assistance of a specialist American supplier.

18 To illustrate this point one banker claimed the reason that Finland, for example, fails to obtain large shares of international markets is, quite simply, that its financial institutions serve a very small domestic market.

19 Paradoxically, by reducing the need for mergers and acquisitions to bring about management changes, these relationships also contribute to the relative weakness of German financial institutions in M&A advisory activity.

20 The requirements of the Solvency Ratio Directive applicable to EC members are very similar to those of the Basle Agreement. The capital ratios of security houses will be subject to the European Commission's proposed Capital Adequacy Directive for Investment Firms.

21 Although 'all German banks are likely to be faced with the need to raise extra Tier II funds to meet capital guidelines' (*The Financial Times*, 23 October, 1990).

22 The fall in profits of Japan's three long-term credit banks (the IBJ, Long Term Credit Bank and Nippon Credit) and the slump in Japanese stock market prices in 1990 meant that all three failed to achieve the 8 per cent BIS guideline. The same two factors helped to ensure that of twelve Japanese city banks only three (Fuji, Daiwa and Kyowa) attained the Basle standards.

REFERENCES

Balassa, B. (1965), 'Trade liberalisation and "revealed" comparative advantage', *Manchester School*, 33, May.

Bellanger, S. (1987), 'Going global', *The Bankers Magazine*, March/April.

(1987b), 'The Japanese invasion', *The Bankers Magazine*, July/August.

(1988), 'The commercial banker as investment banker', *The Bankers Magazine*, November/December.

Bank for International Settlements (BIS) (1985), *Payment Systems in Eleven Developed Countries*, Basle, BIS.

(1990), *International Banking and Financial Market Developments*, BIS, November.

Bowe, M. (1988), *Eurobonds*, Square Mile Books.

Bullock, G. R. (1987), *Euronotes and Euro-commercial Paper*, Butterworths.

Central Statistical Office (CSO) (1988), *United Kingdom Balance of Payments 1988*, London, CSO.

Chu, F. J. (1988), 'The myth of global investment banking', *The Bankers Magazine*, January/February.

Cross, S. Y. (1988), 'The growth and changing character of the foreign exchange market', in Kaushik, S. K. (Ed.), *International Capital Markets*.

de la Mothe, J. R. (1986), 'Financial services', in Smith, A. D. (Ed.), *Technological Trends and Employment: Commercial Service Industries*, Aldershot, Gower.

Dyche, D. (1988), 'Investment banking: what do banks need to compete?' *The Bankers Magazine*, March/April.

EEC (1988), *European Economy: The Economics of 1992*, no. 35, March.

Financial Times (1990), 'Survey of information technology in finance', 7 November.

Gart, A. (1989), *An Analysis of the New Financial Institutions*, London, Quorom Books.

Garten, J. E. (1988), 'Regulating the global stock market', in Kaushik, K. (Ed.), *International Capital Markets*.

Gray, H. P. and Walter, I. (1983), 'Protectionism in international banking', *Journal of Banking and Finance*, December.

Hamilton, A. (1986), *The Financial Revolution*, Penguin Books.

Heller, L. (Ed.) (1988), *Eurocommercial Paper*, Euromoney Publications.

Humphrey, D. (1987), 'Cost dispersion and the measurement of economies in banking', *Federal Reserve Bank of Richmond Economic Review*, May/June.

International Stock Exchange (ISE) (1990), 'Financial performance of ISE member firms', *Quality of Markets Quarterly*, April/June.

KPMG (1989), *International Handbook of Financial Instruments and Transactions*, London, Butterworths.

Kaushik, S. K. (Ed.) (1988), *International Capital Markets: New Directions*, New York Institute of Finance.

Kravis, I. and Lipsey, R. (1988), 'Production and trade in services by United States multinational firms', NBER Working Paper no. 2615.

Lloyds Bank Economic Bulletin (1989), '1992 winners and losers', January.

National Economic Development Council (1988), 'The Single European Market:

issues for the NEDC, sector groups and companies', NEDC (88) 30, October, annex.

Oulton, N. (1986), 'International trade in services and the comparative advantage of European Community countries', unpublished report for the Trade Policy Research Centre, London.

Petersen, J. and Barras, R. (1987), 'Measuring international competitiveness in services', *The Service Industry Journal*, April.

Price Waterhouse International Economic Consultants (1988), 'The cost of 'non-Europe' in financial services: executive summary', March.

Revell, J. (1985), 'The structure of credit systems', *Review of Economic Conditions in Italy*, September/December.

Sherman, P. D. (1988), 'Out from competence: commercial and investment banks in the 1990s', in Kaushik, S. K. (Ed.) *International Capital Markets*.

Smith, A. D. (1989), 'New measures of British service outputs', *National Institute Economic Review*, no. 128, May.

and Hitchens, D. M. W. N. (1985), *Productivity in the Distributive Trades*, Cambridge University Press.

Walmsley, J. (1988), *The New Financial Instruments*, John Wiley and Sons.

Walter, I. (1988), *Global Competition in Financial Services: Market Structure, Protection and Trade Liberalisation*, Harper & Row, Ballinger.

INDEX

THE NATIONAL INSTITUTE OF ECONOMIC
AND SOCIAL RESEARCH
PUBLICATIONS IN PRINT

published by
THE CAMBRIDGE UNIVERSITY PRESS
(available from booksellers, or in case of difficulty from the publishers)

NIESR STUDENTS' EDITION

Published by
GOWER PUBLISHING COMPANY
(Available from Gower Publishing Company and from booksellers)

ENERGY SELF-SUFFICIENCY FOR THE UK
Edited by ROBERT BELGRAVE and MARGARET CORNELL. 1985. pp. 224.
£27.50 net.

THE FUTURE OF BRITISH DEFENCE POLICY
Edited by JOHN ROPER. 1985. pp. 214. £29.50 net.

ENERGY MANAGEMENT: CAN WE LEARN FROM OTHERS?
By GEORGE F. RAY. 1985. pp. 131. £27.50 net.

UNEMPLOYMENT AND LABOUR MARKET POLICIES
Edited by P. E. HART. 1986. pp. 230. £32.00 net.

NEW PRIORITIES IN PUBLIC SPENDING
Edited by M. S. LEVITT. 1987. pp. 136. £27.50 net.

POLICYMAKING WITH MACROECONOMIC MODELS
Edited by A. J. C. BRITTON. 1989. pp. 285. £35.00 net.

HOUSING AND THE NATIONAL ECONOMY
Edited by JOHN ERMISCH. 1990. pp. 158. £32.50 net.

Published by
SAGE PUBLICATIONS LTD
(Available from Sage and from booksellers)

*ECONOMIC CONVERGENCE AND MONETARY UNION
IN EUROPE*
Edited by RAY BARRELL. 1992. pp. 288. £35.00 (hardback,
£12.95 (paperback) net.

ACHIEVING MONETARY UNION IN EUROPE
By ANDREW BRITTON and DAVID MAYES. 1992. pp. 160.
£25.00 net (hardback), £8.95 (paperback) net.

Printed in the United States
By Bookmasters